For Knowing
No Hurt
No Harm

Hidden, Subtle and Obvious Aspects
of
Intimate and Other Partner
Abuse, Violence, and Terror

For Knowing
No Hurt
No Harm

Hidden, Subtle and Obvious Aspects
of
Intimate and Other Partner
Abuse, Violence, and Terror

Angela Brownemiller

Metaterra® Publications

Metaterra® Publications
FOR KNOWING NO HURT NO HARM (2nd Edition):
HIDDEN, SUBTLE, AND OBVIOUS ASPECTS OF
INTIMATE AND OTHER PARTNER ABUSE, VIOLENCE, AND TERROR
Copyright © 2019, 2013, 2002, 2000, 1998,
Angela Brownemiller/ Angela Brownemiller.
Copyright © 2019, 2013, 2002, 2000, 1998, Metaterra® Publications.
www.Metaterra.com
Library of Congress Cataloging-in-Publication Data.
Brownemiller, Angela. Browne-Miller, Angela.
For Knowing No Hurt No Harm/ Hidden, Subtle, and Obvious Aspects of Intimate and Other Partner Abuse, Violence, and Terror / Angela Brownemiller/ Angela Browne-Miller
1. Psychology. 2. Social Work. 3. Browne-Miller, Angela. 4. Domestic Violence & Intimate Partner Violence. 5. Personal Growth. 6. Violence. 7. Abuse. 8. Violence against Women. 9. Batterers. 10. Relationships. 11. Divorce. 12. Addiction. 13. Social Policy. 14. Self Help.
Title:
FOR KNOWING NO HURT NO HARM (2nd Edition):
HIDDEN, SUBTLE, AND OBVIOUS ASPECTS OF
INTIMATE AND OTHER PARTNER ABUSE, VIOLENCE, AND TERROR
Library of Congress Control Number: (see website listed above)
ISBN-13: 978-1-937951-17-7 (Paperback) can be ordered on Amazon.com
ISBN-13: (Kindle ebook) see Amazon.com to order
Published in the United States of America for US and worldwide distribution.
Metaterra® Publications.
Book design by and copyright ©Angela Browne-Miller/Angela Brownemiller.
Ordering information and bulk ordering information available through: Amazon Paperback and Amazon Kindle.
Also contact Info@Metaterra.com.

All rights to all printings, formats, and editions reserved. No part of this book may be reproduced or transmitted in any form or by any means, electronic or mechanical, including photocopying, recording, or by any information storage and retrieval system, without prior written permission from the author, publisher, and copyright owner, except for the inclusion of brief quotations in a review. Additionally, all cover and illustrations, figures, diagrams have been created by the author, Angela Brownemiller, and cannot be reproduced without her written permission.

NOTE TO READERS

The information in this book is provided for informational purposes only, without any warranty of any kind. This book is sold and distributed with the understanding that the publisher, the author, and the author's and publisher's consultants, writers, editors, and artists, are not engaged in rendering legal, financial, medical, or other professional services in this book. If legal, financial, medical, or other expert assistance is required, the direct in-person services of a professional should be sought. The publisher, the author, and the author's and publisher's consultants, writers, editors, and artists, shall have neither liability nor responsibility to any person or entity with respect to any loss or damage alleged to be caused, directly or indirectly, by the information in this book.

Dedicated to humanity.

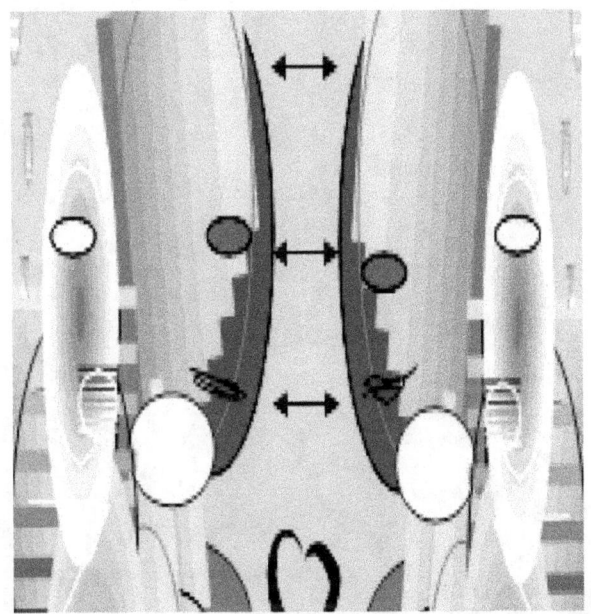

On Micro-Relating
Illustration by Angela Brownemiller

*I've been abused so long
it looks like love to me.*

Table of Contents

Attention Readers	17
Author's Note	19
Note on Stories	25
1. Introduction to For Knowing No Hurt No Harm	27
IPAVT is Complex	30
Conscious Relationships	31
Conscious Relating to Our Loved Ones and Ourselves	32
PART ONE	**35**
2. For Knowing No Harm	37
Intimate Partner Violence is Prevalent	39
Includes Nonphysical Forms	40
Violence Can Be Habit-Forming	41
Violence Can Interconnect with Other Problems	41
Question of Mutual Violence	42
Dangerous Response Delay and Exacerbation	44
Question of Collateral Violence and Abuse	45
List: Collateral IPAVT	*46*
Children	46
Parents, and or Other Family Members	47
Friends, Neighbors, Co-Workers	47
Pets	48
Property	48
Earning Power, Etc.	48
Collateral Terror	49
Terrorization as Abuse	49
3. *Last Time Story*	*51*
4. **All About Intentions**	**53**
Intent is Difficult to Determine and Often Disguised	53
Lines Between Intent and Impulse	55
Violence as a Defensive Response	57
Nuances of Suppressed Fight or Flight Response	60

Violence is Like an Onion	64
Violence and Implied Violence for Dominance	65
When Defending Real and Presumed Power	68
The Need for Power	68
Two Faces of Violence	70
Intents of Partner Abuse and Violence	71
Questions to Ask About Intent	71
Investment in Partner Violence	72
Requires a Deep Honest Look	72
5. What About Consent	**75**
Consent is Misunderstood	75
Enabling the Abuse of Consent	76
Pretended Confusion	78
6. *Power Difference Story*	***81***
7. Precious Time	**85**
Time Passes No Matter What	85
Can We Choose Carefully	86
Choice, Survival, and Finances	88
Control Over Money	88
The Way It Should Be	90
Choosing When There are Unknowns	91
8. Cherish is a Word For	**93**
How We Cherish Each Other	93
Cherish is Not Self Deception	94
When Cherish is a License to Have	95
Element of Ownership	95
Tiny Trades	97
Power Differentials	99
9. *Second Thought Story*	***103***
10. Individual Identity and Boundaries Within a Relationship	**105**
Notice of Bonding	105
When a Bond Crosses the Line	106
Reasons for Formal Marriage	108
Identity and Commitment to What and to Whom	109

11. Meet the IP's Boundary	**111**
Intimacy is Not Physical Nakedness	112
Entanglement is Not Intimacy	112
Intimacy and Mutual Boundary Crossing	113
Boundary Crossing without Permission	114
Intimacy Can Open Doors	115
See The Difference Between Permission to Cross	
and Violation of Boundaries	116
Recognize VIO-lation as VIO-lence	117
PART TWO	**119**
12. Anatomy of the Bond	**121**
Love Can Trigger	121
Bonding and Time	122
Some Bonds Progress Negatively	123
Do Bonds Ever Break or End	124
13. *Messages Story*	***129***
14. Signs	**131**
Slipping Into Boundary Confusion	131
Watching for Signs of Boundary Abuse	133
Vague Free-Floating Discomfort	136
Not Feeling Like Oneself	137
Choosing to Avoid the Truth	137
Sense of Playing a Role	140
Hollow or Unfulfilling Intimacy	140
Feeling Like Something is Wrong	141
Feeling Trapped	142
Denying Signs	143
15. *Any Idea Story*	***145***
16. Denial?	**147**
We Have the Tendency to Not See	147
Denial Sneaks In	148
17. *What Strength Story*	***151***
18. Emotional Abuse	**153**
Tangled and Murky Type of Abuse	153
Signs of Emotional Abuse	154
Hard to See and Invisible Abuse	156

Emotional Abuse is So Complex	158
19. Compromise and Trade (C&T) Abuse	**159**
Compromises and Trades	159
Infinite Trades	161
C&T Abuse	162
Subtle Hidden Triggers	163
20. *Power and Control Story*	**165**
21. Stress, Trouble, Abuse, and Violence	**167**
The Fantasy	167
Some Relationships Do Not Cope with Stress	168
When Boredom or Dullness Plays a Role	169
22. *Who Could Ask for More Story*	**173**
23. When the Person Abusing Feels Abused	**177**
Use of the Word Victim	178
Turning the Tables	180
Trauma of Truth Telling	182
Handling This Turning of the Table	183
List: Remember This When the Tables are Turned	***183***
When the Abuser Nevertheless Tells the Truth	184
PART THREE	**187**
24. *Repeating Story*	***189***
25. Denial and Problem Patterns	**191**
Patterns Can Indeed Be Normal and Good	191
Examine Harmful Patterns	192
Denial Preserves a Problem Relationship	192
List: Anatomy of Denial	***194***
Denial Again and Again, Part of the Pattern	195
26. *Numb Story*	***199***
27. Hollowing to Patterns	**201**
Conflict of Instincts	202
Hollowing to Deteriorating Patterns	202
Hollowing to Patterns of Dominance	203
List: Steps into Positive and Negative Patterns	***205***
Denial is a Pattern	209
28. *Dangerous Denial Story*	***211***

29. Patterns of Abuse in Relationships	**213**
Faces of Abuse	213
Abuse is Violence	214
Violence Can Be Habitual, Even Addictive	215
Habitual "Rewards"	216
Checkpoints Along the Path to Violence	219
Tolerance Can Be Dangerous	220
Conflicting Experience	222
List: Establishing and Maintaining Healthy Patterns and Preventing the Opposite	223
30. *This Time Story*	**227**
31. Pattern Addictions Can Control Our Relationships	**229**
Behavioral Addiction, Love and Sex	229
Habits Sneak Up On Us	230
How We Form Pattern Addictions	231
Running Into Someone's Arms, Anyone's	233
32. *Compulsion Obsession Story*	**235**
33. Emotional Sadomasochism	**239**
Emotional Sadomasochism as a Relationship Pattern	239
Fair	240
Do No Harm Always? Is Harm Ever Alright?	241
Quicksand	242
Was It Good	244
Confusing Pain With Pleasure	250
Like is Too Simple a Word	251
When Relationships Kill	252
PART FOUR	**257**
34. *Cage Story*	**259**
35. Brutal Fiduciary	**263**
Abuse of Dollar Dominance	264
Fiduciary Duty	264
Fiduciary Abuse of Fiduciary Power	267
List: Elements of Relationship Fiduciary's Abuse of Responsibility	269
How Dollar Dominance Arises	271

Institutional Support of Fiduciary Abuse	273
36. *Fiduciary Story*	**277**
37. Related Trauma	**279**
What Trauma Is	279
Intimate Partner Violence Can Be Traumatizing	282
Effects of Trauma	283
Cannot Entirely Erase the Memory	284
Stages of Change	286
Being Trapped in an Unfinished Experience	287
Lack of Closure	288
Completing the Circle	288
Forgetting as Coping	289
Trauma and Dissociation as Coping	291
Trauma Upon Trauma Upon Trauma in IPAVT	293
List: Elements of IPAVT Trauma	**295**
Complex IPAVT Impact Matrix	299
38. *Altered State and Weapon Story*	**301**
39. Long Term Effects	**303**
Tip of the Iceberg	303
Tip of the Reality	304
Co-Occurring Conditions	305
Depression and Anger	306
General, Post-Traumatic, and Other Stress	307
Anger and More Anger	308
Attachment Confusion and Re-Victimization	309
Distorted Attachment Bonds	310
Reliving Past Negatives	311
40. *After the Fact Story*	**313**
41. Child Witness and Victim	**319**
Unaddressed Injuries	319
Carriers of Patterns	320
Teaching Denial	321
Harsh and Painful Reality	321
Children Have a Right to This Information	322
Love	324
Tolerance	326

Special Note: Deplorable Partner Abuse
  Through the Child 327
42. *Cleaning Story* *331*

PART FIVE **333**
43. *Getting Out Story* **335**
44. When Your Skin's Too Tight **337**
  Pressure to Shed 338
  List: Detecting the Shedding Point *339*
  Knowing What You Really Want to Shed 342
  Getting Out 342
  Some Prefer Physical Death to Changing 344
  Growing Numb 347
  List: Numbness May Mean Trouble Brewing *348*
  Seeing the Drive to Violence 351
  We Know These Paths to Shedding Patterns 354
45. Breaking Through **357**
  There is a Way Out of This Pattern 357
  Transcending One's Programming 358
  Those Concerned Ask 360
  List: Conditions for Transcendence *360*
  Phases of Transcendence 363
  Phase 1: Struggle 364
  Phase 2: Paradox 365
  Phase 3: Insight 368
  Phase 4: Elevation or Transcendence 369
  Breaking Through the Shackles of
    Our Programming 370
46. Troubled Couple **371**
  Find the Troubled Couple 371
  Identity, Investment, and Dependence 375
  Taking From Others 376
  Infinite Interactions 377
  Disengaging from Patterns 380
47. Above Violence **383**
  Reaching the Mind in More Than One Way 383
  List: If You are in An Abusive Relationship *388*

48. Wise Elder Plan for Troubled Couple	*391*
49. Coming Back from IPAVT	**395**
50. Love	**397**
Interpersonal and Planetary Peace	397
Love as a Medium of Exchange	398
Violence in Cycles	399
About the Author	**405**

List of Figures

(Note: All Figures and Graphics Designed by Angela Brownemiller©)

Frontispiece: On Micro-Relating	15
Figure 4.1. Examples of Possibly Suppressed Fight or Flight Response	62
Figure 4.2. Blurry Spectrum of Partner Violence Intent	63
Figure 4.3. Graph of Two Ranges of Intent	69
Figure 8.1. Stability, Sanity and Safety Balance	101
Figure 12.1. Anatomy of a Probable Positive Bond Progression	126
Figure 12.2. Anatomy of a Probable Negative Bond Progression	127
Figure 12.3. Example of a Mixed Positive and Negative Bond Progression with Reversals	128
Figure 14.1. Signs Which May Be Telling Us We are Troubled By Our Intimate Partner Relationship	139
Figure 16.1. Whatever Works	150
Figure 21.1. Paths to Violence in Non-Violent and Violent Relationships	171
Figure 21.2. Reaction to Stress (Even Boredom Can Be Stressful)	172
Figure 25.1. Denial Along a Spectrum of Consciousness, Awareness, and Not Seeing	198
Figure 33.1. Emotional and Sexual Pleasure Cycle	246
Figure 33.2. Emotional Pleasure and Emotional Pain Cycle	246
Figure 33.3. Emotional Pain with Sexual Pleasure Cycle	246
Figure 33.4. Emotional Pleasure and Pain with Sexual Pleasure Cycle	247
Figure 33.5. Sexual Pleasure with Sexual Pain Cycle	247
Figure 33.6. Emotional and Sexual Pleasure-Pain Cycle	248
Figure 33.7. Sample Pleasure-Pain Confusion Mini-Cycles Or Subloops	249
Figure 33.8. Sample Discomfort-Comfort Cycle	254
Figure 33.9. Sample Longing for Contact Cycle	255
Figure 37.1. Trapped in the Incomplete, Fractured, Broken Circle	291

Figure 37.2. Fortify the Boundary, Close the Circle   294
Figure 44.1. Stability, Sanity, Safety Balance In and Out of Peril 355
Figure 45.1. Stages in Transcending Relationship Challenges:
                Struggle, Paradox, Insight,
                and Elevation   363
Figure 46.1. Interaction Chart for
                One Couple in One Relationship   378
Figure 46.2. Interaction Chart for One Couple in One
                Relationship Where Each Member of the
                Couple Experiences the Relationship from
                Her or His Perspective   379
Figure 46.3. Degrees of Identity With, Investment In, and
                Dependence Upon, a Relationship May
                Differ For Each Member of the Couple   381
Figure 47.1 Conflict   386
Figure 47.2. Conflicting Conflict   387
Figure 47.3. Rising Above Conflict   390
Back Graphic: Technology of Relating   403

Attention Readers

This book is intended to offer readers insight into healthy and less than healthy—troubled, unsafe, sometimes even quite dangerous—interactions taking place in intimate partner relationships. Many readers will arrive here, at these pages of **For Knowing No Hurt No Harm**, *once someone—either they themselves, or their family members, friends, neighbors, co-workers, therapists, health care providers, faith leaders, law enforcement and court officials, colleagues, or others—have brought them here.*

Of course, where there is a clear, and sometimes less than clear, yet relatively or possibly immediate or imminent danger to self or others, these words in this book can wait, and every step to ensure im-mediate safety must be taken right away. Emergency hot lines, police lines, shelter lines, doctors' numbers, and other contact information must be used to seek and attain information regarding safety and protection.

This book is written for use where there is room and time for reflection and thought, for an increase in awareness regarding what is actually taking place, or has actually already taken place, in healthy relating, yes—and also in possible and actual abusive and violent interactions between partners. So often we are too caught up in what we feel to see in some detail what is taking place in close interpersonal relationships, and to note where there is the potential for abuse and violence—or where there already is abuse and violence underway. Many of us are therefore at times prone to miss signs of nonphysical abuse and even of potentially dangerous physical violence brewing, to only see these after the fact.

Also note that this book is written for adults over the age of eighteen, however much of the discussion on interactions herein is also relevant to teens in relationship, dating, and or other emotional and physical intimacy situations. Readers who are underage, or who are providing this book to someone underage, will please also ensure that young people have adult involvement in understanding and using this material.

Author's Note

Virtually every day we hear of ongoing and new incidents of abuse, violence, and even terror, in homes, schools, workplaces, and elsewhere in our communities and in our nations around the globe. Among these instances are those that too often take place at one of the most interpersonal levels, in the relationship between domestic, marital, dating, intimate, and or other forms of partners connected and sometimes bound by love, law, tradition, and or other personal partnering practices.

What is ever more clear is that people, causes, professions, services, laws, policies, traditions, sometimes even religious practices, tend to not under-stand, or to not recognize, fail to see, refuse to address, consider less important, or even accept, violence and abuse within personal (such as dating, love, partner, spousal) relationships.

This book, *For Knowing No Hurt No Harm*, seeks to help raise awareness of problems that can arise in human relationships, especially in intimate partner, marital, dating, and similar relationships. This book moves the discussion of intimate and other partner violence and abuse to a place the discussion may not visit enough, to the most basic locus of relating, the frequently quite subtle interpersonal communication, interaction, and even moment to moment, *micro-interaction*, levels.

Much of today's excellent work and research on intimate partner abuse and violence overlooks this finer unit of analysis, the minute to minute, second to second, micro levels of interpersonal interaction. Yet it is in the moment to moment interactions themselves that the dynamics of abuse, and even of the steps into all out physical violence, appear, sometimes quite subtly, yet often clearly if we know what to look for.

Hence, this book draws our focus away from some of the more general concepts and issues to the critical and intricate level of interpersonal interaction.

This level is where spoken words, and frequently subtle and hidden, spoken perhaps yet oft unspoken communications, compromises, trades—implicit and explicit, informal and formal, imagined and real—various kept, altered, and broken tendencies, arrangements and agreements—are underway at all times. *(Note: In a sequel to this book, the still finer units of analysis, the brain cell, synaptic, biochemical, and neuro-transmitter levels of all this, are discussed.)*

There is so much to see in interactions between partners, so much so very wonderful, and yes sometimes (in some, but not all relationships) a great deal that is problematic and even dangerous emotionally, physically, and in other ways such as spiritually, socially, economically and financially, professionally, legally, and so on.

And there is also so much more to become aware of even when at first it is difficult to see. Indeed, there is so much abuse and violence that is difficult to see because it is difficult to define, or confusing, or quite subtle, or even purposefully hidden for various reasons.

Therefore this book is written for anyone who will sometime be in, is presently in, and or is looking back upon a previous, intimate partner "and or" love, dating, or other similar form of relationship.

I write "and or" as not all intimate partner relationships are love relationships and vice versa. While these two conditions—love and intimate partnership—frequently occur together, it is all too common that we find people in intimate partner relationships who think there is love there, when there may or may not be love—or when the love may or may not be what the love is assumed to be or mean. Additionally, there is a great deal of confusion regarding intimacy. We must ask: does intimacy guarantee anything—love, stability, safety, truth, clarity, or …? What troubled illusions might moments of emotional and physical intimacy without true caring, commitment, and awareness sometimes foster? Should we wonder?

This book is also written for others—family members, friends, neighbors, coworkers, helping and health professionals—who are seeing and perhaps working to address the needs of spouses and partners in relationships that are working well and in relationships that are troubled or may be troubled.

An additional note….

Various and frequently heated debates have arisen regarding the accept-ability, existence, nature of, and solutions to, violence and abuse in relationships. Interestingly, these debates vary and even differ significantly among different groups, professions and professional perspectives, com-munities, regions, and nations of the world.

Too often, one is forced to "take a side" in these debates, to accept a view or theory prior to looking quite closely at the most subtle and micro levels of relating.

While it is not the intent of this book to take a position on most of these overarching debates, certain realities will be acknowledged here, already on these first pages. Let me begin by making it clear that neither the perpetration nor the receiving of violence and abuse is restricted to one gender (or even to one sexual preference for that matter).

Men can and do abuse women and men, and women can and do abuse men and women. This reality warrants earnest and honest attention. This book, which focuses on interactions between people who are in relationships, attempts to distill interpersonal relationship abuse down to relatively gender-neutral processes. Yet, despite the reality that both genders can and do experience violence and abuse in relationships, there is another matter that warrants equal concern here.

Abuse of and violence against women and girls is a longtime issue, even tradition, of worldwide significance, something that has continued to exist at crisis levels around the globe.

Indeed, one of the signal issues of our times is how to stop violence against women and girls. So much of this violence has been taking place throughout history, and has been virtually institutionalized for centuries. Indeed, over the centuries women were the property or chattel of men in many societies, and where not, nevertheless lived with fewer rights to property and decisions and even freedom than men did, and in some places than men still do.

Descending from this long tradition of seconding women to their fathers, brothers, husbands, and others in their lives, we see even today that abuse and violence against women quite frequently falls into this domain.

Even where women and girls are no longer treated as second class citizens, there can and do remain both obvious and **hidden traces** *of such perspectives. We must remain* ***ever watchful*** *for these. In instances where even these traces do remain, any and all of the possibilities of violence and abuse against, and even terrorizing of, women and girls, can be perpetuated in some way, even magnified or enhanced when and where we least expect this. Even where age old forms of violence and abuse of women may appear to be receding, new and powerful yet subtle even hidden forms may be emerging.*

We must do everything we can to stop this long term, even age old, frequently approved or at least tolerated socially, abuse of and violence against women and girls taking place around the world, to stop the femicide, infanticide, trapping and trafficking, maiming, beating, terrorizing, and the socially, verbally, financially, and other definitely abusive behaviors taking place.

Ultimately, fine-tuning our policies, attitudes, and awarenesses regarding violence and abuse against people by people—no matter who they are, where they are, what their age, what their gender—is essential. This book offers one contribution to the major peace-promoting efforts of our times.

Note on Stories

Several scenarios, labeled herein as "stories," are placed throughout this book as examples of intimate partner abuse and violence, and related relationship conditions and their effects. Some of these stories are rather graphic depictions of violence and abuse, and others may seem to some readers to be comparatively innocuous, relatively harmless along a spectrum of degrees of harm and danger. Yet each story contains within it at least one element of, or potential precursor to, abuse and violence, usually several. And no matter how minor these elements may seem, they can be representative of larger problems.

Also, even the seemingly most harmless abuse events may be signs of other current or emerging abuses that may be still more serious, or that may be increasingly harmful in their accumulation, and should be given attention.

The stories included herein are based upon, composed by combining, hundreds of actual persons' stories. These actual persons exist in a range of sociocultural settings; however, herein all their names, settings, and identifying factors have been changed to protect identities. In some cases but not all, genders have been made impossible to know and or no names have been given. Where gender has been indicated or suggested, this is done with the understanding that gender may be changed for each character in each story.

Any resemblance to particular persons living or dead is unintentional and is the product of the possible commonality of these experiences across gender, race, cultural, socioeconomic, and other groups. Also note that where the names may have been changed to names more typical of some gender and or cultural groups than others, this is not in itself an indication that any particular group experiences these situations more than any other. Readers are invited to substitute for others whatever names and genders they wish as they read along.

Although many of these stories are not happy stories, most of these stop at their own midpoints for instructional reasons. This is not to paint an unhealed or ugly picture of love, but to allow readers to observe potential and actual problems in partnerships and in their interactions, problems that must be seen, recognized, addressed, to be changed. In fact, many of the real stories upon which this book is based have ended well for their participants in their own healing, transformation, change—either within or beyond their relationships. Another book, another time, with another purpose, can tell these other stories.

Clearly, countless other stories could have been included had space permitted. Most readers will have at least one story of their own. We all know relationship stories that are relevant to the following discussion of what hurts and what works. More likely than not, we ourselves have lived or witnessed directly some of these stories and understand them from the inside.

1
Introduction to For Knowing No Hurt No Harm

If these pages could cry, they would shed oceans of tears for those suffering the pain, anguish, confusion, and humiliation of intimate partner abuse and violence. These tears would be for persons being abused, persons who are doing the abusing, their children, parents, other family members, friends, neighbors, coworkers, communities, societies, and worlds. Whether or not we choose to acknowledge this, we all feel the shattering of the hearts, minds, souls, and even bodies of people whose lives are or have at some time been infected with intimate partner abuse in its various physical and nonphysical forms.

A word about the person abusing—frequently described as the abuser, batterer, or perpetrator. Do not think every person abusing is free of the pain, anguish, confusion, and humiliation experienced by the persons being abused. Many of them have themselves been abused or witnessed abuse and violence in earlier situations, frequently as children. And or they have been conditioned to believe that their abuses, or the abuses they are pressured psychologically or socially to perform, are not abuses, or are acceptable and even sometimes required abuses. And, whether or not this is the case, they will have to live (either consciously or subconsciously or both) with the experience of harming others, hurting people, and beating on the bodies and hearts of people they likely love or once loved, for the rest of their lives.

What it takes for these persons to stand up and be counted, to own the behaviors of harm in which they have engaged, and then to change, is immense. Whether standing up to family, social, cultural, traditional, religious, or personal impulses and norms pressing them to abuse, they themselves may face external and internal reprisals that are rarely talked about or acknowledged.

Clearing the legacy of inflicting harm, and lighting the way for others to follow this path, is key to moving past the history of harm and to helping create a world which might someday be free of interpersonal harm.

And a word about the person being abused—frequently described as the abusee (described as the *abusee* in this book), survivor, or victim. We do know that many persons who have been abused by their intimate partners have been so very deeply affected that they will be dealing with the social, economic, professional, mental, spiritual, and physical effects for the rest of their lives.

For these persons, identifying and then healing and moving past the wounds is a large job, which first requires deep commitment to oneself and then to the people one loves. (Note again that even moving past the wounds does not necessarily eliminate all traces of these, as many wounds remain for a lifetime.)

Standing up and being counted, owning the experience, and then owning the recovery process, are all essential. We need to know what human beings are capable of doing to other human beings. We need to know that human beings can sometimes cause, even the people closest to them, often their intimate partners, great harm.

Clearing the legacy of being harmed, and lighting the way for others to follow this path, is key to moving past the history of being harmed and to helping create a world which might someday be free of interpersonal harm.

Each and every one of us is a benefactor and a victim of the human condition. We are living in a world which tolerates and even sometimes glorifies violence as a means of resolving disputes, disagreements, tensions. Just look at the world today, or just see the internet or watch the television.

We have all arrived at this time in history together, facing the pressure to evolve to a higher point of consciousness or to remain a violent species, treating humans violently, treating life violently, treating the Earth violently. What a wonderful place in which to respond to this survival pressure and to help raise consciousness — a close intimate partner relationship with another being!

If these pages can contribute even a little to the evolution of this consciousness, they will. In fact, these pages seek to offer suggestions for:

- getting to better know oneself and oneself in relationship.
- increasing understanding of what takes place in intimate partner, significant other, dating, casual sex, and other sorts of relation-ships.
- raising the consciousness of intimate partners with the goal of reaching highly conscious relating.
- stopping the violence and abuse in relationships by openly and clearly recognizing it for what it is, and…

> by changing it where it can be changed,
> or if necessary, by knowing when to get out
> of it, away from it for a time or for good.

Stopping the clock to look closely at what is taking place when we interact, freeze-framing the process we are partaking in, can allow us to under-stand close up and personally the intricate workings of the energies of two people engaged in pleasure and or harm to themselves and others. The dances people in relationships do are highly elaborate, quite interactive, and more readily understood in very slow motion.

IPAVT IS COMPLEX

Intimate partner abuse, violence, and terror (what this book defines as **IPAV, IPAVT** and **IPAV&T**) is truly complex. *Popular but limited single-theory explanations for these problems say very little about what is actually taking place.*

The various competing socio-political schools of thought regarding intimate partner abuse and violence do best by ceasing the competition and seeing the multitude of factors at work. Reality is not simple, and is not merely a very general or broad social system level issue. So why would we expect relationships or relationship violences to be simple?

Some people spend entire lifetimes mired in very difficult relationships and or the aftermaths of these. For many of them, these problem relationship behaviors become habitual, increasingly difficult, and some-times even dangerous to break away from without guidance and assistance.

What does it take to leave behind the patterns of denial, confusion, wounds, pain, sadness, and agony? Seeing and changing one's role in it all is quite health-promoting, even essential. Owning one's role does not mean voluntarily wearing for life a label such as abusee or abuser, survivor or batterer, and victim or perpetrator. Labels are only labels and not who we are. (*The exception here might be in cases where perpetrators who are highly likely to perpetrate again, perhaps in new relationships, wear these labels to protect others who might become their next victims. Debate regarding this matter is left for other books.*)

Wearing these labels while working to understand and change them, or to leave them behind, is useful. Getting past these labels into entirely new roles and identities is not only moving on, not only healing, but also healthy living.

So, yes, identify one's own relationship to such labels, identify with such labels, as long as this helps to understand what has happened and to heal. Let no one take this process away. Then, when ready and able, move past these labels. For example, if one is a survivor of domestic violence, see this, know this, and deal with this—wear the label as long as it takes to heal, and then move on to new understandings of self and be proud of this progress.

CONSCIOUS RELATIONSHIPS

In the end, the goal here is to help enlighten us regarding what can take place in intimate partner and love relationships, and where even happy and high functioning patterns of relating can sometimes run into trouble. Through the process of examining our own and others' behaviors in relationships, and the ways that we can change our behaviors related to these relationships, we can raise the consciousness of ourselves, of our relationships, of the world around us, and of our children who very much need to see healthy relationships, healthy looking at problems within relationships, and intelligent, aware responses to social, psycho-logical, biological, and biochemical drives.

We *can* enter and maintain conscious relationships in which we do conscious relating to ourselves and each other. *This does not mean that we need endless hours processing and reprocessing infinite aspects of each and every detail and element of our relationships.*

This does mean that we choose to be involved consciously, to know what goes on in relationships, what healthy and unhealthy interactions look like, what unspoken and spoken contracts and promises we make, what various warning signs are, and what it takes to keep ourselves conscious of what we are doing with each other and ourselves.

CONSCIOUS RELATING TO OUR LOVED ONES AND OURSELVES

This book seeks to focus in on the process of **conscious relating**, on what it takes to be more aware of the often invisible, subtle levels of interactions taking place within interpersonal relationships. Conscious relating to these interactions requires close attention to both the spoken and the unspoken contracts we make with our intimate partners, and close attention to the relationship between our own subconscious and our own consciousness.

In the end, we are responsible for learning how to know and then knowing ourselves, and for managing our responses to what life has dealt us. The responsibility for recognizing, changing, overcoming, and or leaving intimate partner abuse and violence is upon us. This book offers a guide for this job. This guide encourages a deep and honest look at the specific interactions, and energy exchanges, taking place in our intimate partner relationships as this is the first and biggest step in recognizing and changing these relationships.

Each individual interaction on this planet mirrors a piece of the whole human story. Each interaction reflects in daily life a piece of the greater human strife and joy on this Earth. As large as the world's population is, it is made up of billions and billions of individual people in billions of interpersonal and intimate partner relationships, engaging in and often struggling with billions of dynamics, including billions of aspects of love and caring, and also billions of little and big physical and nonphysical abuses and violences against others and toward selves taking place each day, at least some of which are touched upon in this book.

Let's say for a moment that violence is cumulative and that all violence affects all humanity. Say that on some level, even if we prefer not to, even if we do not realize we are, we sense, feel, and hear pain of violence coming from the other side of the world. Then, any amount of violence hurts us all. Then, any amount of violence—even the slightest and most invisible—which we ourselves can put a stop to, we must stop.

Clearly there is a great deal of violence in this world. *For Knowing No Hurt No Harm* seeks to help bring about at least a momentary "aha"—to inspire a bit of hookup—to connect us to the larger picture. We can attune ourselves to, feel the link between, our personal and interpersonal behaviors, and those of the whole of humanity, and even of the whole of life on Earth. To achieve this sense of connection is a lofty goal, and readers are asked to contribute to this process, join in connecting the dots.

We can create a wave of change by starting at home, in our own inter-personal relations, modeling intelligent alternatives to abuse and violence. And it is never too late to begin the process of nonviolent relating. Any attention to this process which any one can give and share is much needed in this world.

Part One

2
For Knowing No Harm

Many partner, marriage, and dating relationships are truly absolutely wonderful. Many other relationships are indeed at least quite pleasant, quite worthwhile, handle the realities of life quite functionally, adapt successfully to most changes and challenges. Other relationships are less functional, perhaps somewhat functional yet emotionally and or physically distressing, some unsafe, even abusive. Some other relationships are definitely emotionally and or physically brutal.

Emotionally and physically abusive and brutal relationship experiences are complex. And they are riddled with difficult to recognize precursors, triggers, characteristics, motivations, and often with co-occurring issues.

The effects of troubled relationship experiences can last for a lifetime, sometimes even lifetimes when children and others around the relating are affected and the effects carry into generations. Frequently the abuse in relationships continues for far too long, sometimes throughout the life of the relationship itself, and sometimes even after the relationship has ended. Too many people are dealing with very difficult relationship experiences on an ongoing basis, their pain frequently hidden (hidden from others as well as from themselves).

The love relationship can and usually does bring great comfort, meaning, closeness, tenderness, identity, and many other positive aspects to life. For many, a loving relationship can be central in life, and can become a beautiful and fulfilling way of life.

However, the troubled relationship, which may or may not look like love to one or more members of the relationship, or to onlookers, can also become a way of life in itself. The troubled relationship tends to seek to sustain itself, to do what it takes to dominate processes and lives.

Many times, the drive of the troubled relationship to sustain itself as it is, as troubled, continues undetected.

In fact, many troubled relationships manage to look like good relationships, or at least "alright relationships." When we are caught in a troubled relationship, and have been caught for a while, we may adapt to it. We think things are "not so bad," "nothing to worry about," "worth it."

We think we feel the deep sorrow less and less over time. This adaptation to a troubled relationship is both an individual adaptation and a relationship adaptation. Quite often, this is also a whole family adaptation.

We think we have adapted to it, we think we feel the deep sorrow less. Oh, but we feel it, oh how we feel it. We, either consciously or subconsciously, try to bury awareness of the distress so deeply that we can pretend it is not right before us, there with us every single waking and sleeping moment. We avoid drawing our attention to what is really taking place, avoid asking the questions that might bring answers and awareness—and even safety.

Victims of, and perpetrators of, IPAVT are known to sometimes even avoid seeing bruises and cuts right before their eyes, sometimes even broken bones, avoiding admitting realities that are actually quite easy to see the source of under most conditions.

> Do we really believe we are
> truly ignoring what is truly going on?
> No.
> Are we able to see or sense on a deep level
> what is actually going on?
> Yes.
> Are there questions we indeed should be asking,
> yet avoid asking...
> <u>to avoid having to address</u>
> the violence and abuse taking place?
> Sometimes yes.

INTIMATE PARTNER VIOLENCE IS PREVALENT

Troubled intimate partner relationships can indeed hurt. In fact, in terms of actual physical pain, intimate partner violence results in millions of injuries and deaths around the world each year. And this is before adding on data estimates for countless unreported incidents as well as data for events not typically included in standard IPV definitions *(standard intimate partner violence by formal definitions not including the IPAVT defined in this book)*--such as types of partner rape and some other forms of sexual assault, and a range of abuses and terrors also not considered standard IPV.

These are not always considered events taking place between "intimate" "partners," and or not considered wrong enough, or violent enough to be classed as violent—and therefore these events are quite frequently not counted in standard IPV data.

Ultimately, given abused persons' general reluctance to report the abuse and violence, what the official data do say are vast understatements. Also note that persons, especially women, who have separated from their abusive partners often remain at risk of violence, sometimes even increased risk. However, much of this post partnership risk and perpetration data is not collected. Moreover, victims of violence and threatened violence repeated over time experience more serious short- and long term consequences than victims of one-time incidents and threats, yet these data tend not to be counted.

INCLUDES NONPHYSICAL FORMS

The "hurt" we are talking about has many dimensions. These dimensions also do include nonphysical types of abuse and violence which can be precursors to physical violence, or can be extremely hurtful, miserable, and destructive even in the absence of physical violence. These nonphysical forms of violence are common yet easily mislabeled and can be missed altogether. *For example, threatened violence especially when ongoing, is abuse, and is violence in itself, and is terrorizing.*

Whether threatened violence or another form of abuse, emotional abuse can be so subtle that even the participants do not realize it is taking place. And, where they do realize it, they may not see it clearly as emotional abuse or emotional violence. Emotional abuse wears so many faces and applies so many techniques. (See Chapters 18 and 19.)

Among numerous other forms of "non-violent" abuse is financial abuse, which can seem so natural to the participants that it remains unlabeled. Yet, just like other forms of abuse, the impacts of financial abuse can last for years, even a lifetime. (See Chapter 35.) These and other nonphysical abuses—*hidden violences*—must be recognized and addressed to heal from them and to halt them.

VIOLENCE CAN BE HABIT-FORMING

Here is something people avoid talking about: The many dimensions of violence also include the various degrees to which all forms of relationship abuse and violence can become *habitual*—can take on the characteristics of habits, perhaps even addictions.

Yes, violence can become a habit for the person abusing, who is sometimes described as the batterer or the perpetrator, and even sometimes for the person experiencing the violence, who can be lulled into, forced into, in some way *trapped in a pattern of cyclic abuse*. This "habituation" all too often grows into a habitual, cyclic, way of life for the couple and the family.

VIOLENCE CAN INTERCONNECT WITH OTHER PROBLEMS

Additionally, there are or can be numerous other interrelated, coexisting dimensions of what this book calls IPAVT which can include substance abuse, general anxiety and stress, forms of what is frequently termed PTSD (posttraumatic stress "disorder") and newly understood variations of this PTSD (see discussion in Chapter 39), other psychological conditions, as well as personal histories of abuse prior to the marriage or coupling.

These conditions, some of which are described as co-occurring "disorders," can be so intertwined with partner abuse and violence that it is unrealistic to see and to treat them as separate free-standing problems. Especially but not only in the overlap between substance abuse and intimate partner violence, there is ample evidence demonstrating significant co-occurrence.

There are those who prefer to separate these conditions, not to link these in any way. This is understandable because they want to prevent abusers "passing the buck" for their own violence, excusing their own violence based on other conditions, such as stress, mental illness, alcohol or drug use, or to having been abused as a child. The position against passing the buck is generally described as an *accountability* point of view which is formed to help persons doing the abusing take responsibility for their actions no matter what has contributed to them.

Indeed, this accountability is a noble approach, and persons abusing should be helped to, even expected to, take this responsibility no matter what contributes to their violence. Still, treating their violence without treating the co-occurring conditions is limiting the power of the work being done with and for persons who wish to stop their abusive behaviors.

QUESTION OF MUTUAL VIOLENCE

And then there is the question of *mutual aggression, mutual violence*. What is and is not mutual violence must be examined very carefully, as mutual violence is extremely complex. The old childhood passing of the buck, the "well, you started it" explanation, says very little about who, or which one, is actually at fault—or about whether two people, a few other people, an entire family or community, or no one at all, is at fault. And, the basic meaning of "at fault" is not at all adequately addressed by this "you asked for it" assertion.

The answer to the basic question implied here, the question which asks: *is there typically a dominant aggressor—*

someone who is clearly the initiator and primary enactor of the physical violence between these two intimate partners — is frequently debated. Each case has a different aggressor-victim profile. In fact, law enforcement officers, when arriving at the scene of domestic violence, frequently seek to determine who is the dominant aggressor and take action with regard to this individual. However, when there is not clarity about this, some will say (sometimes perhaps only for convenience' sake) that both members of the couple may be apprehended or at least treated as the primary violent ones, the mutual perpetrators.

Of course, while mutual aggression is quite common, there are countless variations that must be respected. For example, when partners shout or swear at each other, this may be, *may be or may not be,* mutual verbal or emotional abuse. *This in itself is not mutual physical abuse.*

And then, if one of these partners reacts by becoming physically violent against the other (before the other does, or if the other does not), this is *also not considered mutual physical violence.*

Certainly there are instances where the mutual aggression label is ap-propriate. However, too often, this label is used by the perpetrator of the violence (**and by those colluding with, and or defending, the perpetrator**) to obscure the reality that the violence is indeed coming from the dominant aggressor who is indeed the true perpetrator. We can hope that eventually increased awareness of the actual details and subtleties of intimate partner abuse and violence, and any related terrorizing (IPAV&T) will shed further light, revealing light, on the "games" that can be and are being "played" with this issue of dominant versus mutual aggression.

We can also *hope* that eventually we can be quite definite when there is indeed (or is not) a mutual aggressor situation. But what scientific advance will this take? Even when we do develop the ability to fully calibrate abuses and violences, the dividing line among these will likely remain: the first actual act of actual physical violence versus everything preceding this.

DANGEROUS
RESPONSE DELAY AND EXACERBATION

All this being said, there is a serious need for insight into cases of sudden extreme physical violence. Where a partner who is generally the abusee rather than the abuser abruptly grows highly, even shockingly violent against the partner, the history of the abuse and violence patterns in these persons' intimate partner relationship must be considered. While this person who has abruptly become extremely violent will likely be described as the dominant aggressor in this particular instance of violence, there may be a long history of this person being the actual abusee at the hands of the other partner, frequently being abused and or beaten, and or violated in other ways such as sexual forms of abuse and violence.

Always, the question of how much physical abuse and violence this person has experienced at the hands of the person (who is some-times indeed the actual abuser) suddenly now being abused must be taken into account.

Has the response to ongoing abuse been delayed? Has the delayed response been exacerbated by the delay itself, delay while the experience of being abused and violated has continued and perhaps even in-creased in level of danger?

Is there a dangerous backlog of response collected and buried deep within the mind of the person being repeatedly abused over time? Does this back-log perhaps magnify like money in the bank collecting interest?

Are there many instances where the person being abused simply did not respond, or fight back, yet did feel the drive to respond on some very deep, perhaps even subconscious level? Was this drive to respond suppressed, but not eliminated, and left to magnify perhaps? These are questions we must ask. (See Chapter 4 and Figure 4.1 for more on this.)

QUESTION OF COLLATERAL VIOLENCE AND ABUSE

A word here about what this book terms: ***collateral violence and abuse***. This is violence that is expressed by one partner against the other, or by both partners against each other—but indirectly and sometimes out of sight (sometimes unseen by the other partner perhaps, and or some-times unseen by the outside world). *In other words, a person doing the abusing may, instead of abusing the partner directly, abuse someone or something else, in order to threaten or cause fear, pain, expense, or harm of another sort, to the partner. This is abuse.*

Although the significance and gravity of what this books describes as collateral violence and abuse deserves far more attention than it gets among professionals and researchers, collateral violence and abuse is quite serious, and can be quite dangerous, damaging, sometimes fatal. While a separate book in this series specifically addressing this matter looks in depth at many forms of, and severe uses of, collateral abuse and violence, here it is important to simply note that this type of indirect partner abuse and violence indeed does exist.

LIST:
COLLATERAL IPAVT

This collateral abuse and violence includes but is not limited to threatened or actual, implied or explicit, abuse of and violence against:

Children, for example:
- Where children are purposefully or inadvertently neglected by one of both partners in a relationship as part of the overall partner ab-use scenario.
- Where children are purposefully or inadvertently verbally or emotionally abused by one of both partners in a relationship as part of the overall abuse scenario.
- Where children of a partner are abused as a way of implicitly abusing the other partner.
- Where children are used as human shields—thrown under the bus so to speak—in effort to ward off abuse of, or detection of abuse by, one or both partners.
- Where children are used in legal processes as trades or implicit trades for assets or other items.
- Where a parent anguishes over the abuse of her or his child by her or his partner and is not able to stop this let alone get help for this often well hidden, *obscured abuse*—while not able to prove this or be believed about this to outsiders or authorities such as the courts.
- Where a child is shown pornography or involved in pornographic filming, and related media by a parent or relative.
- Where a partner is committing child abuse including child sexual abuse.

- Where a partner is committing child sexual abuse and the other partner is explicitly or implicitly threatened with severe retaliation for exposure of this, or for even the possibility of exposure of this.
- Where child sexual abuse committed by one partner is taking place, and the other partner does not know yet experiences the related stresses and problems of the child and family.
- Where a partner threatens to win custody of a child as a form of abuse of the other partner.
- Where a partner threatens to or actually does take or kidnap a child.
- Where a child is forced to observe or know about other "secret" or threatened, or open abuses being performed against family members.

Parents, and or other family members, for example:
- Where all or any of the same, or similarly or equally abusive, behaviors listed above under the category, children, take place – against children, parents, or other family members.
- Where abuse of and or threats of this abuse are engaged in by a partner.
- Where elder abuse, and or abuse of a person with a disability, and or threats of this abuse are engaged in by a partner.
- Where a partner threatens the safety, well-being, or life of parents or other family members.
- Where parents and other family members are threatened with retaliation for trying to protect the abused partner (or child).

Friends, Neighbors, Community Members, and Co-workers, for example:

- Where all or any of the same, or similarly or equally abusive, behaviors listed above under the category, children, take place.
- Where abuse and or threats of this abuse are engaged in by a partner.
- Where a partner threatens the safety, well-being, or life of friends, neighbors, community members, co-workers, or others.
- Where friends, neighbors, community members, co-workers, and others are threatened with retaliation for trying to protect the abused partner (or child or family member).

Pets, for example:
- Where a partner threatens, steals, or actually directly abuses or kills a pet belonging to, or known by, the partner or family members.

Property, for example:
- Where a partner threatens or actually engages in the stealing, hiding, relabeling, withholding, devaluing, damaging, or destroying of property and assets belonging to or shared by the other partner or family members, friends, and or others around the relationship.

Earning power, etc., for example:
- Where a partner engages in harm to the other partner's career, work-life, etc. via messaging, information withholding or distorting, slanderous or similar reputation affecting activities, paycheck or money withholding—as well as interference with:

Partner's ability to keep a job, to perform on the job, to look good at work, to be at work on time, to utilize the paycheck earned, and so on (*with children, parents, and or others being abused in the same way as part of this scenario*).

COLLATERAL TERROR

The above is a list of just some of the many forms of collateral abuse and violence that may be present in IPAV&T situations. In reading this book, keep in mind that all too often actual, front and center, IPAV&T may be taking place alongside harder to see "background" collateral abuses, violences, and terrorizations. These may be subtle and even hidden abuses, however they are powerful and must be addressed for all involved.

Ultimately, most if not all forms of collateral abuse and violence can be and likely are terrorization of the partner and of all others involved.

TERRORIZATION AS ABUSE

Terrorization is the inflicting of fear of harm and or of actual harm, simply to inflict this fear and or actual harm, and or to *control, retaliate against, persuade, motivate, stifle, or suppress* someone via inflicting fear and or actual harm. Using and abusing children, family members, others, pets, incomes, and so on to control a partner is a common form of relatively indirect terrorization. That this is "indirect" terrorization is that this is done not directly to the abusee but to others around the abusee or to the abusee's property.

This indirect terrorization frequently has as intense and painful an im-pact as does direct terrorization. For example, when the abuser abuses the partner by abusing the child, this is as great if not greater a terrorization than is the direct beating or molesting or raping of that abusee.

Other forms of terrorization of a partner are somewhat more direct and are equally frightening and painful and therefore terror invoking. The fields addressing intimate partner violence must add this form of abuse to the lexicon and description of this violence and abuse: terror, both direct and indirect forms of terror.

3
Last Time Story

In the midst of a loud verbal argument, he yelled, "You stupid idiot, you know I'm right!" He raised his arm as if he would hit her if she did not agree.

She jumped back and yelled, "Don't you dare hit me, you look so stupid doing that!"

In that moment, as she was saying this, he leapt forward, right at her, swinging his arm as he did, this time hitting her in the face, tearing the skin to the side of her head near the eye, and leaving a red mark which would later become a black eye.

Stunned and flinching in pain, she fell to her knees, covering her eye, saying, "Stop! That's the last time you'll ever hit me!"

He grumbled back, "Oh yeah, who's going to stop me?"

"I'll call the police."

"No, you won't. You bitch, get up and go wash your face, it's bleeding all over the carpet. And then, clean this mess up. Or I'll kick you so hard you won't ever be the same."

"This is your fault, you do it," she said. But she finally cleaned it up anyway. She felt this was the safer option.

4
All About Intentions

What is overlooked in many instances, perhaps because it is difficult to determine (or sometimes because one or all of the involved parties prefer not to make it clear), is *intent*. Intent matters very much, yet it is largely misunderstood. Additionally, both actual and manufactured con-fusion—regarding the difference between conscious intent and unconscious intent—exists among onlookers and well as among those involved in the relationship violence.

**INTENT IS DIFFICULT TO DETERMINE
AND OFTEN DISGUISED**

How frequently we hear it said, "I did not mean to hurt you" and "it isn't my fault because I did it on impulse" and "you made me do it" and "I had no intention of knocking your tooth out when I raised my hand at you and hit you, that was an accident."

This and other passing off of responsibility for causing harm and injury is loaded with tricky, elusive, often devious deception—deception of others as well as *self deception*. Deception is used like a weapon although the true nature of the deception is typically hidden from awareness.

The utility of deception to the person deceiving is profound. Lies can be camouflaged in its mazes. A sea of confusion can be pulled in, drowning both the abuser and the abusee in the lies. Basically, deception confuses everyone around abuse.

Persons abusing and then choosing to deceive about their abusing sometimes invest in their lies, in their denial of the abuse they have perpetrated, until they themselves are so very convinced of their own innocence that they have reconstructed—even reconstituted—them-selves as victims (see Chapter 23). Examples of this sort of ***illusion-constructing around abuse*** can be found in families, communities, and even in the courts.

The tables can be turned, sometimes in a split second, with the abusee suddenly and convincingly recast as the abuser, and vice versa. This is where persons around persons who abuse (such as spouses, partners, family members, friends, colleagues, therapists, medical doctors, attorneys, courts) may be unwittingly (largely unwittingly) pulled into colluding with abusers who make this sort of choice—to turn the tables against the true victim, to do this to deny, strike down, the abuse charges against them.

These persons who abuse may do everything to deny that they abuse, be very skilled at doing this, and succeed in pulling others into believing and even supporting their lies. The credibility of the person being abused is then called into question, the integrity of the person who originally reported the abuse is attacked, a tactic frequently seen in court-room strategies. Truth becomes a game or a strategy rather than a reality. A crafty abuser can actually extend the abuse of the partner right into the courtroom, at times even managing to engage some attorneys and judges as colluders.

**Deception itself is deceiving
and unfortunately
can be a useful tool.**

There are areas that are so very difficult to unravel that they are flat out avoided for convenience and simplicity's sake as well as for reasons involving *fear of truth*. Even avoidance or muddling of truth for the sake of simplicity is all too common. Questions such as these can be both ignored and played out by all involved:

> Where is the line between intent and mistake?
>
> Who defines this line, and who should be defining this line?
>
> What should we require of those we expect to define this line?
>
> When does the subconscious mind accommodate its conscious lies by calling certain actions only mistakes, not intentional abuse?
>
> When does the mind fool itself about the use of violence when angry?
>
> How does the abuser find support for the blurring of the truth?
>
> Isn't the abuser's purposeful blurring of the truth itself abuse?

LINES BETWEEN INTENT AND IMPULSE

These are important but difficult questions that require honest answers (where answers are possible). Yet, when it comes to violence, the lines between intent and impulse, and also between intent and mistake, are blurry, and there is significant overlap (see Figure 4.2).

Even in courts of law, these things are not exceedingly clear. Consider the legal concept, *mens rea*, which refers to the mental state when committing a crime. A great deal of debate takes place in courts of law regarding the state of mind a person who committed a crime was in when committing it. Four basic mental states are considered in asking—was this crime committed: intentionally, knowingly, recklessly, or negligently.

At first glance, answers to this question may seem obvious. After all, the person either meant to do it or did not. The assumption is that it is possible to determine whether or not the person who committed the crime knew what he or she was doing and meant to do it. Again, was the crime committed: intentionally, knowingly, recklessly, or negligently. And will the perpetrator of the abuse be honest here?

Where, even in a court of law, intent is debated heavily, the court of the mind is murkier than the letter of judicial law would like it to be. From a psychological standpoint, the overlap among and between these areas of intent can tend to blur the distinctions so much that they cannot be separated successfully.

We might like to say: Of course human beings have developed to a point where it should be relatively easy to make a distinction between willful action and mistake. We know the difference, right? We must ask our-selves questions like this.

How many times have we stepped on someone else's toe by mistake? This is neither impulse violence nor premeditated violence—this is almost always simply a mistake or clumsy error. We know this. (We still care about the toe, still would like to provide assistance with the pain.) What about other injurious acts? What can we take responsibility for and what can we realistically deny responsibility for? Could it be that we should even accept responsibility for our mistakes? (Yes?)

These are complex questions further made blurry by the role of the conscious, subconscious, and unconscious mind in influencing and directing actions people take. On the one hand, there is a range of intent, say intent to commit violence, which is rather obvious, running something like this:

accidental violence→impulse violence→
→purposeful violence→planned violence

And, on the other hand, there is a range of degree of consciousness in action such as this:

unintentional→subconscious intent→
→conscious intent→planned conscious intent

We could draw these as overlapping fields (as in Figure 4.2) or we could graph these two ranges against each other and find actions scattered all over this graph (as in Figure 4.3).

VIOLENCE AS A DEFENSIVE RESPONSE

Typically, but not always, even if both resort to physical violence, one of the partners initiates it, strikes first. Explanations for why this violence was initiated first or at all vary and can differ from each of the partners and from witnesses (if any). Quite often, impulse is the explanation whether or not this is what is said to explain the violence. Impulse war-rants close attention here as sometimes impulse violence is definitely assault and other times impulse violence is something else.

Immediate impulse driven action which may include violence is one of the natural responses to actual and perceived as being actual danger. This response is most frequently described in terms of the "fight or flight" reflex.

Fight or flight is an instinctive response to a situation which requires immediate action—for actual or presumed survival rea-sons.

Fight or flight says: when escaping or simply getting out of a dangerous predicament is not perceived as an option, then fighting back is another response which is available. An animal trapped in a corner, seeing no way to escape a predator, will likely attack the predator.

What other option is there? Perhaps rolling over and playing dead? (Playing dead can be called the "freeze" response, and is almost as com-mon as fight or flight. Freezing is an attempt to hide, blend in, be undetected or not seen, camouflage for safety.) Instinct of course does not require that the animal stop to think the options through.

This ancient fight or flight (or freeze) reflex snaps into place on the spot by means of a **biochemical automatic rapid response system** we carry with us at all times. Biology speaks. (However this biological rapid response system does not always function appropriately or at all for that matter. See the subsection below on **suppressed response** for more on this matter.)

However consistently well it functions, the fight or flight reflex can be and sometimes is an ingredient in intimate partner violence. For ex-ample, during a heated argument, one of the partners may read danger with no escape in the situation, and whether or not this no escape is truly there, allow him or herself to snap (or simply be unable to stop him or herself from snapping) into immediate violent action.

Of course, quite frequently, one of the partners does not "initiate" the violence yet the other one does while using something---something about the other partner's appearance, tone, gesture, or mood, to excuse (or explain, or allow) responding with violence.

However, this using of something to excuse something else is not always purposeful or conscious during the violent event. All too often, excusing the violence takes place after the event, sometimes even in the court-room. Of course, there are also many cases where the perpetrator of the violence does excuse the violence even as it is being perpetrated in a "you asked for it" or "what choice do I have here" sort of assertion.

Now, look a little more closely at the arguing couple. The two of them are arguing, growing louder and angrier by the minute, and gesturing more and more adamantly as they proceed. Suddenly, one gesture one of them makes is seen (or used) by the other as escalation. In this moment, a threat is picked up (or a threat is said to be taking place), and physical danger seems (or is said to be) imminent.

A split second into seeing or sensing this (or pretending to sense this), sometimes without thinking about it at all, reflex may kick in. This person may suddenly perceive this gesturing as threatening and meaning:

Danger!

Now!

Reacting to seeming (or what is claimed to be) immediate physical danger, even perhaps as this danger is manifesting into a real attack, perhaps as it is not, this person swings first.

Now it IS physical.

**Yet now the
first strike is perhaps ambiguous.**

NUANCES OF
SUPPRESSED FIGHT OR FLIGHT RESPONSE

As noted in the Chapter 2 (subsection titled, *Dangerous Response Delay and Exacerbation*), we must consider a largely unaddressed yet quite critical condition in which relationship violence can occur. Note also here the discussion immediately above regarding the fight or flight reflex. Now consider the possibility that there may be instances or cases where this reflex does not fully or effectively function in a timely manner—or does not function at all.

Various other mechanisms can intercede or even block this precious fight or flight reflex. Consider the chart in Figure 4.1. offering examples of where there appears no fight or flight response to potential or actual danger or harm. In this chart, either the flight function is confused or overridden, or the fight function is. These particular victims of this violence either:

- do not realize they are in danger:
- do not see that getting away is NEEDED, or
- do not feel it is WISE to get away from this danger, or
- do not feel SAFE trying to get away from this danger, or
- do not feel that getting away from this danger is POSSIBLE.

For a range of reasons the ability to take flight, to get away from potential or actual danger is thwarted or stalled or blocked by INability to see the NEED to get away, or to see that getting away is WISE, SAFE and or POSSIBLE. Persons who have been abused in extreme ways, or in psychologically repressing or distorting ways, may accept this abuse in these ways.

However, the abuse is indeed being experienced whether or not it is acknowledged consciously. After a while, in ongoing abuse situations, where the victim of this abuse represses or does not tap into the fight or flight reflex, *deep neural memories* of experiencing this abuse and violence can be stored. It may be never or quite a while later when suddenly, unexpectedly, not necessarily logically, the person being abused releases a *mountain of repressed fight or flight responses* and, to speak in common terms, suddenly "loses it" and becomes quite violent with self or others.

To outsiders who have no idea what the mind of this abused person has stockpiled as it has found no previous outlet, this abrupt and often wild behavior is shocking and appalling. Suddenly, the long time and severely abused person appears to outsiders to be the abuser. *Now the abusee's mountain of stockpiled rage and self defense response is seemingly being (to onlookers) ignited for no fair reason.*

Now the person being abused grows abruptly and perhaps virtually uncontrollably violent, releasing a great deal of *pent up impulse response*, all that suppressed and or blocked fight or flight—that backlog of unexpressed yet present somewhere response.

In the particular instance where such an abusee suddenly and fiercely abuses, the abusee is suddenly committing first strike in so far as onlookers may discern.

However this is the long withheld response to the other partner's first strikes....

THERE IS DEFINITE POTENTIAL OR ACTUAL PHYSICAL DANGER, HARM, YET....	FLIGHT does not appear to be NEEDED	FLIGHT does not appear to be WISE	FLIGHT does not appear to be SAFE	FLIGHT does not appear to be POSSIBLE
FIGHT does not appear to be NEEDED	Fight does not appear to be NEEDED, while flight does not appear NEEDED—are these two perceptions interfering with each other?	Fight does not appear to be NEEDED, while flight does not appear WISE—are these two perceptions interfering with each other?	Fight does not appear to be NEEDED, while flight does not appear SAFE—are these two perceptions interfering with each other?	Fight does not appear to be NEEDED, while flight does not appear POSSIBLE—are these two perceptions interfering with each other?
FIGHT does not appear to be WISE	Fight does not appear to be WISE, while flight does not appear NEEDED—are these two perceptions interfering with each other?	Fight does not appear to be WISE, while flight does not appear WISE—are these two perceptions interfering with each other?	Fight does not appear to be WISE, while flight does not appear SAFE—are these two perceptions interfering with each other?	Fight does not appear to be WISE, while flight does not appear POSSIBLE—are these two perceptions interfering with each other?
FIGHT does not appear to be SAFE	Fight does not appear to be SAFE, while flight does not appear NEEDED—are these two perceptions interfering with each other?	Fight does not appear to be SAFE, while flight does not appear WISE—are these two perceptions interfering with each other?	Fight does not appear to be SAFE, while flight does not appear SAFE—are these two perceptions interfering with each other?	Fight does not appear to be SAFE, while flight does not appear POSSIBLE—are these two perceptions interfering with each other?
FIGHT does not appear to be POSSIBLE	Fight does not appear to be POSSIBLE, while flight does not appear NEEDED—are these two perceptions interfering with each other?	Fight does not appear to be POSSIBLE, while flight does not appear WISE—are these two perceptions interfering with each other?	Fight does not appear to be POSSIBLE, while flight does not appear SAFE—are these two perceptions interfering with each other?	Fight does not appear to be POSSIBLE, while flight does not appear POSSIBLE—are these two perceptions interfering with each other?

Figure 4.1. Examples of possibly suppressed fight or flight response.

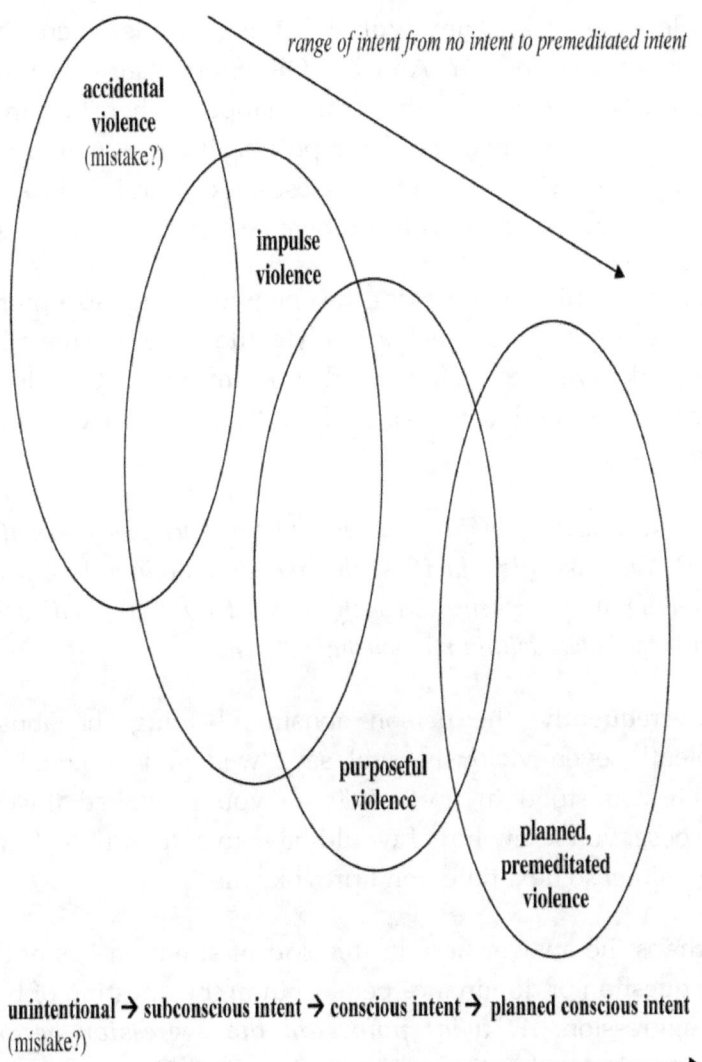

Figure 4.2. Blurry spectrum of partner violence intent.

VIOLENCE IS LIKE AN ONION

But let's go back to any typical fighting couple. There they go again. On and on. And on. OK. Stop. Pause the tape. Freeze. No one move. What really happened here? Chances are each of these persons will report a different sequence of events, a different sequence of escalation, and a different primary aggressor. Will one of them be lying?

Was the dominant aggressor the one who shifted to a highly threatening gesture which actually could have become a hit, or could have become perceived as a coming hit? Or was the one who responded reflexively by hitting first the dominant aggressor?

Does their history of first strikes and previous violence matter here? **Yes, as this clarifies the pattern.** *Seeing the pattern preceding an event helps to clarify it. Most if not all relationship events take place within relationship patterns.*

Too frequently, the person abusing, beating the abusee violently even viciously, will say "well you shouted" or "well you stood in my way" or "you provoked this on purpose, you knew how I would have to respond" or "I'm a big animal so next time don't provoke me."

Perhaps the answer here in this sort of situation lies not in the question of dominance per se, but in the question of type of aggression. *At what point did the aggression become physical?* At the time of the first hit? Or of the first seemingly threatening physical gesture? Is there a point where the gestures or the body language of one or both became truly physically threatening? *(Or, is there a moment when one of the partners **pretends** that the other partner is threatening?)* Again, it does help to ask:

Is there a history here, one of threatened and actual violence and first strikes, a pattern which would explain more?

And what about situations where one partner is more physically capable than the other? Does the partner who can dominate simply by being physically stronger become the actual or implied dominant aggressor al-most naturally amidst conflict or leading up to conflict?

How does this play out when both partners are waving hands and shouting at each other while both know that one is physically more dangerous, or at least stronger and therefore dominant? Clearly, physical dominance brings with it a natural albeit largely implied physical power.

But stop. Roll the tape back again.

Can we get into the minds of members of this relationship to see precisely where the violence actually originated? How fine should our unit of analysis be? How much detail do we want to see? How far back, and back to what, do we go?

Where is the truth hiding? If we continue peeling the layers back, we find more layers. Intimate partner violence is so very layered, its true origins may truly elude us. This complexity and layering make it easy for lies about intent to be believed!

This mix of complexity and layering make it easy for a dominant aggressor to blame the person being abused for the aggression. What a place to hide truth—in the maze of complexity and layering.

**VIOLENCE AND
IMPLIED VIOLENCE FOR DOMINANCE**

Now, let's come at this another way. Let's consider the circumstance where an individual feels—or senses—that his or her **control over and power within** the relationship is being threatened. Assume for a moment that this circumstance involves no threatening gestures or suggestions that actual physical violence is in the wings. *Just see this as a perceived threat to one's dominance—where the ego, or the control over the relationship (or the power one has within the relationship) —is seen as being challenged, eroded, curtailed.*

Sometimes challenges are felt by simple shifts away from a partner's usual or traditional behavior. In a long term (or even a short term where patterns are already instilled) relationship, sometimes one partner changes. This sometimes upsets the unspoken founding contract that apparently "said" that this partner would never change (or change much). Even when this change is personal growth or success, this may be felt to be a breaking of the contract, of the foundation of the relationship. This may even be seen—or not seen consciously but experienced on some level—*as betrayal.*

Let's say a relationship began with one of the partners having more say in decisions. This may have been because one partner was older or had more experience, or made more money. Or it could have been that one partner was a stronger or more confident personality in some way.

There are countless reasons for power distribution arrangements in relationships, many of these reasonable. However there are times when the power distribution is abused by one or both partners.

Let's roll the tape back again. See again: The two of them are arguing, growing louder and angrier by the minute, and gesturing more and more adamantly as they proceed. Suddenly, one comment one of them makes is seen (or used) by the other as escalation. In this moment, a threat is picked up, and some kind of danger seems (or is said to be) imminent. This situation can indeed bring out a fight response. However, quite often something else is being threatened, something other than physical safety.

The danger is now one which threatens to upset the balance of power, or the desired balance of power, in the relationship. Something is said or done that appears to challenge the dominant person's view of his or her right to this dominance and his or her security that this dominance will continue. Something triggers in this person a show of force.

So, is this show of force unintentional, impulsive, or purposeful? Should we call this **unintentional** violence? If this is violence as a defensive response, is this violence defending something which should be defended at all, let alone violently?

Now, there are times when violence (or threatened violence) is consciously—intentionally—resorted to, or applied, to exert, maintain, or demonstrate dominance in a given situation or conflict. Persons exerting violence to maintain power and control over a situation (and or over a person) find no other way to do so. Or they find violence the most certain way to do so.

After all, a vote or a clear conversation about who wants what may not result in what the dominant partner wants. The dominant partner frequently wants to hold onto dominance.

Still, even perpetrators of this sort of violence tend to say that their violence—if they admit to it at all—is impulsive, out of their control. They may go ahead and label this as an impulsive and defensive response (a situation which is further discussed in Chapter 23).

WHEN DEFENDING PRESUMED POWER

Even when the violence is not planned in advance, when it is impulse violence, the use of violence to maintain or gain dominance is rarely entirely impulsive. This is because violence is both physical and nonphysical; violence exists along a continuum (as noted earlier).

This continuum includes many nonphysical violences that are frequently substitutes for, and even precursors of, physical violence. Many elements of violence and abuse are subtle, confusing, sometimes <u>purposefully hidden</u> for the various reasons discussed in this book. These behaviors must be watched by members of the relationship so as to avoid the effects of violence and abuse growing ever more serious.

There is a spoken and also oft unspoken assumption that the use of vio-lence has a "reason" and that this reason is either *self-protection* or *control and dominance over another person*—or both when what is being protected is the abuser's self-defined...

**Entitlement to
power and control, dominance
over the partner.**

Indeed, this is frequently the case. There is usually some form of power (or perceived power) to be acquired (or protected, or regained) by threatening or actually using violence.

THE NEED FOR POWER

This "need" for power in a relationship warrants a whole discussion of its own. In this book, this matter will be addressed as part of several related discussions. Basically, the desire of one partner—or sometimes but less often of both partners—for one-sided power and dominance can drive violence in troubled relationships. Some will even claim that actual efforts to gain dominance—*and or to protect dominance already gained*—are driven by instinct even when the power and control is registering in the conscious mind.

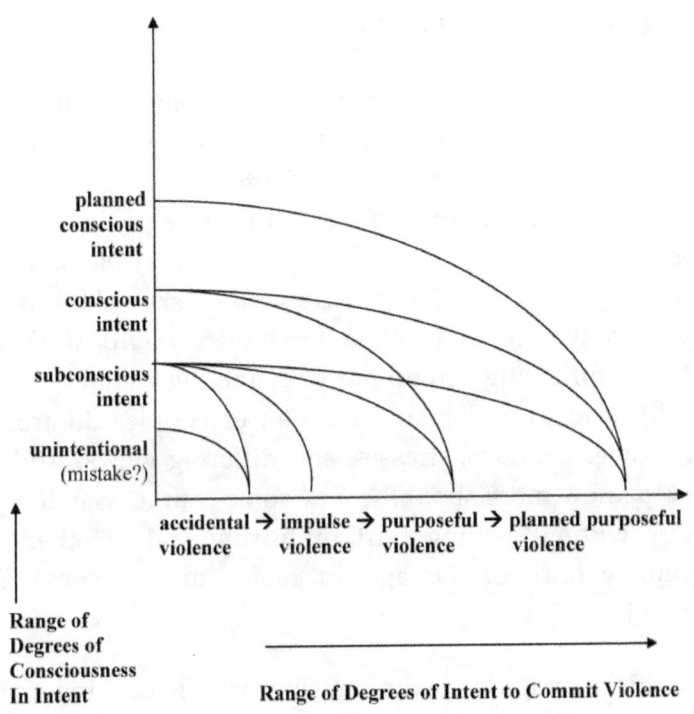

Figure 4.3. Graph of two ranges of intent.

Some will claim that they have a right to the power they seek to acquire via the application of force. This "right" as it is sometimes called is explained in various ways reflecting interpretations of and differences in upbringing, tradition, belief system, faith leader teachings, cultural views of women and men and gender roles, law and policy, and more.

TWO FACES OF VIOLENCE

Intent here can be seen both ways: the abuser's intent and the abusee's intent. Abusee? Does this suggest that the victim intends in any way to be victimized? No. **We do not want to blame victims of violence for experiencing the violence.** This sort of unfair, unjust, and cruel blame is too frequently heard about rape (as per the "she asked for it" excuse), and also about other forms of *boundary violation (VIO-lation)*. Being careful not to blame the victim here, we still do want to understand the dances couples do around their power conflicts, stresses, and differing views. And we want to know more about the way some couples can do their dances without getting hurt or hurting, while others do eventually hurt, or damage, or maim, and or sometimes even kill.

And this damaging, maiming, and killing can indeed be either physical or nonphysical—can be varying aspects and forms of damage, injury, and death. This damaging can truly affect, in the short and the long term, health, body, mind, and spirit, whether or not the physical body explicitly shows this. In this sense, given that the nonphysical aspects of violence and abuse tend to be overlooked and denied, the *invisible* injuries (and costs of those injuries) relationship abuse and violence can bring are perhaps the most insidious and difficult to address.

An entire treatise could be written (as a later book in this series does write) regarding the *invisible—unseen, sometimes denied, other times not recognized by any party*—effects and injuries inflicted or generated by relationship abuse and violence. Here, this book will return several times to this matter, always with the following proviso or caveat: Many abuses and violences immediately or eventually result in one or both of these:

(1) obvious and distinct physical and emotional effects with some of these effects being injuries; and
(2) subtle and oft hidden effects with some of these effects being physical and emotional injuries.

INTENTS OF PARTNER ABUSE AND VIOLENCE

We who have been, are, or will be, members of an intimate partner relationship do well to ask ourselves some of these challenging questions, questions we may tend to avoid. Among these questions is another tough one: what elements of a sort of (what this book calls) emotional sadomasochism (with or without parallel emotional masochism)—or of some form of agreement to allow one member of the couple to intentionally cause hurt (and the other to receive it)—are present or potentially present in the relationship being considered? These are difficult questions, even troubling. (See Chapter 33.)

How can anyone even imagine that the victim of abuse is somehow complicit in inflicting the partner's abuse upon her or himself? Who would intend to do such a thing to her or himself?

QUESTIONS TO ASK ABOUT INTENT

Clearly, intention is a touchy topic here. We must ask:

- Who intends to even sometimes, maybe only once in a while, hurt someone else?
- Who intends to allow someone else to hurt her or himself?
- Who intends to actually hurt her or himself let alone anyone else? Who?
- And who could take pleasure in, or feel rewarded in some way by, hurting another?
- And who could take pleasure in, or feel rewarded in some way by, hurting her or himself? Who?

Daring to ask might give us answers that would help identify dangers before they surface, emerging streams of inclinations, tendencies, vulnerabilities, and dangers.

INVESTMENT IN PARTNER VIOLENCE

Another related and touchy, even unasked, question is this: Is there the possibility that one or both members of the couple may, unknowingly or even consciously, become addicted to a pattern of emotional sadomasochism, or to the adrenalin rush this behavior may invite, or to the emotional/sexual pleasure it may bring on during the acts it involves or after these acts (such as during the makeup sex). We must dare to seek the truths we tend to deny about troubled relationships. (Again, see Chapter 33.)

Now we must ask: *What emotional investment, no matter how potentially self-destructive, do one or both members of the couple (either knowingly or unknowingly) have in the behavioral patterning of the troubled relationship?* Is the pattern the couple is caught in one that carries hid-den rewards such as flowers, hugs, gifts, and sex during make-ups?

REQUIRES A DEEP HONEST LOOK

Key to preventing and or healing abusive relationships is a deep, honest, and unique understanding of the dynamics, not just of abusive relationships, and of habitually abusive relationships, but also of all intimate partner relationships. What elements—or at least traces—of all the above and more are found in both healthy and troubled relationships? (Many relationships do function well and keep these traces at bay.)

What spoken and unspoken contracts addressing these elements are made? What contracts should be made? What contracts are broken? What contracts break themselves? And what contracts are only imagined in the first place? How clear can we be on all this?

And, what about trust—is trust relevant here? How important is trust in successful relationships? Does trust slip into the background, and even dissolve away, in hurting relationships?

Could it be that in some instances troubled partners reach a point where they trust each other, yes, but trust each other to play out the troubled roles they have defined for each other—even when these roles are sad, painful, and dangerous? These are instances of investment in the troubled pattern. (See Chapters 27, 29, and 31.)

Let's explore these and other questions in the following chapters where these roles and some of their troubled interactions are slowed to see them.

5
What About Consent

Welcome to the wilderness of human behavior. Here, we can find great wonderment and joy.

Yet here, in some, not many but some, relationships, we may find perils and monsters lurking in the shadows: anxieties and fears, risks and dangers. And yet, we may say yes, I'm staying.

CONSENT IS MISUNDERSTOOD

If getting at intent is challenging, add in the matter of consent and find a wilderness of human behavior to wade through. When a person who abuses claims not to mean it, or that the person being abused "wants it," what on Earth can this mean? Frequently, this means simply that the person abusing wants to place blame on someone else for the abusive behavior. Sometimes this means that the person doing the abusing did not recognize the abuse as abuse as the other party *seemed to be* participating in the situation, the game, the interaction, with full consent. Seemed to be. Seemed?

All too often, persons being abused who attempt to bring their cases to court are told, "You stayed, so you were consenting" and "You clearly are smart enough to leave if you were being abused, so clearly you were not being abused. THEREFORE YOUR CLAIMS ARE FALSE."

ENABLING THE ABUSE OF CONSENT

In love, sex, and related human behaviors, consent is one of the most misunderstood elements of interactions. Consent is generally defined as agreeing voluntarily, giving permission. Let's stop right here. What a loaded definition this is! First take each word separately: "agreeing," "voluntarily," "giving," "permission."

Agreeing can take many forms, and agreements can be clear and or vague (and or in reality nonexistent). We have all heard the teaching offered to teenagers facing sexual activity early in their lives: "no means no." Yet how often "no" is misunderstood for yes, by both the person being told "no" and yes, sometimes even by the person saying "no." Both parties must understand that no means no and that is that.

What does this messy use of the word "no" do to the act of agreeing? And what does this do to the act of agreeing *voluntarily*? There is nothing voluntary about being forced to do something and this is, of course, simple to understand. *Yet, there are degrees of force, and sources of force.*

For example, someone forcing someone else to engage in sex against her or his will is committing rape. *This is crossing boundaries without per-mission. This is indeed boundary crossing, however quite frequently this is not viewed this way.* Yet, what about social or emotional pressure to do something, including engage in sex, against one's will? Is this force, and if so, is this rape? Again, the law may rightly have distinct categories for these behaviors, and yet these may be far more complex than law may allow. There is no limit to the shades of agreeing voluntarily, and to the misuse of these shades when blaming the victim.

The infinite shades and nuances of consent and non-consent are always at work in human interactions, especially in intimate partner, significant other, dating, and similar relationships.

Now, add in the confusion about "giving permission." "Giving" itself is often misunderstood. How many times do we hear a dialog like this? "Hey, that's mine!" "No, it isn't, you gave it to me." How many times is the act of giving entirely misunderstood by both the receiving party and the giving party?

And what is this thing we call permission? Having permission is generally defined as being allowed to do something, having authorization to do it. This suggests (assumes) that the person giving per-mission is able enough and free enough to consciously allow a behavior, and freely authorizes this behavior. This also suggests (assumes) that the person consenting is informed enough, mature enough, healthy enough, and *safe enough*, to freely give conscious consent.

Now that we have this matter of consent on the table, let's serve it up with intent. How might all this play out in an abusive situation? Does the person being abused give some form of consent—even if it is unspoken consent—to the abuse? Or is this simply a bizarre and cruel distortion of what is taking or has taken place claimed by some persons who are abusing—or who are defending abusers?

Does and could the person abusing abuse with intent to respond to un-spoken yet *assumed consent*? This sounds odd, wrong, and yet this interpretation of behavior—somehow thinking (or at least saying) that consent has been given by the other person, the partner—might be sometimes taken, at least subconsciously (and or consciously yet dishonestly), as permission to abuse.

Yet, "permission to abuse me" is rarely given in words if given at all. The notion that there is such a thing as consensual violence—where one person beats another with that another's permission—is questionable. How often do we hear people directly tell their abusers "please beat me up," or "please hurt me for me." (A later chapter in this book discusses less common yet also important to consider emotionally sadomasochistic relationships.)

PRETENDED CONFUSION

We must look for ways we can get past the confusion in relationships where abuse and violence is taking place. We must also look for ways we can get around the **pretended confusion** in some of these relationships. *Too often, a person being abused is told by a person doing the abusing that the abuse was agreed to therefore it was not abuse. Too often, the person being abused succumbs to the view of the abuser and at least subtly agrees (possibly out of fear or confusion---and or desire for safety or love): "Yes, I said it was alright to beat me" or "Yes, I asked for it. My being beaten is my fault."*

Let's dig a bit deeper into the muddle we call consent. Explicit consent is generally viewed as being expressed directly by means of spoken or written agreement. Implied consent is somewhat more obscure, as it is generally viewed as being expressed indirectly, through actions or behaviors that give the suggestion or appearance of consent. Implied consent is risky.

In instances of implied consent, partners should seek clear, explicit, actual mutual consent after dialoging about what this actually means. *If all parties belonging to the intimate partner relationship have not fully, clearly, and explicitly consented to something, then full consent has not been given for that something.*

The complexity and elusive nature of abuse and violence in relationships is manifested in issues of intent and consent. So let's step back here and look from another angle at this animal—this life form—we call the intimate partner relationship....

6
Power Difference Story

When she married John twenty years ago, Cathy had no idea what her future held. She and John were in love.

From the start, there appeared to be an "almost charming" power difference (and power differential, although the differential aspect which included shifting power issues over time was not understood yet). This power difference seemed to be the result of Cathy being significantly younger than John, as well as earlier in her career.

As the years progressed and they had children, the choices they made tended to be in support of John's career as his earning power was higher than Cathy's. And, his earning power remained higher for various reasons including choices not to relocate for Cathy's career; to have Cathy stay at home with the children when they were young; to have Cathy put her career second to John's and the family; and to not look closely at what was taking place all along the way. All this made sense to John and Cathy. They believed in nurturing the family and closely attending to the children while having which ever parent could bring home the largest paycheck out more hours earning that paycheck.

What did not make sense, and was never discussed between them during the first decade of their marriage, was the emerging of abuse and violence in their relationship. At first, this violence was sporadic, but over time it grew habitual and responded to triggers very much like substance (e.g., alcohol, drug, and nicotine) addiction can.

Looking back much later (and extending the understanding of physical violence to verbal and gestured threats of violence, damaging of items or pets around or near a person, and light pushing and shoving during arguments), neither Cathy nor John can recall the first time the violence took place.

Yet, in increments, the violence escalated, and Cathy suffered several injuries along the way, all of which she told her friends and family were the result of falls and her lack of coordination. She and John both hid the truth about the domestic violence from others and from themselves.

The problem grew worse and Cathy's injuries more extreme. Neighbors, friends, and relatives were increasingly suspicious, and at least some eventually certain, that there was a problem. Eventually, Cathy and John were unable to hide what was happening from their children, who had actually known all along.

Cathy herself, some fourteen years into the marriage, began calling the police about John's violence. However, when the police would arrive, Cathy would be afraid of both social stigma and John's retribution and would say it had been a prowler. The more often Cathy said this to the police, the more they questioned her credibility.

Of course, right to the end—when John had broken Cathy's arm, bruised and cut her face so much she could not cover it up with makeup, knocked out her tooth, and split her lip—when Cathy finally realized John actually could someday kill her and therefore moved out—there were times when John was not only apologetic but even romantic. He loved Cathy very much, she was everything to him, he continued to tell her.

Cathy, who had gone into the marriage with the strong belief that this was a lifelong commitment, was reluctant to leave, yet, when she finally did, she did not want to go back. She actually felt safe for the first time in almost two decades. Yet, this safety was not long lived, as John began stalking her and intruding without warning into her new residence, claiming to desperately miss her and the children.

Eventually, Cathy turned to the court to get restraining orders keeping John away. The entire process was heart breaking as she loved John very much. Furthermore, the children, now older but still wanting the family intact, were also broken hearted.

Yet, once away from it long enough to see clearly, Cathy realized how much she wanted to stop being verbally abused and threatened, hit, and beaten. Only when she was out of the marriage did she realize how very much she wanted her freedom from this troubled relationship, and from whatever her part was in her having continued to suffer its painful and dangerous patterns.

The problem was that Cathy felt more in danger now . . . .

7
Precious Time

You wait to make a change. Wait for the strength, or for a sign, or for the way to change. Wait and wait and wait. But there seems to be no right time. And there seems to be no time to change the way you relate to each other. Years race by, and then years are gone.

It has been said time and again: It is very important with whom you choose to spend the time of your life.

TIME PASSES NO MATTER WHAT

Yes, it is very important, and who would say otherwise. Of few things we are certain, and one of these things is that time passes. Before we know it, days, weeks, months, years, and even decades have sped by like grains of sand slipping through our fingers.

This is a message, the importance of which is difficult to express to the young for whom time may seem abundant. It is typically only after many many years that the gravity of this message is felt. Looking back is easy enough to do. We see so much more with 20-20 hindsight, yet do we actually know so much more after the fact?

What could we do differently if we could turn back the hands of time? Anything? Anything at all? Yes, do more conscious relating.

CAN WE CHOOSE CAREFULLY

Taking care to choose carefully who we spend the time of our lives with…. This is not a very profound concept; in fact, at first glance, this makes complete sense. Of course we are careful about who we choose to spend our precious time with! Yes?

Yet, in the early stages of relationships, especially when we are young, such a question is not only considered to be irrelevant but also inconvenient, even intrusive. Especially when physical sexual attraction is mingled with the emotion we tend to call "in love," our emotional and physical biochemistries color any discussion of the importance of how we choose a partner.

"Don't bother me with such a downer, with such a silly concept. If I weren't very much wanting to spend the time of my life with this person—to spend every second I possibly can with this person—this person I AM IN LOVE WITH—then of course I wouldn't, duh."

And then, if the relationship flowers into the commitments it can bring—marriage, family, and all that goes with it—these signal to the outside world (such as friends, extended family, neighbors, co-workers, the boss)—that what is good to think about is being thought about.

Of course, for the few who then form troubled relationships, thinking about all this may be after the fact, a little bit late to be considering carefully who you want to spend the time of your life with. You're already spending it! You're right in the middle of the process! The few who then find they need to make a change learn that any unraveling of this commitment takes work and often can mean divorce. Divorce itself can be emotionally, physically, and financially costly for the couple as well as for others nearby, such as the children. Yet for some there is no choice.

For many, there are choices every step of the way through staying and staying over time.

And of course, many years, even decades, into the process, long after the kids are grown, long after the first grandchild has been born, when you are finally able to look back and realize how very important it is to think carefully about who you spend the time of your life with, you have already done it—or tried. Precious years have gone by. So make these years good.

Might there be another process which could allow for greater care in selection? We must ask....

Our grandparents and great grandparents, and or other ancestors, may have said so and may even have wanted a say in choosing our mates. This procedure may have guaranteed happiness somewhat more than the mail order bride process. But can it work in our rapidly changing times? Probably not in most cases.

Still, given the high present day divorce rate, who can say which mate-selection procedure creates the greatest chance of lifelong satisfaction with one's significant-other-intimate-partner relationship? (This book can and does say: ***consciously forming relationships and conscious relating all along***.) Certainly, lifelong satisfaction with a relationship is subjective. Satisfaction means different things to different people.

To some extent, complete or near complete satisfaction with one's primary relationship is a luxury few can demand. Simply surviving, having a roof over one's head and food on the table, is already success. And this important element of sheer survival must never be overlooked, especially where children are involved. *Should we want more than this out of life? Can we afford to want more? What do we risk when we want more?*

CHOICE, SURVIVAL, AND FINANCES

While love drives many marriages, we must also see that some marriages are formed and then stay together for economic reasons. Some marriages are formed based upon the perceived earning power or present or future wealth of a mate or of both mates.

Some troubled marriages may even remain in place (or have to remain in place) simply because of one mate's economic dependence upon another, others simply because both mates find the cost of living more affordable when sharing the cost, and others simply because the cost of divorce appears prohibitive. (Not all of these choices are signs of trouble. Many of these choices may make sense.)

CONTROL OVER MONEY

That there is an economic element to marriage and coupling is not in itself a crime. If business partnerships form, at least in part, for economic reasons, why not love, intimate, casual, and similar partnerships? Let's face it, the business of sharing lives, of sharing costs, responsibilities, and chores, is a business. Even a merging of lives, a coupling or a marriage, especially when there are, or will be, children, is an economic relationship.

So, the question is, can we mix love and the business of life successfully? Can we avoid opportunities for the abuse of this love-plus-economic relationship as it is being formed, and all through its years of existence? Yes, of course. (*Note that even after its existence, if there is a break up, divorce, etc., the **post-relationship relationship** is definitely still a relationship, and can, and too frequently does, continue or even exaggerate risks of abuse and violence in relationships where those risks already existed prior to the break up.*)

In businesses, control over the books, the spending, and the money itself, is organized in such a way that the business can survive and even thrive. The organization of this control is indeed designed to help the business survive and thrive. The logical parallel in couples and families is that this same control, although more informal, is designed to help the partnership and the family survive and thrive. In most couple relationships, of course, the organization of control over finances is not as straightforward as it is in businesses. Instead, much of it is casual, even ad hoc.

However, many modern relationship partners do rise to the challenge of clearly and mutually managing, and communicating about, their money.

Of course, love and control over money are not necessarily natural bed-fellows. When control of money is lopsided, control in the relationship can (but does not always) become lopsided as well.

It is best that a love relationship's money management be done by the partners together. And where this is not possible or wanted, then next best is at least a very complete and ongoing communication with each other about money.

Couples deciding who will have what responsibility for managing the money they make, save, and spend do well to take great care to watch that this management does not distort (in a way that could disadvantage one or both partners) the balanced and fair power *structure of this relationship.*

As we all know, power unchecked, unmonitored, does not always but indeed can allow the abuse of power. All too often, when one member of a couple controls more of the financial reality than the other, there is room for that controlling member to have some power which the other does not have, even if this is merely decision-making or information-based power.

A few are tempted to take advantage of this power, to engage in financial abuse. Most choose the positive alternative: equal access to, equal opportunity to use, and equal information regarding, the couple's finances and related financial information. This is the best approach for relationship partners. This is not only healthy, it reduces chances of financial confusion and or abuse.

THE WAY IT SHOULD BE

Clearly, relationship building and maintenance is not a simple under-taking. It is easier for many to just do it and to avoid delving into what is happening while they are doing it. And, there is a strong social directive to just do it, have a relationship, don't look too closely, don't question the process.

There are those who will say "this is how it is supposed to be" and "that's life." Recall the old adage:

> [So and so], sitting in a tree, K-I-S-S-I-N-G.
> First comes love, then comes marriage. Then comes the baby in the baby carriage.

This picture—love then marriage then baby—slips into many young minds as early as the nursery rhyme stage of life, forming a sort of directive, a norm which young people come to feel is most acceptable and most normal.

But what if this is not how it is supposed to be? Or what if this is not how it is supposed to be in this day and age? Or perhaps supposed to be, yet is nowhere as simple as nursery rhymes suggest....

This norm is in reality so complex that while it is transmitted from generation to generation via nursery rhymes, fairy tales, spoken expectations, movies, and modeling done by older generations, no one can say what all goes into it.

No one can say for sure that this is truly "how it is supposed to be" or exactly what all it is that is supposed to be. No one can promise that good and wonderful experiences are normal in, and can be expected of, this sort of supposed to be arrangement.

Nor can anyone say comfortably in our time that the abuse and violence which can take place in some of these arrangements is alright, part of the plan.

It is up to the members of the relationship to maintain a healthy relationship — to regularly communicate with themselves on a mutual, ongoing and open basis.

CHOOSING WHEN THERE ARE
UNKNOWNS
????????????????????

There is so much to be discovered about ourselves and our partners, that we cannot see this all up front. Years and years of discovery may not reveal even the majority of what there is to know. Instead, we must be sensitive to how our relationships play out or evolve over time.

We must be attentive to signs—signs of positive and neutral and also of negative trends—within ourselves, our partners, and our relationships (as discussed in Chapter 14) rather than turn a blind eye (as discussed in Chapter 16).

Most relationships go quite well. Yet, some people miss early signs of potential future abuse and violence. Even where conscious steps into a relationship are taken, relationship partners do best to always remain in the conscious state.

8
Cherish is a Word For

To have and to hold, to cherish, until death do us part, are wordings typical of many traditional marriage vows. What goes into taking these vows or other more modern vows? What do these words mean to us while speaking them, and years after?

HOW WE CHERISH EACH OTHER

Cherish. What does it mean to "cherish"? Do we know? Do we know how to cherish? To have and to hold, to cherish, has been a popular ideal transmitted to young people (and others of all ages for that matter) thinking about marriage.

That we frequently hear this cherishing, or something like this, as a value expressed in wedding vows is to some people perhaps a little unclear. Yet clarity is not exactly what the vow is about—or is it? Most people taking marriage vows have, at the time they take them, no precise idea what it is they are promising in real life and real-time terms, and do not wonder much.

And knowing what cherishing is all about comes with time, is written in our hearts and minds as we learn about it.

This is alright, because it has to be alright, because love is so kindly blind. When deeply in love, it can be difficult to see, let alone want to see, nitty-gritty aspects of reality. In fact, love is a delightful state of mind, heart, and body, a state which is largely biochemical and hormonal. Fortunately, many modern adults understand this and are taking far more interest in consciously dialoging with their future partners.

Love is a sort of drug, and response to love can be lovely.

Yet for some, there can be an addiction-like involvement with the processes of cherishing and being in love. This should not be too surprising. For some people in love, this is what it means to cherish: to be addicted body, mind, and soul (and heart) to another person. Of course this is not the definition of cherish. Yet cherish too often gets played out this way. (And of course, many addictions are quite healthy. Still, it is wise to watch for troubles in even positive habit and addiction patterns as these can at times run awry without our noticing.) *It is up to each of us to look closely and honestly at ourselves and at our own forms of loving, and of feeling loved.*

CHERISH IS NOT SELF DECEPTION

What it feels like to cherish and be cherished can be confused and muddled by a vague self-deception. We can think we are cherishing and are being cherished when we are not. After all, do we really know what cherish looks like? Cherish is not a fixation, addiction, or obsession. Nor is it sacrifice of a life to someone else's will "out of love and dedication."

Nor is it a dominance and submission arrangement, which may be an organization of power and control which has one partner dominating and controlling some or all the other partner's business, assets, time, choices, arrangements, and decisions—or may at times be a more sadistic process in which one partner administers suppression, fear, harm, and or pain either at the supposed request of the other or not upon request. (See Chapters 19 and 33.)

Nor are we talking about
loving parent–child relationships here.

We are, however, talking about
actual adult relationships which sometimes
confuse themselves with parent–child relationships…
…in which one member is
somehow in charge of the other
and has ultimate say, either intentionally or unintentionally.

WHEN CHERISH IS A LICENSE TO HAVE

When is marriage, or any intimate partner relationship, more a license simply to have, and even sometimes to have the sad way: to have and to sometimes hurt, to do whatever good or harm comes about? What elements of this issue are important for all of us, whether or not experiencing problem relationships? Why are these important?

It is all too easy to slip into a painful situation without seeing it coming and then remain unaware of it for a lifetime, or for a long time, or at least until it begins to hurt so much that we notice it.

Thank goodness not all relationships follow this deteriorating route. Most do not! Still, some relationships are at risk of this.

*And every relationship can benefit from a **preventive awareness** of this dangerous tendency to not realize something is deteriorating a little until it has deteriorated a great deal.*

ELEMENT OF OWNERSHIP

The notion of *partner ownership* is, in most settings and societies, seemingly not relevant. However, look again.

Subtle aspects of *ownership of another* may seep in without partners realizing this is taking place. Perhaps this is the sense that one partner "owns" the other's time, choices, reputation, body, reproductive functioning, and so on.

Indeed, sometimes an element of, or form of, this **partner ownership** does enter a relationship—even when undetected by both parties. When this happens there can be an eroding of the equal voice, value and say found in healthy relationships. When this even vague partner ownership enters a relationship, the processes of cherishing and accepting each other can become quite complex, sometimes even convoluted.

What is being traded or agreed to in effort to maintain the relationship? Do the members of the relationship actually know? Do they know the difference between partner boundaries and relationship boundaries? Do they understand that abuse of a partner for the supposed sake of the relationship is not boundary respect? Do they see the difference be-tween boundary respect and boundary trespassing (trespassing where subtle yet very present partner abuse and ownership tendencies can surface)?

A relationship's boundaries can be well protected and respected without degrees of partner boundary trespassing and subtle forms of partner ownership. Yet sometimes people get these confused. *Sometimes one partner feels entitled to cross the other partner's boundaries,* **feels a sense of ownership of this entitlement or supposed right.**

The notion that one person can own another (or can own the right to cross another person's boundaries without that person's informed and freely given permission) may sound wrong or old fashioned. Yet this idea, or attitude, can sneak up on partners in runaway, addictive and or obsessive partnerships—and on partners in healthier relationships. As incorrect and rare as this ownership tendency may sound, partners in relationships must be aware that subtle forms of this can appear in many interactions without people seeing it. Yes…

*this ownership dynamic
can slip into a relationship almost unnoticed.*

*Ownership tendencies
can even be
vague, difficult to spot, in some cases.*

Whether or not ownership is too strong a word for most situations, the **notion of entitlement to control is part of this ownership concept.** Partners must know that they can participate in exchanges in which one person takes over, whether (a) without the other's consent, or (b) with the other's full consent, or (c) with the other fooling her or him self into *not-seeing* this happening, or (d) with the other truly *not-seeing* this happening—*not-seeing this happening until it is too late to prevent this (even where there is abuse of power and control emerging).* (Note that this verb, *not-seeing*, takes on a particular nature of its own, as this is the *act of* NOT-seeing, which will be referred to several times in this book.)

TINY TRADES

Many minor, almost unnoticed interactions take place during a relation-ship. For the most part, we do not focus on these exchanges and do not see their actual nature. Most of these exchanges and interactions are lovely, or at least useful, functional, and or too minor to spot.

Let's return for a moment to the concept of **equal partnering**.

Here, two consenting adults cherish each other as equal partners, of *equal respect, voice, value, and say*, in their relationship. For many, this is the standard by which they measure—or at least feel—the successes of their relationships, and this is good. Yet, applying this standard is easier said than done for some.

The equality standard is all too often oversimplified to absurdity. Expecting people, even partners in relationships, to actually be exactly the same and equal in every way is irrational and denies the value of individuality. Each of us has our own set of personal characteristics, and nothing says we are or should be exact copies of each other in appearance, behavior, performance, taste, or belief system. Equal partnering is not about pretending or talking like we are all exactly the same or equal in every way. It is about allowing, promoting, and desiring equal levels of importance and power in a partnership—fairly distributing respect, voice, value, and say in the business and personal interactions of the relationship.

Even when trying, this model of equal voice, value, and say in relationship takes attention. No matter how much we think we have arranged ourselves in such a way that everything is done in an atmosphere of equal respect, voice, value, and say, there are many hidden trades that take place almost every day and sometimes almost every minute of a relationship.

Each time there is an interaction, there is a choice to feel, say, or do—or not to feel, say, or do—something, a passage in time in which one or the other puts either the relationship first, the partner first, or the self first. While each of these choices can be admirable or at least normal, just know that each of these times, there is a tiny transaction taking place.

These transactions are not in themselves sources of pain, and they can be navigated with sensitivity and appreciation for the process of balancing the give and take required to keep a relationship functional and happy.

Many couples achieve this sort of balance without working hard to do so, and this is ultimately the goal where possible.

At the same time, some couples never reach this balance. Then, as time goes by, they trap themselves or at least one of their members into ongoing chiseling away at or sacrificing of self—and of stability, sanity, and safety. It is then that the vows some couples, just some but indeed some, take can be distorted into traps, licenses to cause pain, hurt, and damage—not because the vows say this but because the vows can be misused, misinterpreted, misunderstood either intentionally or unintentionally.

Two consenting adults can choose to cherish each other as equal partners, with equal respect, voice, value, and say in their relationship. Try to check around. See what various couples say about this….

POWER DIFFERENTIALS

The deck of opportunity is rarely dealt out evenly. Distributions of careers, good jobs, incomes, and other chances to live up to one's potential and or to fulfill one's dreams are uneven enough in this world.

However, in a coupling relationship—even in a loving one fully aware of the issues relating to opportunities and what is sometimes given up by one or both of the relationship members—given up or set aside for each other and or for the family over time—this "giving up" or "setting aside" of opportunity can have long term effects.

What starts out simple—two people coming together based on attraction and love, and perhaps shared dreams, and then *not-seeing* how their differences can be magnified over time—can grow messy where couples do not stay conscious of choices being made every step of the way.

Conscious approaches to the interactions taking place from the start can help prevent unintentional confusion and upset. These can help spot the early warning signs of slight and easily addressed issues, and also the possible signs of budding emotional, financial, and other forms of abuse and violence.

It is in the little steps that

some vague, confusing, challenging,

sometimes even wrong even rocky,

directions are sometimes taken.

Look before you leap, and walk with awareness and respect for each other and yourselves. This is a healthy part of a loving relationship. This makes a big difference in the long run.

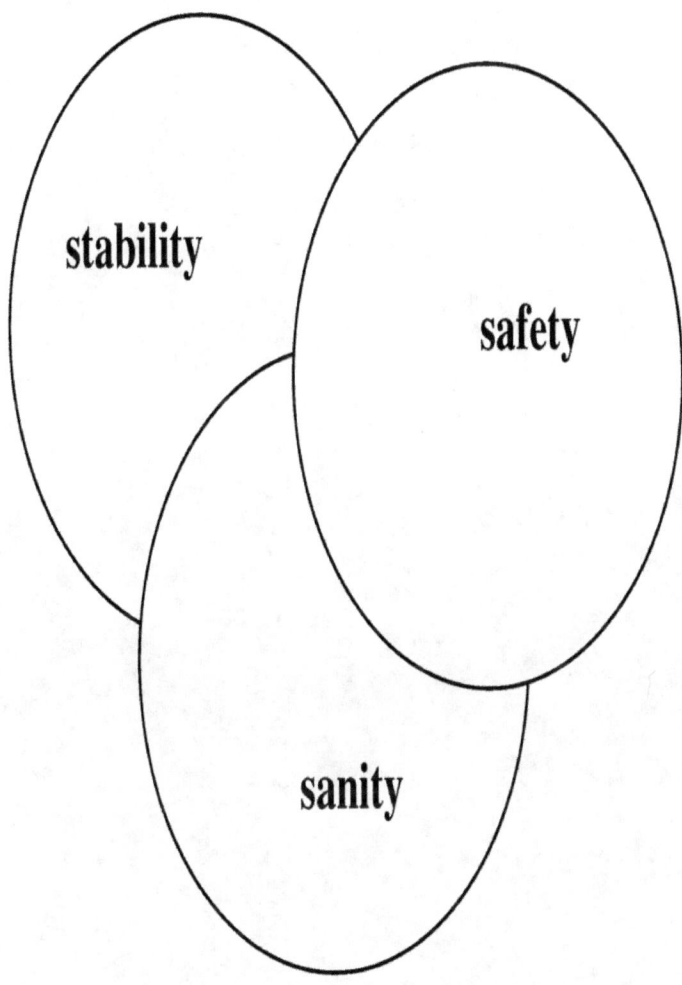

Figure 8.1. Stability, sanity, and safety balance.

9
Second Thought Story

She had heard about these wedding jitters, these bouts of nervousness and restlessness, possibly even craziness, in the weeks, days, and hours before some people's weddings. But never had she even considered the possibility that those jitters she was experiencing could in any way be actual second thoughts.

She simply attributed her engaging in several short, wild, and nearly anonymous affairs, sexual escapades, in other cities where no one knew her, to normal anxiety which would pass.

At least, she told herself, this kind of behavior was acceptable for men right before marriage. So, she asked herself, why not for women too? After all, she thought, "tying the knot" had a slightly binding sound to it, a disturbingly permanent sound to it, a bit like a guillotine about to fall with everyone watching and giving full consent to the termination of her freedom.

She kept herself busy to avoid wondering whether marrying a man she had known for only four months, whose baby she was now carrying, made sense.

She reassured herself that the wedding vows would make it all OK.

10
Individual Identity and Boundaries Within A Relationship

For those who are, or ever have been, deeply in love, a celebration of this love and of the mutual commitments to it is a wonderfully joyous event. This celebration is a wedding of lives and for many, one of the biggest events in their lives, a peak experience. As one of the high points in life, the positive aspects of coming together and committing to share lives have to be acknowledged, respected, and protected.

NOTICE OF BONDING

Yet there exists for some, not all yet some, a great deal of anxiety about relationship commitment let alone marriage for a range of reasons. One of the unspoken aspects of this anxiety has to do with the shift in personal identity that merging lives may bring some people.

Some find this an increase in and a solidification of personal identity, in that marrying or establishing a primary relationship can be the maturation of self and the achievement of a major lifetime goal. And this is fabulous.

Others however are uncertain as to what the effects of this merging of lives with another will have upon their own identities. Rarely is it ad-mitted by those with identity issues that these nagging questions are swimming just below the surface, and rarely do they dare to openly ask:

"Will I lose myself in you," or,
"Will you be taking my life over," or,
"Will I be myself anymore," or even,
"Is this a very good idea, as I do not even know who I am."

Yet there is nothing wrong with openly asking these questions if they are there. Why not talk about these things if they are lurking in the under-currents of one or both partners' thinking? Partners can find safe ways to discuss all of this.

WHEN A BOND CROSSES THE LINE

The wedding or other formalizing of the partnership of love is an explicit notice of what social scientists have called pair-bonding. This wedding of persons is a positive form of formal human bond, a formal bond of love and likely mating. In some ways, like two companies merging, there is frequently a formal written or spoken agreement signifying the intent of the parties to combine or partner in some way. For many intimate partners, the spoken agreement comes in the form of wedding or civil partnership vows, while the license, and for some, the marital agreement, is written and even certified.

All partnerships in love can protect their love by being open and honest with each other, and by being aware of the particular areas they do best by traveling carefully and with great awareness, care and respect. The pair bond is a bond that requires nurturing and protecting to be an ongoing healthy and positive bond.

It is wise to understand that this bond can sometimes cross a line, sometimes through no fault of anyone's, just because life is like this. This crossing can be addressed wisely and well and worked with as it takes place.

Sometimes members of a relationship move beyond a line or boundary without the *full awareness and agreement of both members of the relationship*. There can be risks for these relationships and the partners within these relationships. Yes, past this line are risks, as past this line are potentially dangerous territories. Where partners do not fully see what they are agreeing to do or not to do with their own lives for the sake of their relationship, they risk boundary and identity confusion. They can of course ward this off by bringing as much as they can into the light of conscious choice and conscious behavior and conscious inter-action.

Otherwise, the relationship bond can become more of an agreement to hold one or both partners in a form of **bondage**, bondage to the relationship or to each other. Yes, this bondage is fine where partners are consciously and explicitly aware of their contributions and agreements all along the way. Then this can be a healthy choice for all involved.

Where partners are unaware of the full scope of their relationship agreements, and of their own personal as well as their relationship's identity and boundary definitions, they leave the rules and structure of their relationship vague, ambiguous, and potentially or actually unstable.

Ambiguity in itself is a problem which is generally so ambiguous that it goes on unrecognized while causing relationship confusion and shakiness. Potential and actual destabilizing and deterioration of the relationship can result.

The art of seeing this ambiguous problem of ambiguity coming before it manifests itself is worth studying. Alas, this is not a recognized art. What would we call this?

>Positive bond protection?
>Protection from deterioration into…
>>an unclear, confusing form of bondage?

REASONS FOR FORMAL MARRIAGE

History has evolved marriage ceremonying and licensing for several reasons, among these being that marriage has offered:

- A way to transfer ownership of property (and of women and children in eras and settings where they were legally defined as property, chattel, along with money, land, livestock, and other material things).
- A way to protect property, whatever this property may be.
- A way to indicate, mark, the parentage and lineage of children.
- A way to signify that two persons' sexual intercourse was socially acceptable.
- A way to make sexual intercourse and any children it would bring legally and religiously acceptable and "legitimate."
- A way to protect children produced by the union.

Marriage vows have evolved along with marriage and even today can contain implicit and explicit references to commitment, ownership, and property. Both religious and secular versions of the old "to have and to hold" vow continue to be popular. These tend to include phrases such as "for better or for worse" and "for richer, for poorer, in sickness and in health."

Some vows continue to include an "until death do us part" term as well. The basic message is that "nothing will tear us apart" and "we are committed to this union from this day forward." Permanency and strength of the bond are being promised. And this is good, otherwise, (one might ask) why formalize this bond?

IDENTITY AND COMMITMENT TO WHAT AND TO WHOM

And why not make such promises? Isn't lifelong commitment most often viewed as being the point of the marriage? And why not make such a promise formal and public? Isn't the promise made to not only the partner, but to any future (or existing) offspring and to the community as well? These guarantees are statements of what the community surrounding the couple, and all couples in this community, can expect of those taking the vow.

There is of course a strong ceremonial aspect to the sharing of vows done by couples. Sharing of vows becomes an event, a ritual, a reason for celebration, and frequently publicly marks what would otherwise be a very private rite of passage taking place. This ceremony can serve as official, social, and spiritual approval, authorization, and permission for the union of lives, bodies, and property taking place. And this is usually a deeply meaningful and beautiful ceremony.

Union, yes. Now two individuals unite and in some ways of seeing it, become one. However, they actually become at least three: two individuals plus one relationship—or plus the relationship each of them thinks he or she is entering—which may make it at least four. (See the charts in Chapter 46.) Yes, four: two individuals plus the relationship which each sees there. And this is before adding on additional perceptions each member of the couple has of the other member of the couple. "I am marrying the person I think you are." And this is before any children are added on. *(While some relationships do include more than the two members of the couple, this discussion refers to the couple and to the pair-bond as this is the most common form of primary intimate partner relationship. Readers who wish to extend this information to other forms of relationships will do so with whatever adaptations of this information are involved to do so.)*

Marriage is a vessel of transmission for a culture. When the marriage is an "approved" marriage, legally and religiously accepted, then the culture in which the marriage is performed approves of the marriage, making it an important component of that culture and of the process of that culture's continuation and preservation. Note that little about the institution of marriage is truly aimed at continuation and preservation of the individual. Not exactly anyway. *This remains up to the people getting married.*

Times change, and modern times are changing rapidly. Old values and concepts are being reexamined and in some arenas heavily questioned.

If relationships, love partnerships, couplings, and marriages do not evolve, they may not survive the evolution of the societies where they live. The reverse is also true: societies must keep up with the relationships being formed within them!

So must we all.

11
Meet The IP's Boundary

Although many do, not all relationship partners marry, or bond for life or for years. Some relationships are brief and casual, some are not, yet many may still be flexible and undefined in duration. Either way, once there is emotional or physical intimacy, or both, there is a meshing of or blurring of boundaries.

Intimacy is shared boundary crossing with mutual permission and invitation. To be clear here: The opposite of intimacy is boundary crossing without permission and without invitation, in essence a sort of raping of a boundary, of a person's boundary.

Certainly sex or physical intimacy appears to be intimate. Standing naked before each other, we appear to ourselves and each other to be truly naked, and we feel naked. So naked. Yet, we really are just doing some boundary shedding and boundary crossing. How easy it is to feel that this is intimate.

Most physical intimacy is wanted by both partners (is clearly mutually agreed upon), and is a positive experience for both partners. Where not, partners do best by knowing this, as this is an area where transgressions of oneself, and or of the partner, are possible even when both think they are being sensitive to boundaries.

Intimacy is central in many relationships, hence the label "intimate" partner relationship. It is generally assumed that this term "intimacy" refers to sexual intimacy, however this is not the only form of intimacy in relationships.

INTIMACY IS NOT PHYSICAL NAKEDNESS

Intimacy is indeed far more than only physical. Intimacy reaches well beyond people being physically naked together. In fact, sexual relations may or may not result in any degree of emotional intimacy whatsoever. So, who, other than someone you may get naked with and may have sex with, is the intimate partner? Anyone? Yes, however look closely before answering.

You may have had several persons you would call intimate partners, several who have once qualified or still do qualify. Many readers will have selected one of these, or are in the process of doing so. This is likely the spouse, life partner, significant other, although these labels do not actually capture the deep, interwoven, nature of the relationship we are talking about. *(Some readers will have a life partner and another intimate partner outside of that primary relationship. Where this book does not evaluate choices to or not to do so, again the emphasis here is on mutual agreements by both partners in the primary relationship. Where there are not mutual conscious agreements by both members of a relationship, there can be or already is boundary crossing and therefore a form of abuse ta-king place.)*

ENTANGLEMENT IS NOT INTIMACY

Let's not let this description, "deep and entangled," paint an entirely negative picture. Many highly functional, natural, and very good things are deep and entangled such as: rich positive relationships, fertile beds of seaweed, and neural networks in the human brain. Still, it is in this deep, entangled way that entanglement can bind us, that it can allow us to think a deeply entangled intimate partner relationship is an intimate one.

Entanglement itself is not necessarily intimacy. Entanglement can masquerade as true intimacy and can also serve as the glue holding even a hollow or painful relationship together.

Take another look at intimacy: There is of course something—there has to be something—about the intimate partnership that tends to help distinguish it from other partnerships, such as the business partnership. YES, INTIMACY!

Intimacy.
Intimacy.
Intimacy, whatever that is.

While this answer, intimacy, is of course obvious, it is still hauntingly ambiguous. How can something we can hardly understand and can barely identify be so powerful? Future, present, or past intimacy is one of the great, if not the greatest, influences upon a relationship. Yet we still cannot entirely describe it, fully define its reaches and aspects.

Again and most certainly, when we say "intimacy" here, what comes to mind is usually "sexual" intimacy. Sexual intimacy must be interrogated for its actual effects on human relating. Could it be that this is the ingredient that separates one category of relationship from another and should this be so? Does everything change once two people "have sex" together?

INTIMACY AND MUTUAL BOUNDARY CROSSING

Sexual interaction does help explain acceptable boundary crossing (when that is what the sexual interaction is). Relationship intimacy contains a high degree of mutual boundary crossing WITH MUTUAL PERMISSION—such as what takes place during sex. Note again that if this supposed form of intimacy, sexual intimacy, takes place without mutual explicit permission, this is more like rape than interpersonal intimacy. There is nothing intimate about rape. Sexual assault is not intimate. Boundary crossing without permission hints at assault—hints and shouts assault.

The problem with looking for the clear cut division between sex with and sex without permission is that this matter is not always so clear cut, neither in casual nor in more serious relationships.

Best approach is: where not sure, do not go there. However, this lack of clarity is too often settled for, and then boundaries are crossed without clear permission.

Participating in the sex act can be quite impulsive, as can surrendering to one's own or someone else's sex drive. Furthermore, "no" has many meanings including "absolutely not," and "maybe," "sorta'," " I guess so," "OK yes, yes," and "YES!"

Yes, we are back to consent. Although crossing the line into sexual relation carries a relationship into a certain zone—the sexually intimate zone—the decision to cross is not always a conscious one and is not always deliberate. In fact, some boundary crossings are not wanted but they are not stopped. Some boundary crossings are not wanted by even the *dominant boundary crosser*. And many boundary crossings are entirely misunderstood.

BOUNDARY CROSSING WITHOUT PERMISSION

Although this may seem to be returning to the most obvious, it must be said again and again. So, let's say it again: there is nothing, nothing, nothing intimate about boundary crossing without *clear* mutual per-mission. Without clear and true permission, THIS IS RAPE, isn't it?

And yet, there are forms of and degrees of rape about which many people are confused. Here, sexual intimacy is being discussed because it is more readily seen as intimacy, whether or not it truly is. And then there are some crossings into sexual intimacy which a person wants and does not want at the same time.

This internal conflict is ignored or denied or even acknowledged and then trespassed upon anyway. Where a person consents to sex but does not want this sex, is this a raping of oneself then?

Impulse is fun and liberating, yet impulse can be a problem. So much sexual intimacy is engaged in on impulse. Parents of teenagers know this very well and tend to be very concerned about this. Quite wisely, parents often try to tell their teenagers to think before moving into sexual intimacy. Yet, how many times have these parents themselves given sex as little thought as they are concerned their offspring will?

INTIMACY CAN OPEN DOORS

Intimacy takes a relationship to a new place. Intimacy can open doors to greater depth in relationship, and this can be one of the most positive experiences life has to offer. Deeply knowing and loving another human being is a precious experience, one worth seeking and protecting. Nothing said in this book denies the potential for great meaning and great beauty in intimate partner love.

At the same time, intimacy can open doors to places no one should have to go without understanding first what visiting these places can look like. Walk the intimacy path with respect and awareness, and with open eyes.

SEE THE DIFFERENCE BETWEEN PERMISSION TO CROSS AND VIOLATION OF BOUNDARIES

Do not travel into boundary crossing *without full and clear permission*. Here is where there is risk of rape (boundary crossing *without* permission), self abuse, relationship addiction, interpersonal abuse, and even violence. Here, in these difficult places, interpersonal abuse and violence can occur almost naturally, almost unnoticed at first. Or at least unacknowledged. Here, in this territory of unconscious and careless relating, some can walk a treacherous quicksand, a place where they can lose awareness of their own and others' boundaries, and of their lives. Here is where they can slip away from themselves and fall into problematic patterns of relating.

So, the sign on more than one door says "intimacy," but these doors open to very different places. Meet the brief or long term, casual or more serious, intimate partner here. Yes, maybe this potential or actual intimate partner is opening the door, and if so, hopefully is opening the door consciously.

The partner wants to be clear minded, to love freely and at the same time to remain aware of her or his trades, agreements, and boundaries. Being aware even when in love helps know the possible and for some actual risk of problems that we are talking about in this book: troubled interpersonal issues, interactions, patterns, habits, even sometimes ad-dictions, compulsions, abuses, and violences.

RECOGNIZE VIO-LATION AS VIO-LENCE

Violence? Yes. Having one's boundary crossed *without permission* is having that boundary *violated*. To VIO-late a boundary is to do that boundary VIO-lence. VIO-lation of a partner's boundary IS ABUSE, IS VIOLENCE AGAINST THAT BOUNDARY.

Part Two

12
Anatomy of the Bond

Ultimately, we are looking for ourselves in our relationships as in all else we do. We seek ourselves through our relationships, involving, perhaps even using, other persons as counterparts, players in our searches. The "who am I" question constantly whispers to us.

So, whether or not we catch ourselves doing this, we are constantly seeking mirrors, reflections of ourselves. What better mirror than a love relationship? After all, we might fool ourselves sweetly, "Who I am is who I am when I am with you." But do we hear ourselves when we may also be saying: "Without you, who am I? Much less? Nothing?"

LOVE CAN TRIGGER

Love relationships can serve as triggers for, identifiers of, interactions and bondings that help to bring out in us who we are, and who we are not. Our counterparts, whether or not we want them to or they want to, can trigger all kinds of things within us. Hobbies, interests, tastes, beliefs—also exercising, eating, spending, drinking, and other habits and behaviors—can be brought out in us via our interactions with someone we are close to or around a great deal.

And where particular interests and tendencies are not somewhere with-in us, we can sometimes take them on once in the ongoing close presence of someone who has those interests and tendencies. (Although not at all like the process of a dog owner looking a little more like her or his dog over time, this is an interesting analogy.) *And, in itself, this becoming a bit like each other is not a problem. This can be an exciting and even deeply moving process. Meshing lives, perhaps even meshing selves to some extent, can be a highly rewarding process, a deepening of the self and soul.*

The challenge is to know whether we can take on tendencies, even some real behavioral characteristics, of another without hurting or losing ourselves or our own boundaries. With clear understanding of this process, we can manage to experience some degree of "losing ourselves in each other" (as it is often described) without getting lost. We can benefit by undergoing the bonding, meshing, intersection of lives and selves process with awareness. This can enable us to intersect with each other without losing our own boundaries.

Note: Where we lose too much of our own boundaries, we may do so to the point of weakening ourselves. Then we may reach a place of for-getting who we are as individuals and what we personally need and want. In this sense, we may commit a form of self abuse by being at this point. However, rarely do we choose to do this to ourselves, and rarely do we choose to abuse ourselves like this.

In some troubled relationships, one partner is expected to be more and more the way the other partner expects her or him to be whether this other partner wants to be these things: more attractive, more obedient, more compliant, more submissive in certain activities, more sexual on demand, and so on.

BONDING AND TIME

Intense bonding, even in a very new love relationship, is

natural. Love can be a beautiful bond and a deep emotional engagement and commitment, a truly rich experience making life all the more meaningful. Of course, entering into and then existing as an individual while in an intimate partner relationship is a never ending process.

The relationship changes, just as its members do, as time goes by. The relationship develops a history of its own, a deeper meaning and identity of its own. It truly can take on a personality of its own—not only in the eyes of outsiders who may even come to call the relationship the "Smiths" or the "couple next door" or "those two," but also in the eyes of its members.

When the members of the couple both feel that the evolution of their relationship is generally positive (appearing something like what is depicted in Figure 12.1), then the progression moves something like this although perhaps not precisely in this order: from initial attraction to deeper connection, to intersection of lives to identification with the relationship, to formalization of the relationship to perpetuation of the relationship, to preservation of the relationship to ongoing deepening of the relationship and of the commitment to it.

SOME BONDS PROGRESS NEGATIVELY

Of course there are other less than desirable paths a bond may take. It is important for persons in intimate partner relationships to track, or at least be aware of, the progression of their relationships, the evolution of their bonds, over time. The relationship and its members can maintain an awareness of the direction (or directions) their relationship is taking. They can even influence the direction, if paying close attention—relating consciously and recognizing signs such as those suggesting there may be a need for attention to, and work on, the relationship.

For example, a watchful eye early in a new relationship, when both love hormones and sexual passion can run very high, may help to prevent confusions, issues, and problem patterns from evolving early on in that relationship. Why ignore hints that a relationship might enter or take the path of a troubled or even problem progression? (Such a progression can take many forms, including the one depicted in Figure 12.2. Note that the deterioration of a bond may take paths other than the one depicted in Figure 12.2 and may fluctuate between periods of positive progression and periods of negative progression, as well as have reversals as suggested in Figure 12.3.)

DO BONDS EVER BREAK OR END?

We hear talk of bonds being broken. However, what is frequently taking place is that the nature of the bond is changing and may or may not be deteriorating in quality. If the quality of a relationship is in the process of weakening for some reason (not always a problem reason, sometimes just the result of time and change), there will eventually be a noticeable change in the bond between the partners in this relationship.

Bonds can continue long after a relationship "ends" or thinks it has ended. Of course, somewhere along the line, there may actually be no bond, the relationship may be entirely over, yet as long as there is something between the people in the relationship, no matter how distant they may grow, whether or not it feels good, there is a bond.

There are even those who will argue that years after a couple has ended its relationship, even when there is no contact, a bond may continue to exist. This is not necessarily a positive or comfortable bond, although it may be. It is simply some form of ongoing connection via family or memory, or other human "dots" which remain connected to each.

Figure 12.1. Anatomy of a probable positive bond progression.

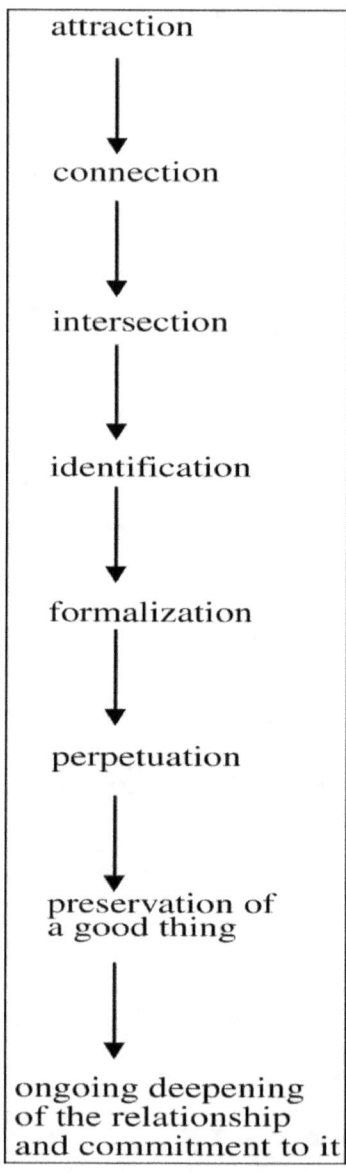

Figure 12.2. Anatomy of a probable negative bond progression.

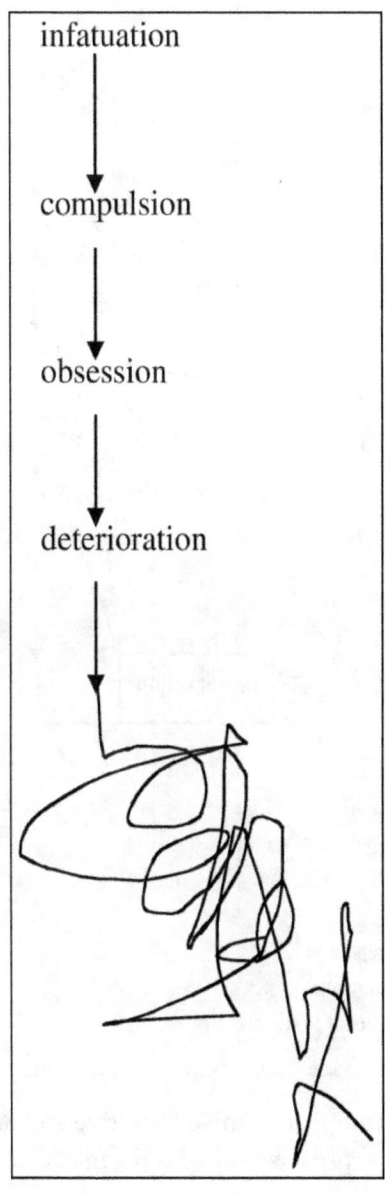

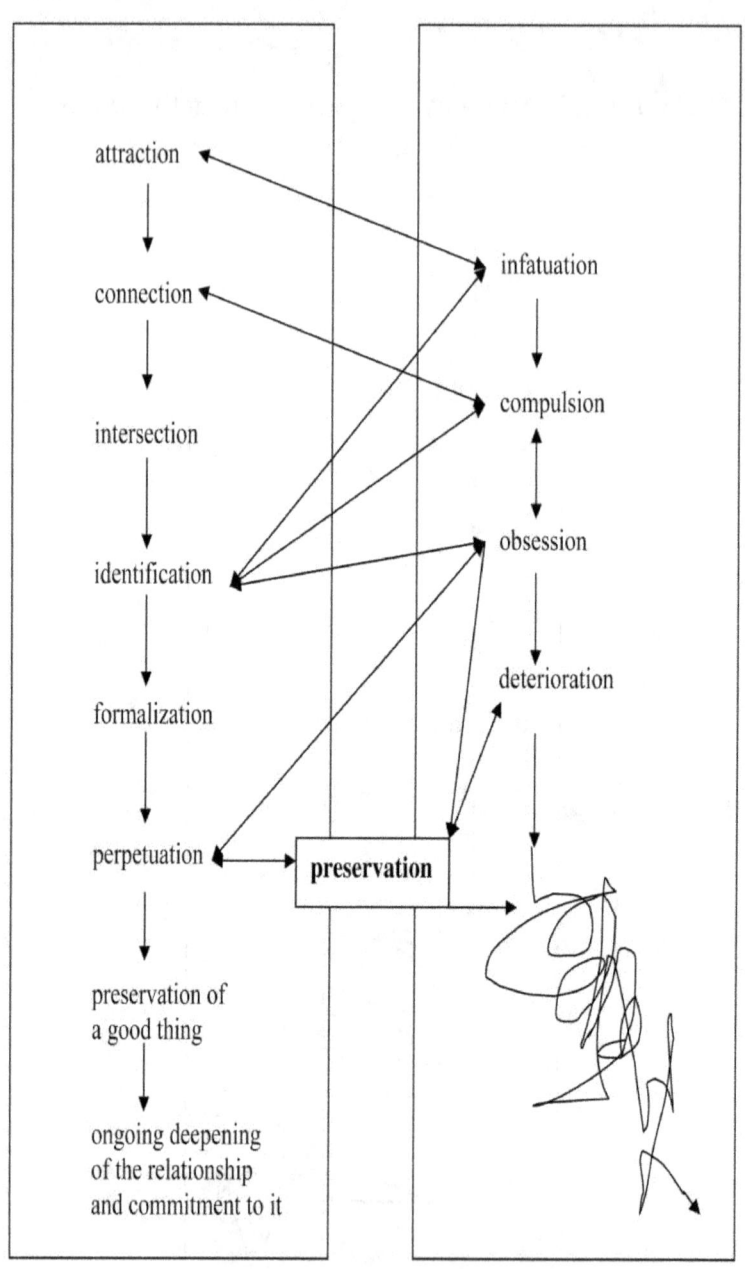

Figure 12.3. Example of a mixed positive and negative bond progression with reversals.

13
Messages Story

There was an eleven month separation leading up to their divorce. About one-third of the way through this separation, Beth was completely uncertain as to what Stewart's true intentions were. She was broke, unable to pay bills Stewart and she had long ago put in her name. She felt financially stranded.

Stewart was the one who had filed for divorce, yet he continued to communicate to her that he was very sorry he had done so and that he did not really want a divorce. He begged Beth for forgiveness many times. Beth was either fooled or confused, or both, and this state of mind continued to plague her for the duration of the separation.

Halfway through the pre-divorce separation, Stewart had his attorney send a letter stating that Stewart had "renewed his commitment to recon-ciliation," and that he assumed that Beth was "in agreement on this." The letter also stated that Stewart had been committed to reconciliation since the start of the separation. Beth was quite confused by this.

Throughout the separation there was mixed communication coming from Stewart regarding their dividing their property without a divorce.

One moment, Stewart wanted to "forget everything and go back to the way things were" and the next he wanted to "legally sever the *property and then stay married."*

And the next moment he wanted out no matter what this meant.

The pressure to sever the property increased as the months went by, but Stewart still wavered on even this matter. Beth really could not make sense out of what Stewart was telling her, and found the idea that they would stay married while severing their finances odd as they had shared everything for so long. As the months wore on, Beth grew very tired, felt that the confusion was not going to end, and that, now that all this had ta-ken place, she could never feel quite the same about Stewart.

Against the backdrop of ongoing emotional pleas made by Stewart to Beth to never leave him, Stewart made concurrent threatening demands (including threats of violence against her and even of killing her) that she agree to whatever financial demands he was making.

Beth found herself increasingly sick, fearful, and wanting to get as far away from Stewart as she could. As she grew more definite about wanting the divorce, Stewart grew angrier that she was.

14
Signs

After two decades of living and sleeping together, a few of you might wake up one morning and find a stranger in your bed—your spouse! How well do we really know the people we sleep with, love, and spend the time of our lives with? Any better than we know ourselves?

When the person with whom you've been emotionally and physically intimate for so many years becomes a stranger to you, is this strange-ness retroactive—does this mean that this person was a stranger to you all along without your knowing this? If so, were you fooled into thinking you ever knew this person? Or were you fooling yourself? Do you know? *Were you having intercourse with a stranger when you thought this per-son was your significant other? Who was fooling whom? Who betrayed whom? Anyone? Anyone at all?*

Who (either knowingly or unknowingly) stepped over the line, masquerading as a known person, as a recognized intimate partner, hiding behind the mask of familiarity and love while secretly remaining a stranger—or eventually becoming one? Or is this just (and most likely) you both simply moving through your lives and now having new parts of yourselves to share with each other? ... Or to not share with each other?

SLIPPING INTO BOUNDARY CONFUSION

We might see this as being about boundaries—whose they

are, where they are, whether they are anywhere, how clear they are—and whether they are wanted. All relationships are at risk of boundary confusions, boundary crossings, whether due to personal change, unbridled enthusiasm, mistakes, carelessness, lies, betrayals, or other positive and less than positive conditions such as problem addictions.

Many partners process these events well, carefully, and grow from them. Boundaries can mature. And partners can grow to further define and respect their own and their partner's and their relationship's boundaries. Even when these all do appear to be the same boundaries, these are not, as the self, the partner, and the relationship are three (at least three) different systems. (See for example Figures 46.1 and 46.2 in Chapter 46.)

However, too many relationships unknowingly slip into patterns of boundary confusions, boundary crossings, and boundary betrayals, and the behaviors which accompany these, the latter of which can be boundary abuses. This is not just a matter of an occasional "Hey wait, that's my toothbrush, use yours," or, "You used all the clean towels in one hour," but more a matter of one partner stepping over the line into the other partner's personal domain, personal territory—or maybe even outside boundaries beyond the relationship's own sexual, emotional, financial, or other boundaries.

This can also be the failure of the relationship to continuously and mutually redefine itself as the relationship moves through life— redefine itself both to its members and to the world.

When the relationship's boundaries are not well or clearly defined, then the boundaries can be crossed (purposefully, or carelessly, or mistakenly) by those within and around the relationship. This can result in extra-marital or extra-relationship affairs taking place without both of the partners clearly knowing and consenting, and or financial deceptions where shared monies are hidden or re-labeled or pilfered without one of the partners knowing the other is so doing, and or other *boundary transgressions*.

(Note that this is not a judgment on the practice of extra-marital affairs. Rather this is a clear statement regarding relationship boundaries and how these are only effective *and real* when *both* partners are clear on these and respect these. Where *both* partners are not clear on the same boundaries, there is actually no shared or respected boundary.)

Again, we come to this matter of boundary crossing without permission. How can it be that so many do not see the problem—boundary crossing becoming boundary abuse—approaching and or getting worse? Some-times we just do not want to see, and other times, we simply do not know how to look—or what to look for.

WATCHING FOR SIGNS OF BOUNDARY ABUSE

Then there is the matter of purposeful boundary betrayal, also a boundary crossing, a more complicated version. This is a partner's knowing breaking of an implied or actual agreement to define, respect, and stick to boundaries which define—form, protect—the relationship. A popular example is secret, undisclosed, infidelity which takes place when an agreed upon, promised, boundary—such as not to be sexually intimate with anyone else—is broken.

> Respecting the relationship's boundaries means
> not crossing them
> unless *both* partners
> clearly, explicitly consent
> in advance of the crossing.

If the basic agreement of the relationship and its own boundaries requires revision, this is best done consciously, directly, no matter how difficult. Honestly rather than secretly treading across boundaries avoids *boundary abuse, and the partner abuse this includes.*

Again note that sexual infidelity can be a ready example of treading over mutually agreed upon boundaries, but in many ways, one of the easier to define. Emotional infidelity—taking the emotional intimacy of the inti-mate partnership elsewhere—can also be betrayal. Some people weigh sexual infidelity as more serious than emotional infidelity, while others say the opposite. *Decisions to cross sexual, emotional, and other relationship boundaries should be those of the partners in the relationship, and these are decisions that should be made by them up front and together.*

Clarifying all this, and keeping partners clear about it, involves having basic and clear founding and ongoing agreements between the partners as they grow and change. Ideally these are explicit, maybe even written agreements, so both partners can take the *founding agreements* seriously—or know when these are no longer in place. This is not to judge fidelity and or infidelity here, rather this is to say that both partners have a right to know what the agreement regarding all this is, and if this agreement is still in place.

Unfortunately, many relationships are formed without very clear, very explicit, very specific agreements about many things such as fidelity. Implicit agreements such as, "Well I thought that is what we meant when we got together, but we never really made it clear I guess" are not sufficient in many cases.

Betrayal and infidelity are only some of the boundary abuses that can take place in vague, confused, and troubled relationships. Almost more difficult are the harder to label boundary abuses. So pay attention. *Love does not have to be blind. There is nothing wrong with falling in love with one's eyes wide open.* Staying alert and watching for signs of possibly emerging boundary confusion and abuse is not a bad thing to be doing. Partners can do this together, consciously, intelligently. And, watching for signs does not have to be hard work.

Watching for signs does require honesty with each other—but first and foremost honesty with oneself! A great deal of focus falls on the problem of members of relationships not being honest with each other, and much less on each of the members not being honest with themselves.

It's pretty much a hot seat, a don't-touch topic: Do we know what it feels like to be honest with ourselves? Can we ask someone else to be honest with us if we are not honest with ourselves? Yes, surely we can. **We have a right to demand honesty in a relationship.** Still, when we are deceiving, or lying, to ourselves about the relationship, we are at risk of betraying both ourselves and the other person. Best to demand truth of ourselves as well as of our partners.

What are the signs that a relationship is a troubled or problem relationship? A combination of indicators coming from within and from around ourselves tells us what we need to know, if we are paying attention. This chapter discusses indicators coming from within. Basically, indicators coming from within are indicators that the person feeling these things is not comfortable—with something.

Figure 14.1 suggests some key indicators and a method of rating these indicators in terms of their significance to us, in terms of their value as signs that we may not be entirely comfortable—and in this case, may not be comfortable in a particular intimate partner relationship, or in some aspect of that relationship.

Keep in mind that Figure 14.1 rates the individual's comfort level and not the quality of the relationship. However, if one or both members are very uncomfortable in these ways, then there is something, some corner of the heart or soul, asking for attention. The following pages discuss the factors listed in Figure 14.1.

VAGUE
FREE-FLOATING...
DISCOMFORT

Everyone has experienced at some point a vague feeling of discomfort, a feeling that something is just not right, something but not anything specific. *This is ourselves sending ourselves a notice. The letters may be faint and hard to read, but the handwriting is on the wall.*

Unexplainable exhaustion, sadness, edginess, confusion, and even more extreme sensations such as nausea, headaches, and body aches—these can be signs from the self to the self. These can be signals saying, "Hey, wake up, there could be a problem here." Of course, if there is a problem, it could be stemming from any number of things, including of course physical health issues, and not necessarily from a relationship.

Still these symptoms are indeed messages from the self to the self revealing that something is going on. *(See a medical doctor to test for health issues. However, where tests show no medical issues, then ask whether perhaps these messages are coming from you to yourself for another reason.)*

The signs do not have to be entirely negative. Within reason, a sign such as increased dedication to one's work or perhaps to one's exercise program can be a good thing, yet it might also be an avoidance or escape from facing reality. When the reality is trouble in an intimate partner relationship, we are not always ready to see this. We may even work to avoid this, to cover it up, to be too busy to see it, to arrange with ourselves to simply not see it. *Not-seeing: this is denial.*

The thing about our subconscious minds not allowing our conscious minds to see what is going on right before our very eyes is that the messages we are suppressing crop up everywhere anyway. We start to know that something is just not right. Something, yes, but not anything specific.... Vague, free-floating feelings of discomfort wander, or even flood, in.

NOT FEELING LIKE ONESELF

Another subtle sign is the sense of not feeling like oneself. "I'm just not myself these days." "Sometimes I wonder what drives me." "I don't know how I feel about that or about anything right now."

Also in this not feeling like oneself category is the *sense of inauthenticity*. "Nothing about what I am saying sounds like me." "I don't really know who I am anymore."

We truly can have times when we truly do not know how we feel. Or we can subconsciously choose not to realize we feel inauthentic. We can lie to ourselves and not realize we are doing so; we can lie to ourselves and fool ourselves into thinking we are not lying. There are so many subtle ways to avoid the truth about something, very likely the truth about our feelings.

CHOOSING TO AVOID THE TRUTH

And, certainly there are times when one consciously chooses to avoid the truth, making a clear and conscious decision to do so.

Why not, we tell ourselves: "The world is full of lies, it runs on lies for the most part, why not my intimate partner relationship too," and, "Too much truth is like taking a medicine which is too strong: it can make you sick," and, "Little lies, well, they save us unnecessary pain."

Choosing to avoid the truth is all too common.

In fact, for many, this is a way of life.

SIGNS WHICH MAY BE TELLING US WE ARE TROUBLED BY OUR INTIMATE PARTNER RELATIONSHIP:
MEASUREMENTS
directions for use:

1. There are several scales listed here in Figure 14.1.

2. Design or add other scales which you feel provide you other signs that you may indeed be in a troubled relationship or at least feel that you are.

3. Give your experience in each area for which there is a scale listed a number – a place on the scale. This number will be from 1 to 10 with 1 being a low level of experience in this area and 10 being the highest level of experience in this area.

4. If you are not feeling anything in the area of a particular scale, give yourself no number or rating, which means this will be a zero for you.

5. Add the numbers for the scales together. A person who is a five on each of these scales will have a total of 35 (7 x 5) if the questions on the left are used.

6. Now compute the average of the responses you gave yourself for each scale on which you scored yourself other than zero: If the chart on the left is used as is, then your total will be divided by 7. If your total was 35, then compute 35 divided by 7=5.

7. Your average would therefore be 5.

8. Any average of 5 or higher *may* indicate that there are signs that you are either troubled by your relationship or you are in a troubled relationship. Even an average response of 3 suggests that something is calling your attention. Whether or not it be your feelings about your relationship, you are telling yourself something.

---

1. Vague Free-Floating Discomfort

free-floating discomfort scale
1--------------------5--------------------10
no or little   maximum

2. Not Feeling Like Oneself

not feeling like oneself scale
1--------------------5--------------------10
no or little   maximum

3. Choosing to Avoid the Truth

choosing to avoid the truth scale
1--------------------5--------------------10
no or little   maximum

4. Sense of Playing a Role

sense of playing a role scale
1--------------------5--------------------10
no or little   maximum

5. Hollow or Unfulfilling Intimacy

hollow or unfulfilling intimacy scale
1--------------------5--------------------10
no or little   maximum

6. Feeling Like Something is Wrong

feeling like something is wrong scale
1--------------------5--------------------10
no or little   maximum

7. Feeling Trapped

Feeling trapped scale
1--------------------5--------------------10
no or little   maximum

Figure 14.1. Signs which may be telling us we are troubled by our intimate partner relationship.

SENSE OF PLAYING A ROLE

What consciously or subconsciously avoiding truth, living with lies, does is create a *hideout from reality*. Wherever truth might shake things up and bring about unforeseen changes, the fear of change may hold back the truth. *Yes, some truths are explosive if and when told. The alternative then, in many minds, is never to tell them.* Similarly, many people prefer to be lied to and even tell their partners, "Of course I don't want you to, but don't tell me about it if you go to bed with someone else," and, "Some things are better left unsaid."

This sort of warding off of the truth casts the real life one is leading into a sort of stage set atmosphere. Everything is an act, because everything must avoid the truth which is not being told. Everything is scripted, even if done subconsciously, designed to speak around what is not being said. *Out of this comes a sense, sometimes a deeply buried sense but nevertheless a sense, that one is playing a role rather than being entirely real.*

HOLLOW OR UNFULFILLING INTIMACY

All of the above effects are some key elements of discomfort—with something. These signs can be telling us to pay attention—to something, and this can be to ourselves, to our relationships, or to something else. The same is true for intimacy issues. These can be signs of many different things and not only that there is a problem with an intimate partner relationship.

Hollow and or unfulfilling physical, sexual, emotional, and or other intimacy (whatever of these intimacies are part of a particular relation-ship's life) may well be an indication that something is not quite right. Experiencing these, we may be sensing something about ourselves or about our partners and not realize that we are doing so. For example, engaging in sexual intimacy when not wanting to, or not wanting to very much, or not enjoying it, is a sign that a person is doing something a least a bit alien to her or his best interests at that time.

Recall the earlier discussion of rape being crossing boundaries without permission. Here, this person "willingly" engaging in sex without wanting it, or while feeling that something is not quite right, is in a sense allowing her or his boundaries to be crossed without her or his own per-mission. This is almost a self-betrayal or yes, on some level, almost a self-rape sort of event. Being willing to do this to oneself is a sign that some-thing is awry. This calls for some deep introspection:

What value do we place on our own personal boundaries, on ourselves, and on our relationships when we allow this sort of thing to take place?

Whether this sense of hollow intimacy comes on this profoundly, or simply takes the form of a lingering but vague feeling of hollowness during intimate interactions, there is a message from self to self in the experience. Anything which we continue to engage in after it becomes hollow and unfulfilling deserves at least some of our attention. Why are we doing this while feeling this way? Do we feel good about doing this while feeling this way?

Might this hollow, unfulfilled, self-betrayed feeling be a sign that we need to stop and look deeply in order to acknowledge that some kind of dis-connect is taking place?

FEELING LIKE SOMETHING IS WRONG

Reaching far beyond free-floating discomfort, this nagging,

haunting sense that something is wrong, perhaps very wrong, works its way into our consciousness quite slowly, creeping in from the vague subconscious realm. This sensation may be with us for quite some time before we recognize it. Or it may be with us for quite some time while we choose to ignore or deny its presence.

Sometimes we just do not want to know that something is wrong, as once we know this consciously, we may call upon ourselves to actually do something about it.

And frequently, the sense that something is wrong is not attached to any-thing specific.

Yes, this could be denial at work, or it could be that we are not fully understanding what this discomfort or "wrong thing" or "wrongness" might be. Nevertheless, this sensation must be respected and given attention. Stop and feel. That's all it takes. Stop and feel that something is going on, and that that something may be confusing, uncomfortable, or wrong—or not, and that that something may be something which cannot be labeled as of yet.

FEELING TRAPPED

And then there is the sensation of feeling trapped. This can register with us as stagnation, confusion, depression, frustration, tension, claustrophobia, anger, or other troubled emotions. An animal in a maze with no exit does not know what the maze is, does not know why he or she was placed there, and does not imagine that perhaps he or she created this maze or at least willingly entered it. But, eventually the animal does come to feel trapped and does demonstrate this in any number of ways including being lazy, or frantic, or aggressive toward itself or others.

The looming sense of being trapped must be listened to. A "no exit" sensation is not healthy and, if unaddressed for too long, can lead to problematic mental and physical conditions, and even abrupt unexpected outbursts of depression, anger, rage, and or violence.

If you feel trapped, pay attention to the feeling. Feel it, and feel it more. Find safe places and friends with which to share what is going on.

DENYING SIGNS

How often do we ignore these signs, especially the early warning signs, in hopes that things will simply get better? How much of this ignoring, which often continues on while a relationship does NOT get better, is part of the larger problem of denial?

A person living with or in a troubled relationship, or who is feeling troubled about that relationship, if paying attention, can note many signs that there is something to be looking at. When there is something to be known, the signs are all around, yet quite frequently hard to see or not seen. Denial again. It's that same old denial! Denial serves its purpose—it denies the existence or reality it seeks to deny. Meanwhile, vague free-floating feelings of unlabeled discomfort and agitation follow us around, nag us, until we turn and face them.

A troubled relationship is usually troubled long before the trouble is addressed or even recognized.

15
Any Idea Story

Chris and Jan were together over ten years before one of them, Chris, quite suddenly decided to leave the relationship.

This came as a complete surprise to Jan, who had had no idea that there was a problem. They had come together in the early stages of two up-swinging careers, had had no problems or disagreements along the way, and found living together not only convenient but a good idea. They liked the same foods, the same colors, and the same music, and they kept the same hours. Very early on, they decided they were extremely compatible and that was that.

What Jan had not realized was that Chris was not entirely happy with the arrangement, because Chris did not really like health food that much, longed for red meat which they did not eat, hated the persimmon color they painted their walls, definitely hated classical music, and really needed much more sleep.

That Jan had not realized this was surprising, but not as surprising as the fact that Chris had not consciously realized any of this either, not until the moment the entire relationship ended. From one moment to the next, the denial fizzled and reality set in. At least for Chris it did.

While this was powerfully freeing for Chris, this was debilitating and demoralizing for Jan who felt that the investment of over a decade of time in this relationship had virtually been what Jan now decided to call a "complete lie."

And while this accusation made Chris very angry, Chris knew that this was actually true, that Chris had been lying all along. However, Chris had been deceiving Chris at least as much as Chris had been deceiving Jan.

16
Denial?

Denial is a dangerous drug. Denial is an illusion supported by those in denial and quite often also by those around them. Denial is a way of seeing something other than what we truly see before us. Or better stated, denial is a way of thinking we are not-seeing what is right there before us, and instead seeing what we choose to see.

WE HAVE THE TENDENCY TO NOT SEE

If this book were restricted to but one message (a message which is in-deed repeated in various forms several times herein), this would be it:

We have this tendency to not see what is going on around us when we do not want to know about it. And this tendency can be damaging and dangerous.

But first, an important note: Yes, we can fool or lie to ourselves. And we can also be fooled by others and be lied to by others. There is no denying this.

We are not guilty of telling the lies which others have told us when we thought they were telling us the truth. We cannot be expected to detect and decipher each and every lie, every hidden truth behind each lie, and every detail about that truth. How can we possibly filter everything coming at us from outside ourselves? (Or maybe even from inside?)

Yes, we can also be lied to by people other than ourselves, and we can simply not realize or not see this. Yet, while this is going on, we can nevertheless feel on some level, in some way, there is some sort of problem. We may not be able to give ourselves a detailed description of this problem, however we may have a general sense that there is something off, unclear, or maybe wrong.

However, all too often, the person sensing this something, if attempting to ask the partner about it, is shut down, ridiculed and sometimes even beaten verbally or physically just for asking, for doubting.

As a result, the person simply feels that something, something not easy to pinpoint, but something, is terribly askew. This nagging feeling is often ignored, suppressed, denied, and sometimes even denied out of fear of danger. In actual and or potentially physically violent relation-ships, the risk of this denial (denial of danger or possible danger) is definitely a physical risk and can include injury, even serious injury or death.

This process of not-seeing is a looking away from reality. When an intimate partner relationship is entangled in a web of deception, the relationship is for the most part not with the other person but with the web of deception that has been built.

(What, I'm not involved with you? I'm involved with what I tell myself is who you are, with what I tell myself is going on here? Or maybe I'm in-volved with the person you tell me you are, not you.)

DENIAL SNEAKS IN

So, denial has many faces and masks itself in many ways. At first, denial sneaks in, largely unseen, or under some other label such as: cooperating, being considerate, adapting, compromising, going along with things, doing what is best, giving in, doing what works—whatever works. Let's be clear: none of these things is so bad in the form of a single incident, even as a string of incidents, and many of these things can be components of a relationship that works well.

Problematic denial creeps in when we take steps down a path where we get lost, get damaged, die inside, die in some way—and where the denial process blocks awareness of emotional and physical safety.

In troubled relationships, problem denial, even dangerous denial, can find its way in through every crack in the wall, every chink in the *armor of the relationship*. Denial creeps in and wants to stay in. Denial itself becomes the glue holding things together. The composite, the whole picture, is then ...

a facade not a relationship—
a false front—an act covering over a lack of awareness...
buttressed by denial upon denial ...
facilitating the not-seeing of
the steps toward participating in, allowing...
anything needed to preserve the relationship.

Again, this relationship by now is not really between two people but between their separate perceptions of themselves in the face of what they think is taking place. Frequently, this transition into denial is relatively innocuous. (See Figure 16.1 here below.)

cooperating/ being considerate

adapting / compromising

going along with things / doing what is best/ giving in

doing what works – whatever works

doing what works – whatever works

doing what works – whatever works

doing what works – whatever works

doing what works – whatever works

doing what works – whatever works

absolutely whatever works

Figure 16.1. Whatever works.

17
What Strength Story

She had carefully prepared yet another gourmet dinner and was about to put the plates in the oven to warm them to the perfect temperature so that the meal could be served on perfectly warm but not hot plates.

He had just then arrived home.

Immediately, for no clear reason, they were in the midst of yet one more angry and loud discussion about something minor. The debate went on for several minutes, and then, as was his usual behavior, he suddenly turned and walked out.

She waited a while, in fact for three hours, for his return, trying to keep the meal warm but not let it dry out, as she had done so many times before.

Tonight was different, she felt different, although she could not say why. Hungry, she finally ate her share of the meal and put his in the garbage.

An hour after that, he returned home and looked for his dinner. Finally he asked her where she had put it.

She told him she threw it away.

Upset and shocked, he tried to put some dinner together for himself, pulling what he could out of the garbage, slamming refrigerator and cabinet doors, and calling his mother long distance on the kitchen speaker phone as he did. When his mother came on the line, he complained about how his wife had thrown his dinner into the garbage just because he was a few hours late.

The speaker phone crackled with a long distance sigh as his mother replied:

"WHAT STRENGTH. I SHOULD HAVE DONE THAT TO YOUR FATHER YEARS AGO."

18
Emotional Abuse

Now you see it, now you don't. So tangled and murky it defies us to sort it out is the elusive matter of emotional abuse. After all, actual physical abuse can be difficult enough for some to detect and identify. Emotional abuse leaves vague traces of itself, many twisted tracks leading in different directions all at once. Questions about--when it is serious, what of it is damaging, who causes it, who feels it, and what the reason for it is, are painful, disturbing, and challenging.

TANGLED AND MURKY TYPE OF ABUSE

Emotional abuse is taking place all around us, affects almost every one of us at least in a minor form at some time in our lives. Emotional abuse is so very common that we practically take it for granted, as normal and acceptable. Emotional abuse tends to take a back seat to concerns about physical abuse as physical abuse is seen, at least by law enforcement and the courts, as more damaging, more dangerous, and more specific.

In fact, many persons who are being abused emotionally but not physically do not recognize this abuse as there appear to be no physical signs of it. And of those being abused physically, many do not include emotional abuse in their descriptions of the abuse they are experiencing. However, the effects of some emotional abuse can be just as powerful as the effects of some physical abuse.

A note of reminder here. The discussion in this book deals with emotional (and physical) abuse *of adults by adults*. When children experience abuse, and far too many do, a host of highly critical factors not ad-dressed in this book are present and require specific attention. Here the discussion focuses on what is behavior taking place between two adults in a love, marital, dating, and or sexual relationship. *(This book can also apply to persons near adult age, teens, as in too many instances teens in relationships can also experience many of the issues discussed in this book. Refer to the Author's Note at the opening of this book.)*

SIGNS OF EMOTIONAL ABUSE

Even adults experiencing emotional abuse may not see that this abuse is taking place. They may experience general indicators that something is awry (such as those indicators listed in Chapter 14). Again, those general indicators or signs may or may not be related to being the victim of emotional abuse. Yet it is important to know that emotional abuse can cause, bring out, or magnify where already present, general indicators or signs of general discomfort or distress.

Beyond the general feelings of discomfort listed in Chapter 14, people who are actually experiencing emotional abuse may also experience more specific feelings of discomfort such as these listed here below. These signs may or may not be caused by, or attributed to, emotional abuse (not even in instances of high levels of emotional abuse), however these are quite common responses to emotional abuse in intimate partner relationships:

- Embarrassment.
- Confusion.
- Instability.
- Fear.
- Identity doubts, not feeling like oneself.
- Worthlessness, low self esteem.
- No or low level of confidence.
- Sense of complete or extreme failure.
- Depression.
- Isolation.
- No sense of control over what happens.
- All encompassing self blame—for every problem.
- Humiliation.
- Pessimism, a negative outlook on the future.

And eventually, persons being emotionally (including but not limited to verbally) abused by a partner over long periods of time may add to this list:
- Feeling that the criticisms of oneself being made by an abusive partner are correct, even believing them.

And even . . .
- Defending these criticisms to others.

And sadly, sometimes these self abusing behaviors also arise:
- Joining in on the emotional abuse of oneself.
- Amplifying the abuse being experienced by working to hurt oneself even more than the abuser does.
- Allowing, even inviting, physical and sexual abuse of oneself to take place unprotested or weakly protested.
- Hiding the pain of the abuse in substance abuse or other detrimental habitual behavior.
- Bottling up of rage.

- Hurting oneself emotionally or physically.
- Showing tendencies to suicidality.

And of course, what deserves entire volumes and is reported in depth elsewhere, as well as noted here in brief in Chapter 41, is the risk that the abuse being experienced is then transferred onto others such as children.

HARD TO SEE AND INVISIBLE ABUSE

Countless other feelings and attitudes can be found in persons experiencing emotional abuse. However, what is taking place during emotional abuse is in large part invisible as the abuse is occurring not only explicitly, such as audibly (verbally) and visibly, but also quietly, invisibly, and often quite implicitly, even in many cases secretly.

It is perhaps the implicit, invisible abuse that is most difficult for the person being abused to deal with, as there is little if any validation that it is taking place. Other people (for the most part) do not see it, so they do not acknowledge it is happening, and in fact, they may if asked deny this is happening.

This can be a confusing, disturbing, even so-called crazy-making experience in that the person being abused is not only suffering the abuse but also feels that there is no reality to the experience—a potentially dangerous combination for one's mental and physical health.

(Note: While this is similar to self or others' denial, this may indeed be something else such as: lack of knowledge regarding abuse and violence; particular denial-like childhood experiences with and messages from parents; lack of self-awareness; poor self-confidence; self-destructive tendencies; etc.)

Abusers administering emotional abuse tend to prefer to do this out of sight and earshot of others and tend to deny that such abuse is taking place—deny to themselves, to the persons they are abusing, and if asked about it by others, to others. After all, emotional abuse, no matter how harsh, is a form of abuse that often can be rather easily hidden. Hiding this abuse to invalidate the abusee's issues and claims of being abused—to in-validate the abusee—is often part of the abuser's process.

Comments such as, "She thinks I don't love her, but she's very wrong," and, "She feels so badly about herself, I just can't get through to her that all this is her imagination," and, "She's making it up because she wants people to think I'm mean and cruel, but you know me, I'm not that kind of person," are heard all the time. How often are such comments:

> *masking something taking place behind closed doors where no one else can see or hear?*

Hidden emotional abuse is painfully common and rarely addressed. Many people just do not get help for something this elusive, something even the reality of which they themselves are frequently forced to wonder about, no matter how intense the abuse is. In fact, an added level of emotional abuse is a sometimes present and quite convoluted aspect of this abuse—where the person being abused risks "looking crazy" when talking about it, trying to tell anyone it is taking, or has taken, place. In fact, many abusers include in their abuse their *skill* at making the abusee "look crazy."

Being abused in private, either directly or by implication, is not easy to report to others, especially when others may not want to hear, may not believe what they hear, may have contradictory and positive impressions of the abuser, may have a (personal, familial, financial, professional, legal, or other) stake in the abuser not being viewed as the abuser.

EMOTIONAL ABUSE IS SO COMPLEX

The complex matters of intent and consent were introduced in Chapters 4 and 5. And of course, their introduction only served to show how complex these aspects of intimate partner relating are rather than to simplify them. Truly, stopping abuse and violence requires more than knowing about the many faces of this abuse and violence; it also takes seeing that the faces themselves are masks for layer upon layer upon layer of intent and consent, confusion about intent and consent, and abuse of consent and intent.

When there is no physical violence, emotional abuse between two adults in a significant other intimate partner relationship is difficult to point to because it typically appears to be taking place with both parties' per-mission. (If it appears to anyone to be taking place at all, that is). After all, others may say, "They both show up for the abuse event and stick around for it," "The two of them pick on each other, this is just the way they are," and, "There is no physical force compelling one or both to be this way, so how can we call this abuse?"

Certainly, emotional abuse can be mutual; however, quite often it appears mutual when it is not.

Woven throughout the following chapters on abuse is the recognition of this pervasive and powerful yet all too invisible cruelty, emotional abuse. Other terms for this form of abuse in intimate partner relationships include but are not limited to: psychological abuse, mental cruelty, "gas lighting," and quite often the slang description: "mind-f---ing."

19
Compromise and Trade (C&T) Abuse

It is truly a challenge for onlookers (those outside of the intimate partner relationships they are observing) to capture in words, to de-scribe entirely, and to understand in full, the intricate process of other persons' intimate partner relating. There are an infinite number of subtle and obvious interactions and communications, and endless day to day, even moment-to-moment events, agreements, compromises, trades, and exchanges taking place.

Even the actual members of relationships do not entirely see and under-stand what all is going on in their own relationships.

Indeed, so very subtle are the undercurrents and under-messages driving the processes of relating that it is even a challenge for the members of the relationship itself to identify their own intricate communication, and compromise and trade (what this book calls C&T) processes in progress. As per these C&Ts, while these are natural and essential, they can sometimes go quite wrong.

COMPROMISES AND TRADES

A relationship is more than the sum of its parts, and or

perceived parts at any one time. It arises out of ongoing human interactions—many many, an infinite number of interactions over seconds, minutes, hours, days, weeks, months, frequently even years.

Were we able to play back any of these interactions with the timing of a slow motion movie, we would see how many micro-mini-steps there are even in any one minute's process of relating. Every millionth second, breathing patterns, facial expressions, postures, vocal inflections, body language, looks in eyes, and more vary. We do not see ourselves seeing or hearing all this, nor do we consciously feel ourselves reacting to each miniscule shift and change in expression, but we take it all in.

We may not see ourselves *not consciously seeing*, but we nevertheless see and react to what we see and also to what we *do not see ourselves seeing*.

Yet sometimes what we see is the slightest shift in body stance or posture. When this posture is leaning toward us with shoulders hunched, we may subconsciously interpret this as an ever so subtle but nevertheless very real threat. We may snap into self protective mode, without a conscious tracing of the steps triggering us. We may not want to attack or flee, but we want to do something, anything, in response. Quite often, what we do in response is respond to, by accepting, trades and compromises being offered to or subtly forced upon us:

I will agree to this if you do not do that to me. I will give in here if you give in there, with this "there" maybe being not to hit me, or hit me so hard, this time. Sometimes this "there" is yet more extreme, being "not to beat me, or rape me, or otherwise terrorize me."

There are definitely even cases where the C&Ts themselves are so very risk laden that whatever safety or security is being presumably C&T'd for is not at all what is actually being offered or given. Thus, com-promises and trades in highly troubled relationships are frequently quite ineffective, even dangerous.

INFINITE TRADES

Human interaction is indeed at least a series of perceptions plus actions, often also trades and compromises, a never ending series of responses and decisions. Of course these are not all threat based and of course these are not all negative. Clearly there are fabulous aspects of inter-acting in many fine intimate partner relationships.

Let's call a relationship a *life form*, an entity which develops a life of its own, with characteristics of its own, and rules of its own, forming all this out of its own history. Eventually, the relationship grows and is such a large part of our lives that it requires a financial, an energetic, and an *emotional budget* to function, and room to breathe. *Many a relationship consumes more of everything than does the sum of the individual members.*

Amidst this relationship's virtually infinite number of interactions are the almost infinite number of large and small, even minute, trades and compromises. These are essential parts of the process of relationship-defining, relationship-building, and relationship-maintaining. And yet, right there, right within the body of all those trades and compromises, lurks the very thing that can hurt the very relationship these are defining, building, and maintaining: the hidden trigger.

If we were to dissect a relationship into steps, millions and millions of steps, each step being composed of millions and millions of sub-steps, we might be able to see what that relationship was made of. Might.

Again, even though we may not see ourselves seeing, hear ourselves hearing, feel ourselves making each and every little shift in facial expression, posture, body language, vocal tone, pause length while speaking, volume of speech—shifts in the expression of emotional positives, negatives, and neutrals—both we as individuals and we as relationships are on some level picking these up and responding to them at all times. (Note that even a non-response is a response). Among these difficult to detect, tiny, micro-minishifts are infinite signals, triggers, that trigger responses in us.

C&T ABUSE

Let's back up and look at the abuse of C&Ts. Every relationship moves through many strings or series of C&Ts. These C&Ts can definitely be key building blocks toward positive and successful relationships. And yet there is a point in *some* relationships' C&T processes where the process is at risk of downgrading into increasingly negative patterning. Can we slow the process, see what is taking place and catch ourselves in a troubled C&T process as it begins to wobble, before it heads in the direction of downgrade? Yes, if we are paying close attention.

C&Ts which are dominated by one of the partners in an intimate partner relationship are at risk of becoming one-sided C&T processes. Can we slow the process to see where a particular C&T may not be relationship-preserving in a positive way and where instead the opposite is taking place?

Might it be that some persons in C&T processes are actually un-knowingly—or at least are rather unconsciously—giving away their rights to have a significant say in how they live, what they do, who they see, what risks they take, what forms of intimacy they engage in, and how they spend the time of their lives, their energy, their money? Might it be that their partners sometimes see this unconscious giving away of rights taking place and sometimes even take advantage of this?

Could it be that inadvertent (or perhaps somewhat purposeful) confusion about what consent should look and feel like is again the culprit, and at play in the muddling and muddying of functional C&T processes? Might one or both of the partners in a troubled relationship feel on some level that he or she or they benefit by deficient C&T processes? By lying to themselves in some way?

Embedded in C&T interactions are all of the gives and takes found in relationships. Persons in troubled relationships can benefit by choosing to carefully and explicitly make clear what C&Ts they have made and are making every step of the way. Unravel this C&T process, pull out the magnifying glass, and look very very closely.

SUBTLE HIDDEN TRIGGERS

What triggers those unspoken micro level compromises and trades? This is the level where the real action, the real compromising and trading is taking place. What *small step in one direction or the other is vulnerable to confusion, dominance by one or the other partner, and maybe even abuse*? We have to allow ourselves to ask such questions, to sharpen our awareness, or at least intended awareness of this micro level of interaction.

20
Power and Control Story

M.J. had maintained a fierce, force promoted control over their joint earnings. But now Bee's usually smaller separate side income grew to the point that it was far larger than what M.J. gave Bee out of their joint earnings. Now Bee wanted to stop working with M.J. and build a separate business.

Another threat to the power structure in their relationship arose. Bee's separate income was growing and Bee was now maintaining control over it. Bee continued to spend all of this on the family, an arrangement that had been instated early in their relationship, but now Bee worked hard to maintain complete control over these separate earnings. Now, Bee did not turn any of it over to M.J. any more.

Bee then quietly began putting bits of her earnings away for herself.

M.J. found out and grew increasingly resentful about this. The tension built beyond its already heavy level.

M.J. began flamboyantly threatening to kill Bee.

Bee started wondering if M.J. meant this, and whether M.J. was actually dangerous. Bee was unsure how to take M.J.'s threats of death.

21
Stress, Trouble, Abuse, and Violence

How many times is something like this said: "He says just because he doesn't love me the way I think I should be loved doesn't mean he doesn't love me. I can't tell whether he is right or I am right in thinking I am not being treated well at all, or being loved. I mean, is any of this abuse really love?"

THE FANTASY

That any relationship can be entirely problem- and stress-free is almost a fantasy. Real life has its challenges—financial, parental, health, work-life, schedule, neighbors, and so on—and these can affect relationships, even when the relationships are themselves not troubled relationships.

A relationship can get itself into trouble quite suddenly; however, for the most part, there are many steps into trouble along the way. For example, how the members of the relationship cope with stress, as individuals and as a team, is one of the key factors in determining the well being of the relationship.

There is a stress continuum ...
      ... a range of stress related states within relationships.

Many significant other relationships typically move back

and forth along this life stress continuum as they respond to the individual and joint variations in their lives and the world:

*normal life stress←→slightly elevated life stress←→
←→unusual degree of life stress←→high stress

SOME RELATIONSHIPS DO NOT COPE WITH STRESS

Some significant other relationships experience, as individuals or as a team, a more problematic continuum, a stress-abuse-violence continuum, one which overall, no matter what its fluctuations might be, be-comes more stressful, abusive, and violent as time goes by:

stress→trouble coping with stress→→
→→increasing stress related abuse and violence

Ideally, we want to be primarily at the normal life stress location at the starred (*) far left end of the first continuum diagram (at the bottom of the previous page). Of course, we are not always there, as life has stressors and we respond to stressors with stress feelings, behaviors, and experiences. This first continuum (at the bottom of the previous page) is the normal (and therefore presumably healthy) response to life stress continuum (as per the discussion in this book). Any point along this first continuum is possible in life, however, note that on this first continuum there is no abuse or violence as response to stresses in life.

And we do want to avoid leaping or falling into the second continuum (seen at the top of this page), as this is the place where the normal stresses of life can become triggers for abuse and violence in a relationship.

Too frequently, members of relationships which contain

abuse and vio-lence blame each other for the fact that their relationship exists along this troubled (second above) continuum. They blame each other for compounding the experience of even normal life stress, let alone variations in life stress, far more (see Figure 21.1).

Sadly, both the perpetrator of the violence and the recipient of the violence are responsible in some way for finding themselves there. Each of them is there, present, for this problem. They travel into and through the realms of Figure 21.1 together. *Stress does not always lead to abuse and violence, but it is good to watch for the signs that it might.*

WHEN BOREDOM OR DULLNESS PLAYS A ROLE

And then there is the problem of under-stress. There are degrees of relatively normal stress, such as the stress typically involved in navigating daily life. (This normal stress helps keeps us awake, alert, alive, and functioning because WE HAVE TO BE).

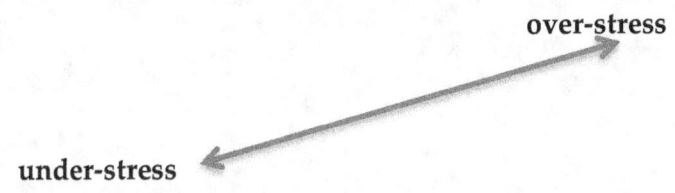

Under-stress can be dangerous and even boring. One who is under-stressed may be at risk of depression, anxiety, and other problems. We all handle under- and over-stress differently (see Figure 21.2).

Under-stress can also affect relationships. A relationship in which there is no stress whatsoever may be in another kind of wobble, a flat line of day after day after day of nothingness. This may sound like peace, but the lack of any of the typical ups and downs of life whatsoever can invite deterioration similar to the way too much stress can be destructive. Boredom itself is stressful.

There are times when members of relationships are driven to abuse and even destroy their relationships rather than deal with the problem of boredom (and or of life's stresses) within the relationship or within the lives of one or both members of the relationship.

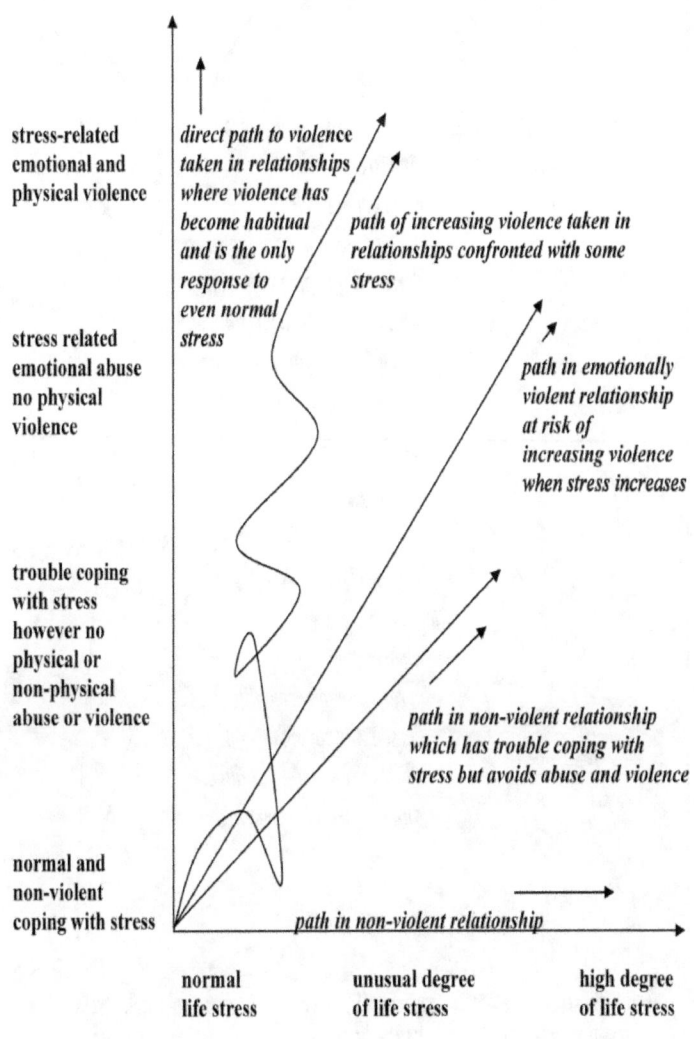

Figure 21.1.
Sample paths to violence in non-violent and violent relationships.

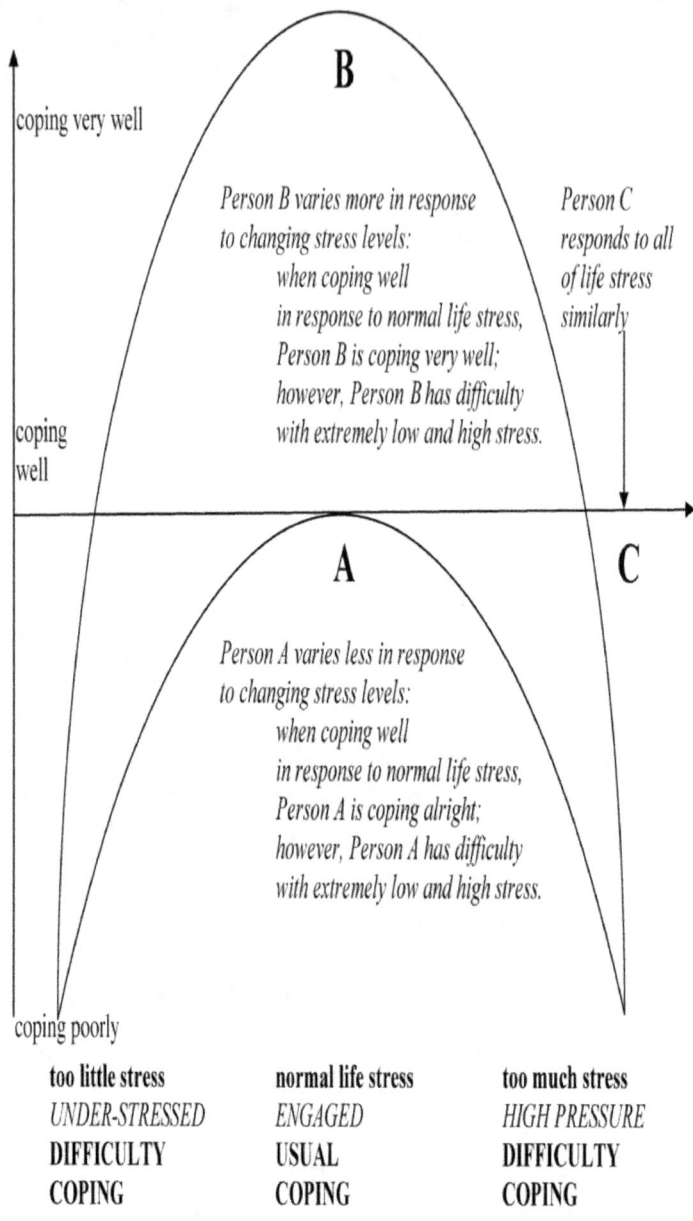

Figure 21.2. Reactions to stress
(even boredom can be stressful).

22
Who Could Ask for More Story

Marta fell in love with a wonderful man she admired very much and looked up to in every way. When he asked her to marry him, she was ecstatic and of course said yes. She felt like the luckiest woman in the world. Who could ask for more, she wondered.

On their honeymoon, Marta tried to explain to Jed her deep spiritual views. He seemed to be open, as they discussed this in bed after making love, feeling very close. She poured her heart out to Jed, revealing a deep commitment to her beliefs.

But, the next month, at home and back into the swing of life after their honeymoon, she mentioned this discussion in a moment of sweet reminiscence. Now, he seemed to go through a total personality shift from understanding to critical. He told her she could have her "little fantasies about God or whatever it was," but that she should keep these "fantasies" to herself and "never ever" let their friends or colleagues hear about them.

Instantly, she began to abide by his dictum, perplexed, but wanting very much not to rock the boat. In that moment, she began, if she had not already started, to work to fit his views of the perfect wife.

They eventually moved into a very nice house, and Marta further accommodated Jed's views of the perfect wife in every aspect of her behavior, looks and thinking. He did not acknowledge her efforts to please him, but Marta told herself that perhaps this was because he did not realize she had to try very hard to make herself this way, that this did not come naturally for her.

And she was actually glad he did not know she was not as perfect as she worked to appear to be.

What she did not see, or did not let herself see, is how self-centered he was in their daily interactions, in his use of time, in his lovemaking, and in every way. She also did not let herself admit to herself that he surrounded himself only with people who admired him, and that he expected his wife to be one of these people and to serve him in the way he "deserved."

She appeared to him to be one of these admiring people, because when they first came together she surely was. And over time, where she was less admiring, she knew not to show this admiration diminishing even the slightest bit. Too risky she felt, although she never really gave the risk serious thought. She was still very committed to this marriage and to this man whom she thought she still deeply loved despite the fact that he looked more and more human to her every day.

Eventually pregnant and still committed to their marriage, she pushed not only her dwindling admiration of him but also her own spiritual beliefs into the background. And she pushed her own career into the background as well, in part because she knew that her success would not be welcome should she ever equal or outshine him in anyway.

It was a year or two later that she belatedly realized that he was becoming (or had been for quite some time) both sexually and emotionally abusive. "Becoming" was not the appropriate word for this, she knew this on some level, as he had been abusive all along.

Yes, increasingly abusive over time, but abusive from the early stages of their marriage. But, she had not recognized this behavior as abuse and, in a sense, had behaved in such a way that she seemed to tolerate or even OK it.

An old friend of hers came to town. Marta saw him and told him how tough her internal emotional struggle was, perhaps owning it for the first time. Her friend was clearly worried about her, and reflected to her that she had changed and now seemed very tense and fearful. Marta denied the tension and the fear.

Marta's husband found out about that meeting, perhaps because in his free time he followed her around without her knowing. At first, he did not tell her that he knew about this visit, but he became more abrupt and cold in their conversations and more aggressive in bed. His violent ugly side broke through now, and he began to push and shove her, and hurt her during sex.

As she was pregnant, he now accused her of being pregnant by her old friend, which was in no way the case. This baby was for sure Marta's husband's; she never slept with anyone but her husband, not even once since they had married.

His anger and cruelty increased, and he told her she was its cause. She changed. One day, she finally really stood up to him in ways she had not done previously, now insisting on her right to be believed by her husband—to be believed that she was pregnant with his child—and also on her right to have her own friends and beliefs.

Hearing her talk like this, his expression changed, and he went immediately out of control—as she continued to say more—he hit her in the belly very forcefully and repeatedly.

She stared at his changed face—and cried out for him to stop. He seemed to be temporarily crazy, as he hit her and shouted at her until she crumpled in a corner, then kicked her in the back several times and finally stomped off.

She lost this baby. Their marriage continued along the same path.

23
When the Person Abusing Feels Abused

What happens when the person who is most definitely the abuser claims to be the actual victim of the abuse? What is going on when others believe this? How can something so seemingly straightforward be turned around to the point that the entire story is backward? How can the truth bury itself so deeply that all involved, including the physically abused and injured one, may feel the need to pretend to wonder, or even actually begin to wonder, who the dominant aggressor is.

Before proceeding here, it is essential that we understand that, in a world where violence is so common, we are all victims of this human condition. In this sense, both the abuser and the abusee can be said to be victims of cultural and biological parameters, which allow (or at least look away from) some forms of interpersonal abuse and violence to re-solve interpersonal disagreements, disputes, and conflicts.

Also note that at least some IPV is indeed mutual, where the partners are equally violent and there is no first strike in that there is no dominant aggressor. In other IPV there is a definite dominant aggressor and a definite victim—there is a definite instance, or pattern of instances, where one partner is violent with the other who is the victim of this violence.

All variations exist. This chapter focuses on the situation where there is a dominant aggressor, a distinct abuser, and here one that feels or at least claims to be to be the abused one.

USE OF THE WORD VICTIM

Where most discussions of victimization are relatively simple, if we look closely we see this concept is complex and perplexing. Hearing the person who has been abused and the person who has done the abusing both describe themselves as victims of the abuse confuses us and brings to mind many questions. Who hurt whom? Who started this? Who is the dominant aggressor here? Is there one? This experience also brings to mind the question of who is telling the truth. One tends to think: they both have such opposing stories, one must be lying! But which one?

As noted earlier, unfortunately, all too often the person being abused (the person stepping forward to admit she or he is being abused) is treated like the liar even in a court of law—likely revealing some deep bias against members of our social family who dare to point out to us that there is a problem.

The world can be very rough on a truth teller. And the world can some-times favor the abuser.

On a very broad scale, we can see many examples of (what this book defines as) *institutional bias* against persons who report they are being abused. And, we can see these examples in courts of law (among other places) every day! (See also Chapters 4 and 35.)

Clearly there are significant *institutional biases* against persons, especially spouses, taking domestic violence, IPV, claims to court and to law enforcement. (Just examine the data on courts' frequent denial of re-quested IPV-related restraining orders, and the failure to fully enforce these, the too frequent failure to take these seriously.)

Even without persons who are doing the abusing claiming the word "victim" for themselves, there is much to be confused about when using this term. And persons who are doing the abusing who wish to hide, to deny that they are abusers, take full advantage of this confusion, frequently with great success. Suddenly, competition for the title of victim is apparent all around us and most frequently perhaps in the courts, such as when persons who abuse deny their abuse and violent actions.

VICTIM?
WHY VICTIM?
WHO IS THE VICTIM?
IS THERE A VICTIM?
IS IT A GOOD IDEA TO THINK OF ONESELF AS A VICTIM?
CAN THE ABUSER BE THE VICTIM?
CAN BOTH THE ABUSER AND THE ABUSEE BE THE VICTIM?

So much is associated with the word victim that its meaning is controversial and largely misunderstood. As noted earlier, law enforcement tends to speak in terms of the victim and the perpetrator of violence in domestic violence situations. In fact, persons being abused can expect to be called victims by law enforcement and may benefit by this label in that law is more likely to respond to a victim.

Terms such as *victim* and *perpetrator* have extended in use past law enforcement to some therapeutic, treatment, shelter, and other settings, but there these terms have largely evolved to other forms. Other professional terminologies apply different terms, for example domestic violence programs may call victims of abuse *survivors* to emphasize the importance of recovery from the abuse. And programs treating perpetrators may call these perpetrators *batterers*.

While words are only words and mean only what is attributed to them, the word, victim, has taken on a particularly troubled meaning in numerous circumstances. Victim sometimes has associated with it something permanent and irreparably damaged. For this reason, many domestic violence and other treatment and therapeutic services have chosen to apply the word victim to those who have died at the hands of their abusers and the word survivor to those who have survived the abuse and sought to find or form a new life past the experience or experiences of abuse.

This framing of this understanding that one need not become permanently mired in the role of victim of abuse and violence is powerful. Being a survivor can mean not being a victim forever.

Being a survivor means moving past, finding a way out, being stronger for making it past the experience of abuse. Use of the word survivor allows for hope and a future, while use of the word victim may allow for less and can carry with it a sort of dead-ended, trapped feeling.

TURNING THE TABLES

We do find that some perpetrators of abuse step forward and call themselves the victims of the abuse, as if competing for the label, hiding behind the label, and in many cases, accepting the label as they may indeed be victims of abuse—victims of some abuse somewhere along the line, at some time in their lives. Having experienced abuse, especially as a child, it is easy to find oneself carrying traces of this abusee experience through life. Sometimes these traces are deeply buried, so deeply buried that their effect on current behavior is not recognized.

When the abuser calls him or herself the abusee, he or she may be telling it like it is, or may actually be turning the table—claiming that the hurt and pain he or she is described as causing is really not as it is being reported or appears. The roles may then get reversed in the listener's mind, with the perceived abusee being depicted as the actual abuser!

While this turning of the table and reversing of the roles is at times right on, quite frequently this table-turning is *grossly deceptive*. All too frequently this is a way of denying, of not seeing (NOT-SEEING), and or not owning the truth. How easy it is for the abuser to blame another for that abuser's own less than desirable actions.

How easy it is for that abuser to muddle the truth, to make reality conform to whatever this dominant aggressor wants it to be.

Yes, the dominant aggressor is likely to have just enough dominance over the situation to define it! And law enforcement, the courts, society at large, may believe the dominant aggressor because of that person's dominant control over the definition of the relationship's reality (and even of the funds to make a case in court)!

Hence the abusee loses the protection and response so very much needed—and loses this to the abuser. *(Watch for this when in divorce, family, court during debates regarding the presence of IPV in a marriage. Appearances regarding the dominant spouse, who also often happens to be in control of the family funds or most of these funds, may not always be what and who the dominant spouse is projecting and paying attorneys to argue.)*

TRAUMA OF TRUTH TELLING

Regardless of who tells the "real" truth about an abusive relationship, and regardless of whether or not the so-called truth being told is actually a lie about the source of the abuse, truth telling can be quite traumatic for both parties.

When the actual abusee becomes the truth teller, the actual abuser can feel attacked, even victimized by this truth telling. After all, telling the world that this abuse has been going on was not agreed to, not part of the deal.

Typically, truth telling about intimate partner abuse and violence feels to the person abusing a lot like the abusee has broken a contract. And yes, if the abusee somehow promised never to report the abuse, this may in some way be viewed as the breaking of the contract— but of course this is not a valid contract. Or shall we call it one? Might there be cases where the consent to receive the abuse is valid consent? Is this logical?

The self perceived as victimized person, the one who is actually abusing, may grab the role of victim and be far better at projecting the pain of this victim experience than the actual person who is being abused. Here the label and even the perceived role of abusee shift from actual abusee and truth teller, actual victim of the abuse, to person abusing.

The tables can turn this quickly, this bizarrely, in the blink of an eye!

This reversal by the abuser, when the abuser is self labeled the abusee, is all too common although too often entirely undetected, or at least entirely unacknowledged as a reversal. This reversal of the roles of abuser and abusee finds a way to express itself during arguments, family encounters, beyond the home out in the world, even in courtrooms. Hence there can be a great deal of confusion regarding who is indeed the perpetrator of the abuse.

HANDLING THIS TURNING OF THE TABLE

Here is one place the defensive response claim can surface. The person abusing, not yet ready to take responsibility for the abuse, chooses to grab the role of the person who has been the recipient of the abuse, in an almost greater abuse.

Now the fact that the abusing person ever abused is being denied and the abusee is called crazy, dishonest, attention seeker, liar — even abusive.

Addressing this threatened or actual turning of the table is tricky, as truth is not necessarily supported by those around the actual truth teller who sometimes finds truth telling a lonely path to take.

The truth teller must be prepared for this possibility. For those who do come to this painful twist of reality, with support and knowledge of what is taking place, the truth can still be unearthed.

LIST:
REMEMBER THIS WHEN THE TABLES ARE TURNED

When the person being abused is being recast as the abuser, or as a "nut" or "liar" for reporting the abuse, it is important for this person to:

- Hold steady: continue to know and remember what the truth is.
- Know that truth tellers can be ostracized.
- Know that many people do not want to hear the truth.
- Know that truth telling is a doorway to leaving the imprint of being abused behind.
- Keep in mind that agreeing to support and defend someone else's (even the abusive partner's) lie is lying.
- Know not to get lost, not to lose oneself, in the process of defining and defending the truth.
- Continue to raise questions about other persons' views of what is going on.
- Put truth on the table for all to see, and keep telling the truth.
- Continue to break the unspoken contract to support the lie, to protect the abuser.
- Be strong, be very strong, and seek support from others who are strong and have walked this challenging path.
- Know that you are breaking a cycle of abuse and that breaking troubled cycles can be like this.
- Be a cycle breaker.

WHEN THE ABUSER NEVERTHELESS TELLS THE TRUTH

The above list is addressed primarily to the abusEE, the person actually being abused, when this abusEE is being miscast as the abusER by the actual abusER. This abusEE-blaming is common among abusERS.

Let's shift focus now to the case of a different abusER, one who does not blame the abusEE. This particular abusER does not call the abusEE the abusER, and instead seeks to admit to the abuse, to do the opposite of blaming the abusEE for the abuse:

What a watershed experience it is for a person who has abused a mate, an intimate partner, for many years, to step forward, to own the abuse. (Note that these watershed moments are frequently achieved in Batter-ers Intervention and Batterers Treatment Program Groups.)

What a powerful breakthrough it is for the abuser to (a) admit to the abusive behaviors; and (b) perhaps to help make the damage which has been done easier to repair, if in no other way then at least by validating it, agreeing that it really has taken place.

Owning participation in harm is a big step, and support and information may be required. Shedding the lies which may have been carried for too long is a powerful experience. Reversing the denying of the violence committed against a (present or past) intimate partner is stopping the violence which lingers in the lies about the violence.

Part Three

24
Repeating Story

The two of them went through three bottles of wine while trying to make a decision. No progress was made, both were frustrated, and abruptly she got up and walked away.

Sometime later, John found her crying in the bedroom. He yelled at her, out of the blue, with no conversation preceding, "You just won't cooperate, will you? I've asked you again and again."

She said nothing, just cried.

"I'm fed up. I'll break you," he went on, "I'll make you cooperate around here!"

He marched away, but then turned around and came right back in, suddenly acting somewhat apologetic. "Look, I think we can fix this, just go along with me, and see how this can work. Just have sex with me three times a week and go back to cooking for me, and this whole situation will get a lot better."

Desperate, and worried that he would do something crazy if she did not, she complied with his wishes. This was difficult for her as now he became unusually aggressive and abusive during sex. But, at least he was nicer to her for a while.

A few months later, she realized that they had cycled through exactly this pattern many many times before. And then she forgot they had—all over again.

25
Denial and Problem Patterns

We all fall into patterns—patterns of life. This patterning can be and usually is normal and even healthy. In fact, patterning in behavior has a certain amount of survival value. For example, it is good that we can become patterned to simply go onto automatic and stop at a red light when we come to one.

It is good that we automatically fasten our seat belts. It is good that we automatically get out of the way of danger such as a moving car or a falling object. Patterns of instinct can allow us to detect or sense danger and move to quickly protect ourselves from danger when we need to.

However, when emotions are at play, self-protective gut level instinct, sheer split second awareness and response, may take a back seat. Other behavior patterns, which may even be contrary to basic survival, can surface. Some of these other behavior patterns may even masquerade as survival oriented.

PATTERNS CAN INDEED BE NORMAL AND GOOD

How does this understanding of patterning apply to relationships? Relationships often build into themselves patterns, some of which sneak in without being recognized.

And, many of these patterns are nice, even wonderful, for example: a shared good night kiss; a "have a good day" in the morning; a "how was your day" in the evening; a "can I help you with that;" an "I'll do this chore—you do that one, and we'll get this work done quickly."

EXAMINE HARMFUL PATTERNS

When relationship patterns are harmful, or potentially harmful, to us or to others, we must examine them. This takes, of course, a willingness to look—specifically a willingness to look at behaviors which are detrimental, unsuccessful, and in some way imbalanced in their repeated compromises and trades. Simply doing what supposedly works is not always healthy. Not paying attention to patterns as they form and continue can be problematic.

Yet, we often forget to pay attention, or perhaps even choose not to pay attention. All too often, instead of examining patterns of relating—of compromising, making little and big trades, and doing what seems to work—we do what it takes to ignore troubled patterns or downplay their importance, or just plain deny their existence.

We look away to avoid seeing the truth, to help us avoid rocking the boat. Truth can sometimes be very unsettling, so we bury it. It's that denial again. And again and again and again.

DENIAL PRESERVES A PROBLEM RELATIONSHIP

Does denial about harmful patterns preserve a troubled relationship? Yes. Does denial about being in denial further help to preserve this troubled relationship? Yes, for a time—sometimes for too long a time. Relationships can establish an uneasy form of stability by living in denial.

However, when the denial is actually burying ongoing suffering, the damage festers and grows. The damage may grow for years, even de-cades, before it is so extreme it is addressed. Some people are even willing to take their denial to their graves! This is how very scary truth may seem to some.

Sometimes we engage in this denial out of lack of information about the existence of patterns or the signs of these patterns. Sometimes we engage in this denial out of insecurity and fear of change. Other times we engage in this denial out of actual fear for our own safety.

Recognizing and addressing the truth can be unsettling, especially in an environment where truth is repressed and punished if told.

We see this scenario many times around us, where someone speaks up about abuse or other interpersonal problems which were expected to re-main secret, and the person speaking up is the one who then suffers and pays!

The role of truth teller, perhaps better described as truth revealer, may be a dangerous role to play in a relationship, a family, a group of friends, or a community where abuse and violence is not supposed to be revealed. Powerful unspoken agreements "not to let outsiders know things" are made and can even be carried from generation to generation.

Just keeping the peace can therefore be quite a popular motive. Whether this just keeping the peace motive is subconscious or conscious (and it can be either or both at any given moment), it is powerful. This **keep the peace, no matter how painful this peace may be**, motive fuels the denial it takes to remain in the problematic or dangerous situation or relationship.

LIST:
ANATOMY OF DENIAL

We can think of this monster we call "denial" as having several very related, overlapping, characteristics. Their very overlap is part of what makes denial work so well in covering over the reality of what is actually taking place in a troubled relationship.

Characteristic One: How Conscious One Is

Denial can be entirely unconscious, or it can be rather subconscious, or it can be quite conscious. Being conscious of something usually means that we are consciously aware of it and know we are aware of it.

Characteristic Two: How Aware One Is

But awareness itself is shifty. Sadly, awareness and consciousness can be worked against each other to help us lie to ourselves. Sometimes we consciously choose to be unaware of a problem, choosing to not see it taking place. Levels of awareness therefore do not always match how conscious we are of something.

Characteristic Three: How Much We See and Do Not See

And what we think we see of what is going on around us is colored by our conscious choice not to be aware of it all—and by our awareness of this choice. Seeing and not-seeing can be used as tools by a conscious-ness that wants to lie to itself, to be somewhat or even entirely unaware of what is taking place—to deny the very existence of what is taking place.

These characteristics of seeing and denial are interlinking levels of consciousness, awareness, and seeing. These levels run parallel to each other at all times, even in highly conscious relating processes (see Figure 25.1). We can actually consciously make an effort to be more conscious, more aware, and to see more of what is going on around us.

We actually can have this much say in the workings of our minds, no matter how driven by biochemical and neurological programming we may be or may think we are!

**DENIAL AGAIN AND AGAIN,
PART OF
THE PATTERN**

In that denial serves to preserve many a relationship, even many a wonderful high functioning relationship, perhaps denial is not in itself so bad. If the only challenge in a relationship is that one partner wears a plaid shirt, or maybe a color of nail polish, which the other partner thinks is a little out of style, it may be that letting this matter go, choosing not to see it, helps.

However, far greater issues can be ignored in relationships. Ignoring, not-seeing, problems, so as not to rock the boat may feel like the only option, the only thing to do. And again, the matter of remaining in denial out of fear of the truth steps forward.

Quite often, popping through denial brings on questions, unsettling questions, discomfort, and agitation, and sometimes results in change, whether or not change is wanted.

One way to overcome denial in a relationship, to realize that denial is taking place, is to keep being told what denial in relationship is. So, let's give ourselves this message again and again:

>Denial happens.
>Denial denies its own existence.
>Denial grows the more it denies what is taking place.
>Denial increases the more the presence of this denial is denied.
>Denial helps sustain what is being denied.
>Denial can have positive or negative purposes.
>When denial is preserving something negative or detrimental,
>denial can be quite stubborn.

>Note that denial of danger is dangerous.

So, we do see that denial can have a stabilizing effect, *preserving what is*—preserving both the relationship and the patterns that have become it. Denial can also prioritize issues and postpone, back burner, or simply eliminate attention to problems.

Again (and again), when these problems are serious and potentially damaging problems, denial itself is a problem. People can see the black eyes and bruises on their own or their partner's faces and say nothing about these for years and years! When asked, even when looking right at these wounds, people can not-see them! How much of this is a conscious lie and how much of this is a subconscious lie?

Rocking the boat rocks the boat. And the tendency is to avoid sha-king things up, to preserve the status quo, good or bad, whatever this may be. Lies keep the boat from rocking, yes, until the boat springs a leak, or sinks, and one or more of its passengers drown.

Being too dead to tell or support a lie about one's violent intimate partner relationship is not the most desirable form of truth.

Figure 25.1.
Denial along a spectrum of
consciousness, awareness, and not seeing.

26
Numb Story

Having been beaten many times, eyes now closed, the burning slaps to the face and the hard knocks to the side of the head feel like more of the same. Almost all the hits and slaps and kicks feel the same now. And here comes more and more of the same. And then a fist to the stomach, and a slug to the shoulder, then a hit so hard somewhere—where?

Eyes flicker open and shut. Things start to spin and get darker. Down, falling to the floor. Being kicked now, again and again and again. Each impact making every cell in the body shudder, each cell echoing the thud. Every cell takes each hit and kick, every cell takes it in.

Feeling like nothing but a slab of meat, a beaten, bruised slab of meat. But then, wait, I'm not here, I'm not in here. This doesn't hurt. Hurt is too much to take now. No pain. This isn't happening, I don't feel it. I don't feel anything but the jarring impacts through and through. . . .

Hit, hit, hit. Wait, I'm being beaten as I curl into a ball on the floor. I can make it.

Just go blank.

27
Hollowing to Patterns

Patterns abound. Patterns are normal. Patterns are a way of life. We need to establish patterns to live. So do relationships. Relationships build patterns of relating and eventually become dictated by these patterns.

In fact, some relationships hollow to nothing but their patterns. These pat-terns then appear to be the reality of the relationship, as these patterns have then existed long enough to take on lives of their own. Together, these patterns are now the relationship for all intents and purposes.

This can work for partners, especially partners in and for life. Establishing healthy patterns can be healthy, so it is good we have this pattern establishing instinct.

But there is a fine line between preserving what is good and preserving what is. Preserving something just to preserve it (no matter what it is) takes a particular mind set, especially when what is being preserved is detrimental or dangerous to the self or others. The old adage "I'd rather fight than switch" takes on new meaning: "I would rather die than switch." This is how much we can resist change.

This is how some people who are able to get out of dangerous situations, relationships, stay: Change appears more frightening than the clear and present danger. And even exit itself appears dangerous.

CONFLICT OF INSTINCTS

We all engage in some not-seeing of patterns, whether desirable or less than desirable patterns, because instinct tells us to go onto automatic. Now a conflict of instincts looms: the powerful instinct to establish and then to preserve patterns may override the instinct to avoid danger!

Basically, when we are receiving two conflicting messages from ourselves, we might let one override the other. Amazingly enough, we can endure exposure to a negative experience better when this negative experience is part of an ongoing pattern. Being part of a pattern we have grown used to, we are less shocked by the negative experience.

We see this in ongoing troubled relationships. Partners can grow quite used to problem patterns and accept them, perhaps not-seeing any escalation (such as escalation in the degree of violence) or deterioration (such as increasing obsession).

One-time abuse incidents may be upsetting. However, repeats of the same abuse over time can be less upsetting. Actual yet subtle tolerance of the abuse may increase with its ongoing repetition. A dangerous numbing to the ongoing reality emerges.

HOLLOWING TO DETERIORATING PATTERNS

This function—enduring something more easily because it is part of an ongoing pattern—allows us to slip unaware into deteriorating patterns, patterns which start out positive and deteriorate into destructive ones, even dangerous ones.

For example, if this pattern is one of intimate partner violence in which one partner hits the other repeatedly, and continues to do so over time, the intensity and danger of the violence may increase. Little by little, or maybe abruptly, the situation can become dangerous, perhaps even life threatening.

Sometimes neither party sees the danger of serious injury increasing, even when the danger is there right before their very eyes! Denial? Denial? Could be denial. Blinded by pattern? Yes, quite likely.

Denial as part of this dangerous pattern? A pattern of denial itself? Of course.

HOLLOWING TO PATTERNS OF DOMINANCE

It is similarly quite easy to slip into patterns of relationship arrangements where one partner repeatedly dominates certain decisions or processes. This dominance may feel quite natural to both members of the partnership, as one may be more of a leader or extrovert than the other, or may have more knowledge about something than the other, or perhaps be more experienced in certain decision areas than the other.

There is nothing wrong with a person who has knowledge or skill in a particular area offering to take the lead there. This can be both efficient and logical. What can take place though, when partners are not aware of the permission being given and the power being allocated in this process, is a general transfer of overall power from two people to one of them. This is quite a subtle step, and one which is frequently not seen.

A pattern of dominance can sometimes grow into a pattern of dominance and control. Now the process is not just dominated, it is controlled.

While dominance and control may seem one in the same, they are not. A person may dominate a discussion by speaking more loudly than everyone else. However, this person may or may not run the con-versation. Someone may have the control over the topic, or over the amount of time for the conversation, or even of the means by which people are allowed to speak.

For example, sometimes people complain about how a town meeting has been run and hold the chairperson responsible for not keeping time, for not maintaining control, and for not being fair and impartial to all participants. This chairperson may have maintained control but allowed the person speaking most loudly and most often to do just this: talk the most. Here, the person in control allowed someone to abuse the power, to talk too much.

Unlike a town meeting, there are fewer people, usually only two, in the intimate partner relationship, the IPR. Here, if the overall transfer (or surrender) of power becomes an overall transfer of dominance, power, and control to one of the partners, we have a potentially dangerous situation. Or do we, some will ask, saying: Of course, intimate partner relationships are run like democracies where everyone is supposed to have equal respect, voice, value, and say (as was discussed in Chapter 8), right?

Wrong. There are no guarantees that intimate partner relationships automatically guarantee anything close to equal respect, voice, value, and say to the members of this relationship. This is up to each participant in the relationship and is something which deserves conscious monitoring. *A relationship which does not want to discuss the matter of mutual and equal respect, voice, value, and say is avoiding conscious relating. Why?*

When power is becoming unevenly and unfairly distributed in a relationship, it is good to stop and take a look at what is happening. Monitoring the use of power in a relationship is a good thing. This does not have to be a moment-to-moment dissection of each and every action and decision in a relationship, which is likely far too much processing. But it should be part of the awareness of the members of the relationship and a healthy piece of ongoing dialog.

LIST:
STEPS INTO POSTIVE AND NEGATIVE PATTERNS

As the old adage tells us, "Power tends to corrupt, and absolute power corrupts absolutely." And this is the risk. Power within a relationship can be abused and can be a tool of abuse, as can power's sometime partner, control.

Let's think about the steps that may be involved in an increasing and potentially abusive overlapping of one-sided dominance, power, and control in a relationship. This abusive overlapping can become a problem pattern in the relationship.

This warrants discussion; however, let's first begin by keeping in mind that *all relationships have patterns.*

1. Sometimes patterns are formed around one partner's expertise, seniority, confidence, or strength in a certain area which we can call his or her domain. This can be a useful and logical step.

2. This person will have certain power (and likely control as per this power) in a particular area. This can make sense.

3. This person may naturally be in a position to exercise some degree of dominance in his or her domain. This in itself is not harmful.

4. This dominance is a form of **control of power over** information per-haps, and or over an activity. There is nothing wrong with power in itself.

    Power is often distributed between partners in a relationship in a way that is useful and efficient for both of them.

    One partner has this power, the other has that power. One partner may therefore have more control in this area, more control amplified by more power, the other in that.

5. This power can be distributed and used well, even further developed, to the benefit of both the individual members of the relationship and of the relationship as a whole.

6. It is important to be highly aware of the distribution of power in the relationship and to see the compromises and trades which help to form that distribution of power.

7. It is important to be highly aware of places where specific areas and actions of specific dominance, power, and control may extend and affect (or, where problematic, *infect*) the entire relationship.

8. The dominance of power and control can change over time or can change quickly. It is

important to continue to be aware of this change in the use of power and control in the relationship.

9. Sometimes this power and control is not distributed well and or fairly and is not used well and or fairly. Dominance and control are then being abused.

10. Sometimes this power is distributed well and fairly at the outset, but then over time, things shift. Old compromises and trades (C&Ts) still in place are not quite applicable anymore. New and always mutual compromises and trades (C&Ts) which address these shifts are essential. Yet these new compromises and trades are oft not consciously created.

11. The power, or the *distribution* of the power and related control, can thus become imbalanced. Sometimes this problematic distribution of power spreads to (infects) other parts of or even the entire relationship.

12. Sometimes this power is abused. Sometimes the abuse of this im-balanced power spreads to (infects) other parts of or even the entire relationship.

13. Being unaware of all the above points—from the beginning and for the length of the relationship—is risky and can be damaging or dangerous. Being aware is healthy.

14. It is best for members of a relationship to maintain an open and on-going dialog, and

open eyes from the start, so that they can see clearly:

- the C&Ts which establish themselves early as well as later in the relationship.
- whether these C&Ts are being made consciously.
- the way these C&Ts can indeed be made quite consciously.
- the way C&Ts need regular and mutual review over time.
- the way C&Ts form patterns.
- the patterns which establish themselves in the relationship.
- the way patterns in the relationship change over time.
- the way power is distributed in the relationship.
- the way these patterns of power may organize the overall power in the relationship.
- how patterns of power can become general dominance of power and control.
- the patterns of dominance in the relationship.
- when the use of power and control in the relationship is risky, damaging, or dangerous.
- when the use of power and control becomes the abuse of power and control.
- when to address any possible potential or actual abuse of power and control.

DENIAL IS A PATTERN

The pattern-establishing instinct can run awry. Choosing (either consciously or subconsciously) to allow the downgrading or abuse of pat-terns can allow a relationship to dwindle to nothing but problem pat-terns. A hollow life fraught with senseless emotional and physical (and often also financial) risk emerges and becomes a holding pattern.

Like a jet plane circling an airport in a storm, waiting for the weather to allow a landing, this holding pattern can be in place for a long time. Sadly, for some troubled relationships, the storm never clears and the holding pattern never ends.

28
Dangerous Denial Story

High power advertising couple, a real "alpha" or "power" couple, Vitz and Kat, had been married fifteen high speed years. By the time Kat realized how serious their situation was, both Vitz and Kat were testing HIV positive.

Kat had been entirely monogamous and also, by the way, drug-free all fifteen years.

Vitz, on the other hand, had been for several years "exploring" his sexuality—mostly on the sly when he was high, but not keeping this activity entirely from Kat, his best friend and partner in life.

Indeed, Kat knew about Vitz' activities to some extent and felt Vitz was behaving like this as a result of his tendency to overuse certain drugs rather than out of a desire to cause pain or threaten their relationship. However, Kat just trusted that Vitz would practice safe sex extra-maritally because he promised he would.

Oh, and by the way, Kat had also just assumed that Vitz would of course always use sterile needles when he would shoot up.

29
Patterns of Abuse in Relationships

Tending to sleepwalk through portions of our lives, through portions of our waking hours, the significance of the fact that we are creatures of habit, including less than desirable habits such as abuse, may evade us. And it is when we examine these patterns, the existences of which are often hard to admit, that we must call a harmful and sometimes quite dangerous problem what it is: dangerous.

FACES OF ABUSE

Let's step back and think about how often true abuse is not considered abuse, let alone a form of violence. This is because violence in relationships has many faces. Let's look at some of these faces and some of the patterns in which these faces show themselves. The many types of relationship abuse and violence are frequently categorized along these lines:

Emotional abuse;
Verbal abuse;
Physical abuse.

Although these categorizations are indeed oversimplifications, let's work with them a while. These types of abuse and violence can be placed along a spectrum like this, depicting the steps some relationship abuse and violence patterns follow from emotional and verbal abuse to physical:

> emotional abuse→verbal abuse→physical abuse

We might want to add in threats of physical abuse. These can be threatening words or threatening gestures, or implied hidden but very real threats, and should have their own category:

> emotional abuse→verbal abuse→→
> →→threats of physical abuse→physical abuse

ABUSE IS VIOLENCE

One of the first things that this spectrum suggests is that, where we might call what takes place on the far left end of this spectrum "abuse" and what takes place on the far right end of this spectrum "violence," all take place along the same spectrum and all are forms of the same sort of people-abusing-people behavior. These all are violences as these all do **VIO-LATE BOUNDARIES**. Hence, we can call emotional and verbal abuse as well as threats of physical abuse—violences. And indeed these are violences.

While today this list of abuses has become common, and many of these abuses are considered possible precursors to physical violence, not all of these abuses are themselves considered violences.

One reason for this is that many people who do not think of themselves as violent are abusive in other ways, ways that they and society may deem less harmful than actual physical violence.

Much emotional and verbal abuse is highly subtle, some virtually invisible, most of it not seen for what it is by its recipients or by its perpetrators. (Let's be clear here: physical violence *is* definitely physical violence, and nonphysical violence *is not* physical violence.)

In some relationships, there is never physical violence but there is a great deal of other violence taking place. Sadly, these often damaging situations can be entirely overlooked because there is no actual physical violence ta-king place.

VIOLENCE CAN BE HABITUAL, EVEN ADDICTIVE

And while there is surely growing understanding that sometimes emotional and verbal abuse are signs of physical abuse, or signs that physical abuse is coming, there is less understanding of the matter of **HABITUATION TO ABUSE AND VIOLENCE**. Intimate partner abuse and violence, which is all violence of some form, can become cyclic, and can become a habit, even an addiction! We must therefore be on the lookout for damaging habits and behavioral addictions—and the invisible pat-terns which form these habits and addictions—in our relationships.

The potentially habitual, even sometimes addictive, nature of actual pat-terns of abuse and violence in relationships remains largely hidden to us, perhaps because we shy away from this understanding. Understanding this could be disturbing, could call far too many behaviors into question.

Bottom line: we must admit that ***people can become addicted to pat-terns of intimate partner abuse and violence*** the way they can become addicted to just about anything else repeated over time—anything which has either, or both, positive and negative sensations associated with it.

Where such a pattern is experienced on a regular basis, it has its built-in and predictable sensations (such as relief of built-up tension). These built-in sensations work like rewards—things that may seem to feel good—positive reinforcements which are typical in addictive patterning. These so-called rewards are easy to reap, in that they are natural parts of the cycle.

A sad example of positive reinforcement of a dangerous habit is the habit of makeup sex after a dangerous level of intimate partner violence has taken place.

Couples have even been known to engage in their habit of makeup sex after a bout of abuse and violence instead of going to the doctor or the hospital for stitches! (And then to return to the violence after the sex!) How very much like the picture we have of severe drug addiction—craving the drug during withdrawals—then using and getting high and using again despite the damage and injury this is causing. Even using while needing to get medical attention for a wound inflicted while high or while desperately seeking the drug! The general script reads like this:

> **undergo suffering, then feel relief and or pleasure,**
> **undergo suffering, then feel relief and or pleasure,**
> **undergo suffering, then feel relief and or pleasure,**
> **undergo suffering, then feel relief and or pleasure,**
>
> **and so on.**

HABITUAL "REWARDS"

People go for rewards for many reasons. When it comes to intimate partner violence, the reward can tie into the addiction to the pattern of this violence. There is a potentially addictive *pain no-pain pain cycle*. Yes, the cycle of abuse and violence often (but not always) ebbs and flows. And when it does, it may bring with it the simple reward that there will at least be breaks, whether momentary or hourly or weeks long, from cyclic extremes such as physical violence and possibly from the physical pain it brings.

Note that sometimes it is only after the violence stops that the physical injury and pain it causes is felt. On the other hand, in many instances, suddenly, the person abusing stops hurting the person being abused and there is new relief — the beating has ceased. This fleeting so-called relief is a form of reward (albeit a "cheap" reward), a positive reinforcement for this pattern.

Let's be very clear here: *there is nothing in these words that says the person being abused likes being abused*. Instead, these words say that even momentary relief from abuse can be looked forward to or longed for; that tolerating abuse from which there seems to be no escape is facilitated by anticipation of even brief relief; that when this situation becomes a pattern, both the person abusing and the person being abused can become habituated or programmed to it:

Pain, then relief from pain →
Pain, then relief from pain →
Pain, then relief from pain →
Pain, then relief from pain → and so on.

Of note here is that there is potential addiction to a specific reward. Many relationships' patterns of abuse include what has been called a "hearts and flowers" or "make-up" stage. During this time, no matter how long- or short-lived it may be, there can be politeness, or emotional caring, or gift giving, or makeup sex.

Each of these stages brings with it not only the positive effect of the respite from the violence, but also the positive experience of the makeup activity.

Addiction to the highs and lows themselves—to the very behavioral pattern—is quite natural. Highs and lows are experienced as—in terms occasionally used to describe the experience of drug use and addiction—a roller coaster ride. This ride itself can become addictive, as it can produce biochemical shifts which in themselves produce something similar to cycles of:

>**Seeking stimulation**—*then relief by excitement, adrenaline rush;*
>
>**Tension building**—*then relief from tension in some form;*
>
>**Pain building**—*then relief from pain in some form;*

and even a

>**Longing for relief from discomfort**—*then comfort in some form;*
>
>**Longing for the sense of contact with someone or something**—*then contact with something or someone in some form.*

In an emotionally or physically violent relationship, hidden unrecognized habituation of, addiction to, a pattern of highs and lows has distinctly detrimental effects. Prolonged addiction to roller coaster rides of stress and violence increases the probability of more and more damage and of more and more instances of severe damage and injury, with the potential of these additional last phases* being added onto the general spectrum (spectrum of abuse, as was described earlier):

physical abuse→physically damaging abuse→→
→→physically disabling abuse→murder*
*murder or risk of
homicide or suicide

Also in terms typically used to describe patterns of drug addiction is the concept of the co-addict. Transferring this term, we might say that in some relationships, when one partner is hooked on, addicted to, vio-lence, the other could play the role of co-addict, riding the other's roller coaster.

CHECKPOINTS ALONG THE PATH TO VIOLENCE

And somewhere along the line, usually from the very start when attraction is intensely biochemical, we may cross checkpoints on a path which for some (not all yet some) could be traveling from:

interaction to →
→ **habitual nonphysical abuse to** →
→ **habitual physical violence to** →
→ **addiction to the highs and lows of the pattern of relationship abuse and violence.**

Prior to this section on habituation and addiction to violence, earlier chapters have discussed warning signs (Chapter 14), emotional abuse (Chapter 18), and denial (Chapters 16 and 25). This is not to say that all or even a majority of relationships follow this path into addictive behavior.

This discussion is to emphasize that everyone in a relationship can benefit by knowing about these paths, warning signs, and checkpoints. To say that anyone has a relationship which should not look at these matters is to say we support the not-seeing approach.

TOLERANCE CAN BE DANGEROUS

Sometimes people experiencing relationship violences—whether these be emotional or physical or both—*grow numb to the pain*. This numbing to pain can take place because the emotional and physical pain is too much to bear. However, this numbing or detaching behavior as a coping skill is terribly dangerous.

This numbing causes us to not only not-see how serious the situation is but also to not-feel the intensity of the pain! We humans are supposedly pain averse, pain avoiding, animals, programmed to avoid pain in order to keep ourselves safer.

But hah! We sometimes risk our safety by numbing to the very pain which would allow us to sense the true level of danger!

Unfortunately, detrimental habitual behaviors bring with them not only the continuing of the damaging and dangerous behavior, but also the potential for numbing to (detaching or even disassociating from) the effects of the detrimental behavior itself.

Repeated, prolonged, exposure to a stimulant (such as violence) can diminish our reaction to it. Habituation to abuse and violence does not make it less damaging or dangerous, instead the damage and danger may increase as we grow less and less aware of its severity, more tolerant of it. (Moreover, ongoing IPV patterns tend to grow more physically violent over time.)

When our physical, moral, and or emotional responses to experiencing and receiving abuse and violence diminish, we have developed a tolerance to the abuse and violence. (The same is frequently true for persons doing the abusing, as they may develop a tolerance to their own perpetration of violence, thereby missing realization of the danger and damage they are inflicting.)

This tolerance emerges much the way a person addicted to a drug will eventually require more and more of the drug to feel or achieve the same effects—and also much the way a child who has watched thousands of hours of violence on television grows accustomed to witnessing violence and may be less and less shocked or emotionally (even morally) taken aback by it.

What tolerance can look like in intimate partner abuse and violence is a numbing to the experience of being abused as well as to the experience of abusing. Again (and yes, again and again), we must remember that numbing to violence does not prevent the damage it causes, rather it can allow the violence, danger, and damage to continue and even grow worse.

Addiction to a neuro-stimulant (such as cocaine, methamphetamine, or even caffeine) offers an example of tolerance. A person addicted to a drug with stimulating effects will crave the stimulation and energy increase—feel the "need" for the drug when not "on" it, when not "high" on the drug. Over time, when not high, the energy drop will become increasingly low and miserable. Each time the stimulant is taken to relieve the low, brain cells may open more receptor sites (something more complex than this, but for simplicity's sake, let's describe it this way) which fit, recognize and receive the stimulant's neurochemical effects.

Tolerance emerges. These brain cell receptor sites eventually "expect" the stimulant. And during phases when there is no stimulant available, the brain cells are hungry for the stimulant, more and more of the stimulant, while the individual is very tired, more and more tired, without it.

Tolerance means, in this case, that the highs get lower and the lows get lower. The brain cells require more and more of the same stimulant to feel the high. Even with more and more and more of the same drug, the highs eventually get lower. Then, the addictive behavior hollows to robotic repetition, even more dangerous, even more detached from its damaging effects.

CONFLICTING EXPERIENCE

If we transfer this thinking to the experience of violence, we might say that while the intensity of the violence may increase, the conscious sensation of "receiving" the violence (or of "giving" the violence) decreases over time.

The word "conscious" is used here as we may turn off to pain consciously, grow more and more numb to it, while suffering immensely deep inside. The suffering is taking place whether or not we allow ourselves to recognize it: we can fail to consciously feel our own pain.

Such conflicting messages we can give ourselves! And this applies to both persons abusing and persons being abused. Being either the cause of the pain or the recipient of the pain is painful. This does not in any way say that an abuser who on some level suffers as much as the abusee is therefore OK'd to abuse or is off the hook for the damage and injury caused.

Persons who abuse must hold themselves, and be held, accountable for their behaviors. Accountability is healing, just as is understanding what has taken place while asking for accountability.

LIST: ESTABLISHING AND MAINTAINING HEALTHY PATTERNS AND PREVENTING THE OPPOSITE

Most relationships can establish a healthy holding pattern, a way of life which stabilizes and promotes not only stability for the relationship but also safety and healthy living for its members, and for the people, including the children, around them. However, some troubled relation-ships *may stabilize in holding patterns which on the surface work, but which are laden with risks lingering like time bombs waiting to go off.*

For example, a "little bit of hitting" or "getting mad and throwing things sometimes" may be alright for partners and may work for quite a while. Still, if there are time bombs lurking, it is generally best to detect and diffuse them before they become more damaging and dangerous. It is best to work together to make a conscious and shared decision to:

1. Protect the relationship from deteriorating into ongoing problem patterns which once in place are more difficult to change.

2. Try to spot, in the early stages of their formation, possibly difficult or troubled patterns which could grow into problems.

3. Weigh the risks of doing nothing preventive about patterns which may eventually become problem patterns.

4. See the risk of certain potentially abusive behaviors and patterns, spotting these before they exacerbate into clear abuse and violence.

5. When spotting abusive behaviors, even very subtle ones, be ready to call them—admit these are—abusive.

6. Understand that even emotional, verbal, social, economic, and financial abuses are violences.

7. Direct and change patterns and behaviors in a direction away from potential and or actual abuse and violence.

8. Be highly alert to the process of numbing to pain and of avoiding, not-seeing and not-feeling, pain.

9. Do not let the relationship tolerate certain levels of violence, as there is no OK level of violence.

10. Recognize that the above-listed efforts can be made along the way, and acknowledge yourselves, as members of a partnership, for choo-sing the path of conscious relating.

11. Know when one or both members of the relationship choose not to participate in the above-listed efforts, acknowledge this reality; and consider seeking outside assistance to participate in the above-listed items—or if not, then perhaps outside assistance to plan for safely exiting each other's company.

12. If exiting each other's company, have a clear and safe plan, and agreement about a clear and safe plan, for so doing.

13. If a clear and safe plan for so doing is not possible, the individual member or members of the relationship, and the children and other dependents, if any, whose well being and or safety is in question or peril, *must get away*. Seek assistance in exiting the relationship where

the safety of the exit process is in question. Exit does not necessarily mean leaving, it may mean that the other individual in the relationship leaves; however, when safety is at stake, exit does mean leaving whenever required for safety's sake.

14. Do not sacrifice personal or children's and other dependents' well being and safety for the preservation of the relationship.

15. Knowing whether, when and how to get away from each other is also conscious relating.

30
This Time Story

"Stop shouting at me and get away from me!" Ann said, shoving Karl away from her body with more force than she had ever before shown him.

Karl was surprised that Ann had shoved him so hard. The force was so unlike her. This angered him even more. He grabbed her arm and shook her viciously. "Don't you dare touch me, Ann. I talked to a divorce lawyer and he said that once our voices are raised in anger, if you so much as touch me, that's an act of violence."

"Leave it to you to find a legal excuse for beating me, you bastard." She pushed him away again.

He slapped her face, then grabbed her by the neck with both his hands and shook her, his thumbs pressing in on her wind pipe.

Ann tried to free herself, hitting his sides.

Karl laughed at her and let go.

Ann turned to leave the room.

Karl kicked her, hitting her tail bone with his knee.

She fell onto a carton of papers, cutting the side of her leg. As she was falling, she reached out to grab something to stop the fall and snagged her arm on the corner of a tall metal sculpture, which then fell, hitting her on the forehead, knocking her unconscious for a moment.

Karl swore and then shouted from the door, "Go to Hell!" Karl headed out.

Ann came to when Karl slammed the door. She tried to stand, but fell over. After several minutes of struggling, she was on her feet, trembling. There she was again, exactly where she had been so many times, countless times, over the past twelve years. At least the kids hadn't been home this time, she told herself with a bit of sad relief.

31
Pattern Addictions Can Control Our Relationships

Let's talk further about addiction to a troubled relationship pattern, a discussion many avoid addressing, many want desperately to avoid, and others simply do not know they are avoiding. One reason for avoiding this discussion is that some troubled (troubled here meaning addicted to troubled patterns) relationships go beyond any generally habitual pat-terns that may be positive and healthy (and most are)— to quite specifically problematic emotional, physical or other patterns—compulsions, addictions, even obsessions such as what tend to be referred to as *love and or sex addictions*. (Note that other intimate partner relationship addictions which may or may not center on sex may include addiction to cycles of many forms, even extreme cycles including complex forms of serious habitual emotional abuses and emotional sadomasochisms, as discussed in Chapter 33.)

BEHAVIORAL ADDICTION, LOVE, AND SEX

Quite naturally and normally, both emotional and physical interactions between two people can release hormones and other biochemicals in the bodies of those people. And of course, most love- and sex-related behaviors are normal and healthy. Just thinking about certain physical and emotional activities such as sexual attraction and sexual intercourse can cause the body to release certain hormones and biochemicals. Pleasurable sexual experiences, and even the imagination of these, can be somewhat habit forming, even rather addictive. This is the result of a simple process which involves a form of positive reinforcement, when each time the same or a similar act is preformed, the same or a similar pleasure is experienced.

For example, repeated exposure to the pleasurable experience rein-forces the internal awareness that this act brings on this pleasure. A slight hunger for this pleasure is established, and the hunger desires to be fed, maybe even fed and fed. This is the way even a gentle and harmless addiction is born: of course a person will do repeatedly some-thing he or she likes a lot.

Usually the ongoing desire for contact with, or sex with, the person who was involved in the pleasurable experience is a positive drive.

However, there are some instances when such a positive drive begins to dominate other life activities to the point of negative or even destructive interference. Now there is an interference or harm to self or others taking place. Now, when the individual cannot stop, a detrimental addiction is born, frequently assuming the form of a bad habit, problem com-pulsion or obsession, or serious problem addiction (as referred to in Chapter 33).

HABITS SNEAK UP ON US

Destructive habits sneak up on us. Because positive patterning is desirable, we do not necessarily screen for negative patterning, something to which all people are at risk of being addicted. As noted earlier, some people may develop destructive dependencies on certain eating habits or foods, others on sexual behavior, others on the people in their close personal relationships, and others on drugs or alcohol.

Destructive dependencies, or negative addictions, are those habitually repeated behaviors that are detrimental and dangerous to self or others.

The reality of human existence is that a "little addict person" lurks within all of us, waiting for the opportunity to turn healthy patterning behavior into addictive behavior. This tendency can even affect some intimate partner relationships, resulting in relationship addiction itself, alone or coupled with other addictions such as to drugs.

HOW WE FORM PATTERN ADDICTIONS

As noted earlier, so much of what goes on in an intimate partner relationship is patterning, and positive patterning for that matter. And, as noted earlier, some patterning is not positive and has detrimental effects. Where this patterning falls into the category of negative habit or problem addiction behavior is where the repeated behavior is harmful to self or others yet perpetuates itself. Pattern addictions sneak up on people. Take, for example, the development of a relationship addiction. You may even be in a relationship addiction right now and not realize it. Note that a relationship itself is not a relationship addiction. Note that a relationship addiction IS an addiction. (And note again that not all addictions are problem, troubled and or negative addictions.)

An addiction to a behavior usually begins with casual behavior. Casual behavior is brief, occasional, and a sort of emotional experiment, seemingly without deep consequences. For example, perhaps there is stress in an intimate partner relationship, and one of the partners may on occasion get into bed with someone else outside the relationship thinking that this is coping. Of course, this and other casual escape behavior can become regular behavior:

Casual Behavior→Regular Behavior

Again, not all casual behaviors which become regular behaviors are problem behaviors. However, some are problem behaviors. At some point, when casual problem behaviors become regular problem behaviors, they become a bit too regular. Thus they can become troubled behaviors, even form patterns of negative or detrimental behaviors. We may understand this more clearly about alcohol and drug addictions than about addictive relationship problems:

Problem Regular Behavior→→
Problem (Troubled) Behavior Pattern

People who are exhibiting troubled behavior continue to do so in the face of adverse effects to themselves (their health, their mind, their work), their intimate partner relationships, their families, their businesses, their communities, and or their societies. It is easy to slip from regular behavior to troubled behavior because the early signs of troubled behavior are subtle, often go undetected, and tend to be denied if detected.

Again, consider drug use as a blatant example. Someone who has a few drinks at a bar on the way home from work is already driving "under the influence"—however slight that influence may seem—of alcohol. Of course, driving home may be entirely possible. Yet, unmonitored, in some people (in just some, yet indeed some) this casual drinking may increase, may become a regular pattern, and sometimes a habit growing into a troubled behavior. May.

Many who are in a state of troubled behavior do not consider the risks that their use of this alcohol on the way home (or of other coping behavior) is posing to themselves or to others. They are not even aware of how easily they can, if they have biochemical programming or tendencies in this direction, slip from casual to regular to troubled behavior into full blown addicted behavior.

Casual→Regular→

Troubled→Addicted Behavior

Fortunately, not everyone who tries a behavior which might be addictive travels this troubled and sometimes even tragic path. Some of these persons, these persons we can call here "casual behavORS," try a behavior once or a few times and then consider the experiment completed. Or, they engage in the casual behavior very rarely and this works.

But all too commonly, casual behavORS unwittingly slip into a sort of regular yet compulsive behavior. We hear people confidently tell them-selves, "It can't happen to me. I'm too much in control of my life to develop an addiction to any behavior." We may think statements like these are true. In reality, we are deluding ourselves. We can indeed become addicted to harmful behaviors, including to patterns of abuse and vio-lence in relationships.

RUNNING INTO SOMEONE'S ARMS, ANYONE'S

So when a feeling like that "let me go have sex with someone, anyone" feeling sweeps a very lonely or otherwise troubled person, there is a possibly a need or deep need driving a behavior which will not address that need. Stepping back from this level of desperation to see it, we get a picture of a driven yet vague desire, a longing for something, an emptiness or loneliness even within an intimate partner relationship, and this being difficult for some persons to cope with. There is a need, yet for what exactly? *Need is a word for so many things, a sort of garbage pail diagnosis (or excuse).*

Look at the relationships you see around you. Can you find a relationship in which one or both partners are seeking to have met and meet deep needs for something which no other person can ever really give anyone?

What does "need" really mean here?

32
Compulsion Obsession Story

On the first day of the semester, student Williams became a student in assistant professor Dr. Sanford's class. Both student Williams and Dr. Sanford recognized immediately that they were intensely physically attracted to each other and also knew immediately that, regardless of any official college rules against their interacting romantically or sexually, they were going to secretly break the rules. And they did right away. Within 24 hours of their first meeting, Sanford had invited Williams to dinner, and Williams had accepted.

Although Sanford was practically a gourmet cook and had prepared a fabulous dinner in anticipation of William's arrival, they never ate that meal. Instead, five minutes after sitting down to eat, they were in Sanford's bedroom and engaging in fierce intercourse which they continued to engage in all night. Barely stopping for anything, this went on all weekend and became a nightly activity for the next several weeks in a row.

Sanford had to attend a brief conference out of town, and they were separated a few days. When Sanford returned, they returned immediately to their frantic sexual behavior. This went on nightly another several weeks. The two of them had an insatiable appetite for each other.

Then, one night, when Williams arrived at Sanford's house, there was no answer to the knock on the door. The house was locked and no one was home. Williams waited about half an hour and then headed home. But Williams turned around and decided to wait a while longer. Two hours later, Sanford had still not appeared. Four hours later, Sanford had still not appeared. Williams went home, worried that something was wrong and not sure what to do. It was Friday night, and none of this made sense. They always spent the weekend together.

Williams was miserable all weekend and remained in bed, trembling, awaiting a telephone call that never came. That Monday, in class, Williams saw Sanford for the first time in days. Sanford was of course not available to say hello or discuss any of this, as this had been a secret liaison. It was against the rules.

That night, Williams went to Sanford's house, knocked and was let in. Williams wanted to know why the strange treatment.

Sanford had no real answer, except to say that there had been an emergency. The conversation deteriorated to flirtation, a somewhat desperate flirtation on Williams' part, with Sanford's response to this flirtation being to drag Williams to bed and rip Williams' clothes off and have intercourse without further conversation.

Their intense nightly lovemaking continued but now there was even less conversation than they had been having before this turn of events. And now there was no dinner included. Just sex.

Williams would arrive, find Sanford in the bedroom, and they would have sex for hours and then sleep, wake up, have further intercourse, sleep, awake and engage in more, then sleep, get up and dress and leave.

Williams felt increasingly hurt by the distance Sanford was now keeping, although, in some way, Williams felt that they were deep into a profound relationship. Still, as time went on, Williams wanted to engage emotionally and Sanford clearly did not.

What had seemed to be a remarkable love affair now transformed to a hate affair of sorts. The sex was still intense, they continued to spend the night together almost every night, but grew increasingly tense with each other.

Williams began having crying bouts on the way home from Sanford's house each morning. Williams was suffering more and more. Sanford was simply engaging in what seemed to Sanford to be an ongoing and highly charged sexual affair.

They moved into a phase of more intense and more violent sex, with some hitting, and mostly with more forceful intercourse. This moderate use of force during sex allowed them to express their tensions with each other or with their lives without speaking much. Months went by and they continued in this manner, hardly sharing feelings or ideas, or conversation at all. Williams began to experience depression at all times they were not engaging in sex.

The depression increased.

During Sanford's brief trips out of town, Williams got into bed and shook and cried the entire time Sanford was gone. Sanford did handle the situation better, as Sanford simply did not think about what they were doing when they were not together. At least this is what Sanford said.

The resentment between the two of them grew. Sanford resented Williams having a difficult time with this situation which Sanford viewed as simply a harmless mutual sex addiction which would eventually pass. Williams resented Sanford for never discussing any of this, and for failing to respond to any of Williams' attempts to communicate about the situation, and for failing to see what a negative impact this was having on Williams.

One day, after a particularly intense sex session, while they were still in bed, Sanford asked Williams never to come back. Williams was stunned and began to cry. Almost hysterical, Williams pulled clothes on and demanded an explanation. Sanford grabbed Williams and put Williams outside, then locked the doors to the house, went out through the garage, and drove away.

Williams sat in the yard and cried all day. Sanford did not return that night. Williams could not understand what had happened and could not imagine living without Sanford. About midnight, Williams left. Sanford did not reappear for days. When Sanford did reappear, there was another person on Sanford's arm. Williams was out and that was that.

Williams checked into the hospital claiming possible appendicitis. But Williams' actual motive was to have someone around, serving as a suicide watch without this being said.

Williams lived through the experience but was virtually shut down and nonfunctional for several months.

33
Emotional Sadomasochism

And now a word about the sadomasochistic relationship. This is a challenging topic for a number of reasons. Because people tend to assume that sex has to be involved in this sort of relationship, with the person being described as the sadist taking sexual pleasure when causing someone else pain or suffering—and sometimes (although far less frequently than assumed) with the person being described as the masochist taking sexual pleasure in suffering or responding to the abuse someone, usually the sadist, is inflicting.

Yes, for some purposes, these definitions of physical sadomasochism and masochism are close to accurate. However, there are many variations on what are called sadomasochism and masochism in daily life and daily relating, many of these not necessarily linked to sexual pleasure or even sex, and more often linked to emotional pain and pleasure. Rarely are these variations clearly described as sadomasochisms as full under-standing of *emotional* sadomasochism has yet to emerge.

EMOTIONAL SADOMASOCHISM AS A RELATIONSHIP PATTERN

Therefore, a special discussion of the sadomasochistic relationship is useful at this point in this discussion of emotional and physical abuse. A sadomasochistic relationship may or may not be one which includes the above referred to sexual sadomasochism, but it does include elements of emotional sadism and or masochism.

Emotional sadomasochism is a relationship pattern that is often hidden although existing right before our very eyes, with major components of the sadomasochistic process themselves invisible, nonphysical, emotion al, and even non or pre-emotional (still buried deeply enough in the subconscious that they are not registering consciously with any emotional or recognizable impact). In fact, these unseen elements play powerful roles, far more than we give them credit for. *These hidden patterns are composed of intricate and often quite subtle energy exchange processes.*

As discussed earlier (see Chapter 19), most C&T processes are neutral and constructive building blocks toward positive and successful intimate partner relationships. Also discussed earlier is the painful reality that some relationships' C&T processes are at risk of downgrading into increasingly negative patterning.

These deteriorating C&T processes are occasionally steps into highly troubled emotional or even pre-emotional (as described earlier) sadomasochistic relationship behaviors, whether played out physically or non-physically.

FAIR

Now, right out the gate, we must agree that there can be healthy arrangements when two fully aware, fully consenting, equally mature adults engage in a specific relationship in which there is a power balance.

These adults may freely choose to engage in emotional and sexual arrangements which:

- Definitely cause neither of them harm.
- Definitely cause no one, including children, outside their direct inter-personal relationship, harm.

When the no harm clauses are clear and equal, it can be said that these adults have some rights to practice their own relationship behaviors and beliefs. Again, this refers to instances WHEN THESE PRACTICES ARE MUTUAL (AND FREELY CONSENTED TO BY FULLY INFORMED ADULTS), AND MOST DEFINITELY DO NO HARM TO ANYONE. The moral and legal discussions attending this matter are left for others working in those fields. Here, we briefly look at:

- What harm is.
- How harm works.
- What harm is in terms of where it may actually be or become abuse.
- Where this abuse can be recognized and prevented.

DO NO HARM ALWAYS?
IS HARM EVER ALRIGHT?

Recall the discussions of the complex matters of intent and consent in relationship behaviors (found in Chapters 4 and 5). When we talk about doing no harm, intent and consent, along with certain relating to intent and consent, come into play.

Do we understand what *do no harm* looks like here? The question of legal, constitutional, and even religious rights aside (as this would require a treatise on moral and civil law which is beyond the parameters of this book), we must ask about the matter of consenting adults' rights to privately harm or hurt each other. This is a highly sensitive topic as it invites us into several normally treated as no trespass zones, where we must carefully differentiate among:

- An adult's right to hurt another adult.
- An adult's right to hurt another adult when that other adult has NOT given consent.
- An adult's right to hurt another adult when that other adult SEEMS to have given consent.
- An adult's right to hurt another adult when that other adult HAS CLEARLY given consent but may not fully understand in sufficient detail what giving consent truly means, including but not limited to what the implications of whatever is being consented to are, both now and in the future.
- An adult's right to hurt another adult when that other adult HAS CLEARLY GIVEN CONSENT and DOES FULLY UNDERSTAND what this giving consent means, including but not limited to what the implications of whatever is being consented to are, both now and in the future.

As well as:

- An adult's right to harm her or himself.
- An adult's right to harm her or himself by giving someone else clear consent, permission, to do this.

QUICKSAND

Immediately, we step into the quicksand of definition, a sort of now-you-see safe ground, now-you-don't situation. There are several understandings of this concept. Among these are the special definitions of hurt and of the overlap between pleasure and pain.

First, the definition of hurt. Many readers have heard the phrase, "but it hurts so good" used either jokingly or seriously or both. Here the shifty overlap between the sensation of pain and the sensation of pleasure is identified.

Basically, for some, feeling anything, anything at all, is preferred to feeling nothing. Therefore, whether it be pain or pleasure, both of these experiences fall into the category of feeling something and thus are thrown together.

Second, sexual relationships—upon and around which many intimate partner relationships are built—can generate both pleasure and pain:

- at the same time.

- and or, in such close sequence that they are felt to go together.

- and or, in a sequence which places one as a threshold to the other; frequently with some degree of emotional or physical pain being the precursor to some degree of emotional or physical pleasure (and or the reverse).

This is an especially troubled area as many find discussion of this sort of thing difficult and even offensive. Yet, whether the pain–pleasure linkage is played out physically, emotionally, or via some combination of both, it is safe to say that many emotional relationships play out these sequences in their own ways (which might be one or more of those pictured in Figures 33.1 through 33.7 or some variation of these).

Emotional sadomasochism may never apply the actual tools oft used in sexual sadomasochism, but the sadomasochistic role parodies, role distortions, and the bondage-like handcuffs and whips are nevertheless metaphorically present.

Situations in which emotional pain is seemingly invited and inflicted and endured can follow sadomasochistic patterns or versions of these.

> *We may not want to see this as a reality…*
> *…in fact the not-seeing of*
> *emotional sadomasochism is common.*

WAS IT GOOD

There are likely as many patterns as there are people, as individuals experience even the same let alone different instances differently.

Recall the old adage: "One man's meat is another man's poison." In fact, any of the various patterns diagrammed here, or perhaps an infinite number of variations of these, might be experienced by the different members of the same couple at the same time. A poignant example here is the "it was good for me, was it good for you" question.

The flaw in this wishful thinking is of course that just because "it" was good for one of them does not guarantee that "it" was good for the other—whatever it was. In fact, "it" is not always good for both members of the couple—even when both tell each other that it is. Furthermore, in some cases in which one member of the couple dominates the reality for both members, the dominant member's pleasure is the only pleasure noted.

Ultimately, "good" is not experienced in the same way by any two people, even those experiencing the same thing at the same time.

We all see colors, taste foods, feel temperatures, experience the world somewhat differently.

Good is just a four letter word for a feeling or sensation which may have some positive characteristics in the mind of either the person experiencing it or someone assuming something about the experience.

A superb sexual encounter may even be superb for both participants. Yet even they live in different bodies, with different bio-chemistries, hormonal makeups, emotional and physical sensory systems, personal histories, minds, and needs. They are therefore registering what they may feel to be a shared superb experience quite differently....

Figure 33.1.
Emotional and sexual pleasure cycle.

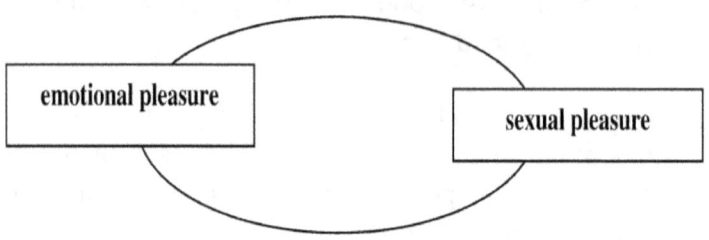

Figure 33.2.
Emotional pleasure and emotional pain cycle.

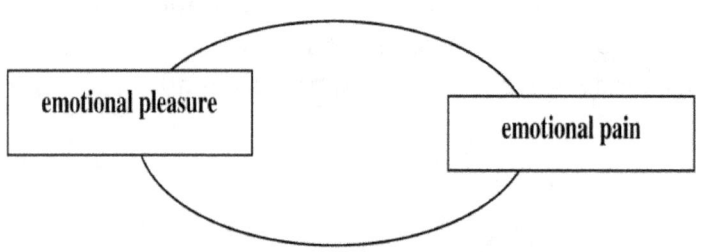

Figure 33.3.
Emotional pain with sexual pleasure cycle.

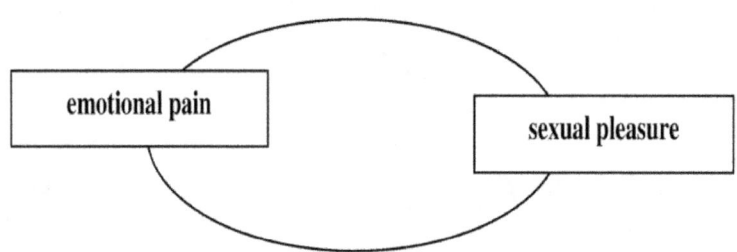

Figure 33.4.
Emotional pleasure and pain with sexual pleasure cycle.

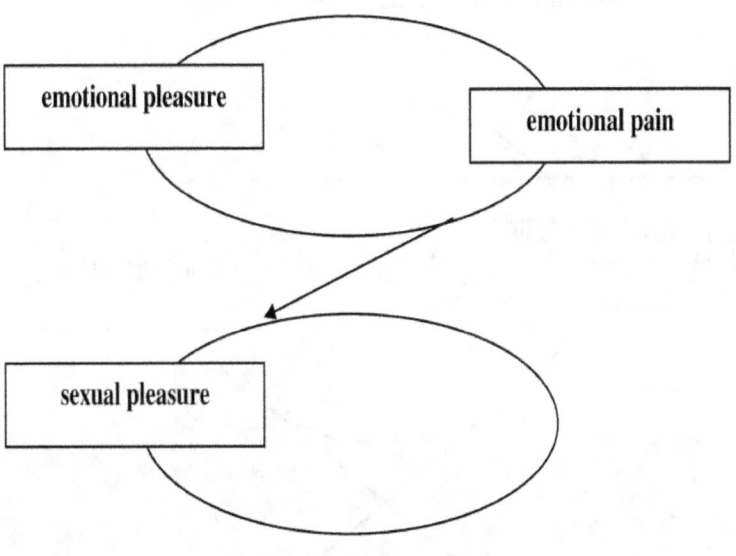

Figure 33.5.
Sexual pleasure with sexual pain cycle.

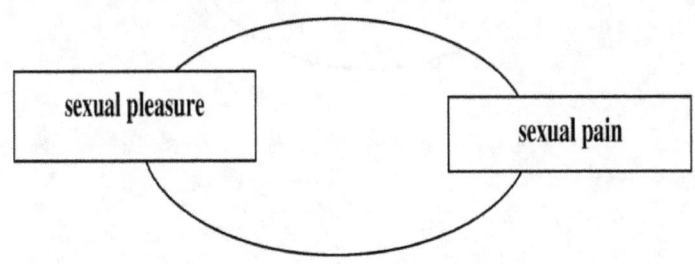

Figure 33.6.
Emotional and sexual pleasure-pain cycle.

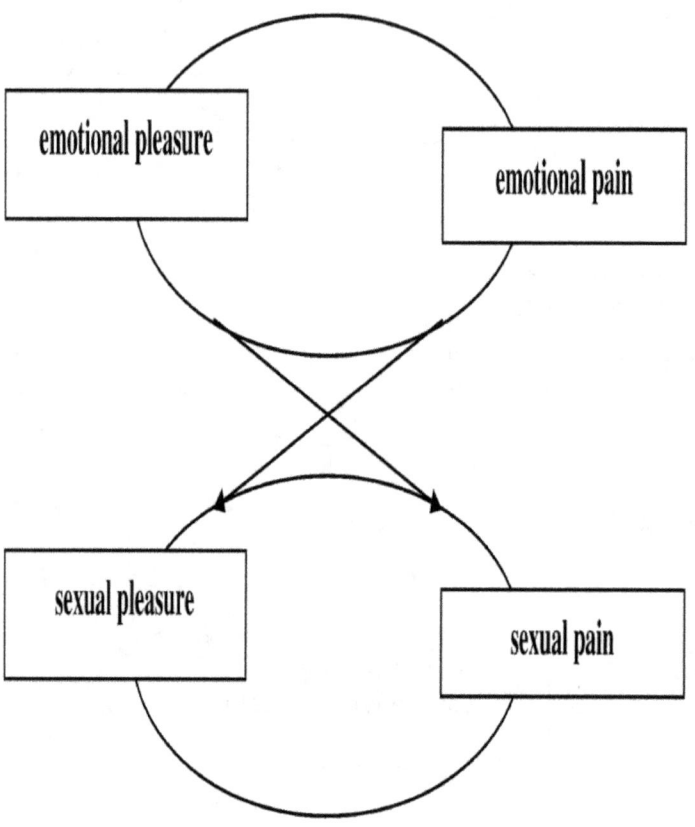

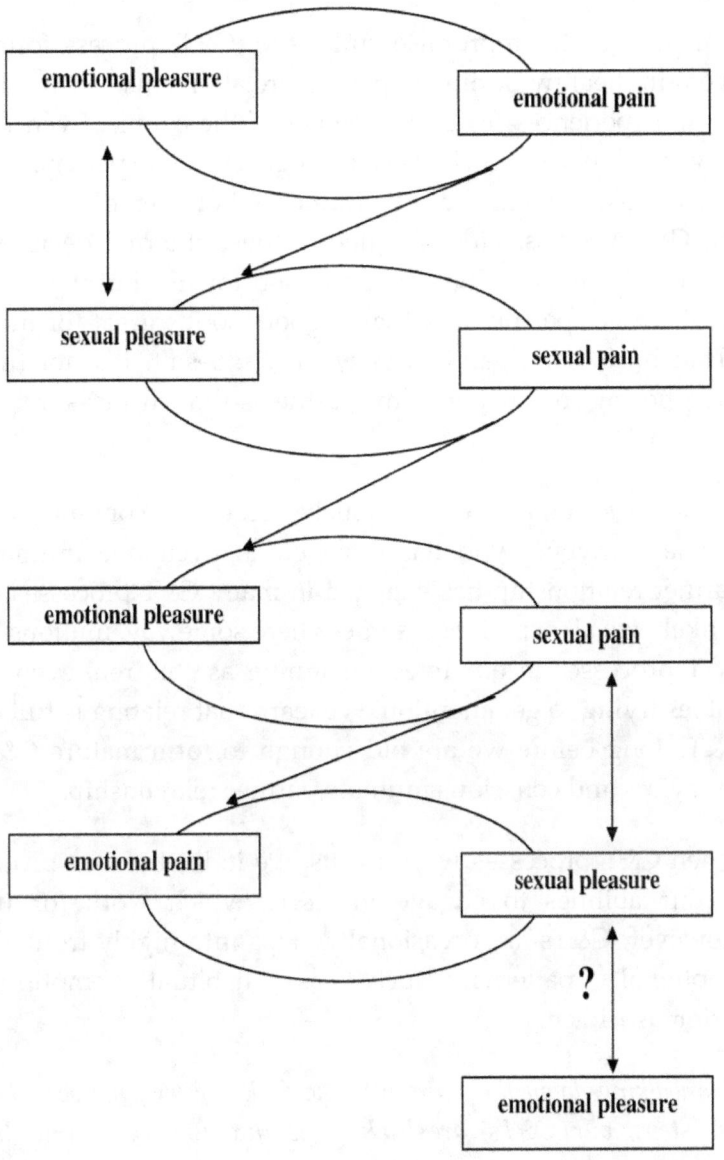

Figure 33.7.
Sample pleasure-pain confusion mini-cycles or subloops.

CONFUSING PAIN WITH PLEASURE

The perpetual compromise and trade, C&T, process found even in healthy intimate partner relationships can color entire experiences for each member of the couple. Even the way an individual chooses to register an experience as pleasurable or painful can be influenced or even dictated by the C&T process. How frequently these internal decisions are quietly made: "That's not so good for me, but it's great for the other person, and that is good, so it's great for me." "That hurts some, and even when it doesn't, it's not fun, even boring, but it gives my partner so much pleasure, so why not?"

As noted several times previously, C&Ts are common and normal. Anyone who has engaged in even one intimate partner relationship has engaged in many C&T processes. It is likely we all experience, some-where someway, millions of C&T processes in our lives, beginning as children, even as babies trying to get attention. We learn that relating is full of C&Ts long before we are old enough to form mature C&T behaviors and conscious intimate partner relationships.

When C&T processes work for us, we indeed can be proud of our abilities to engage in C&Ts which work for us. However, C&Ts are occasionally steps into highly troubled emotional patterns such as habitual emotional sadomasochism.

Like walking down the stairs into the dark, we may not see what our steps, our C&Ts, are leading us into until well into the situation.

What sheer irony it is that all the while we are compromising and trading—interacting in any way—with our intimate partners, we are actually living in our own worlds, experiencing our own perceptions—not anyone else's—of what is taking place.

Hence, we travel through our own personal emotional cycles all alone, even when keeping company with another who may or may not be on the same emotional ride!

Take, for example, the discomfort–comfort cycle depicted in Figure 33.8, and the longing for contact cycle depicted in Figure 33.9. Do you see someone you know in either of those cycles? Do you see two people in either of those cycles? Clearly, an individual can be taking these cyclic rides virtually alone.

The longing for contact and discomfort–comfort relationship experiences depicted in Figures 33.8 and 33.9 may not be anything like what the other member of the relationship would know or say is taking place.

LIKE IS TOO SIMPLE A WORD

Another reason that discussion of sadomasochism is touchy is that, quite rightly, there is a concern that persons who are being abused by their intimate partners like it or consent to it and therefore stay. ***This is not the case.*** "Like" is too simple a word here. For example, longing for con-tact is not liking abuse, and taking any form of contact as a form of comfort is not liking abuse.

Emotional sadomasochism with masochism may involve, among other things, the overlapping of emotional abuse with perceived consent. Permission to hurt me, even to break my heart, to destroy me, seems to have been granted although it has not. Hearing that consent has been given is just thinking that it has or pretending that it has.

Additionally, some partners who are not extremely clear and caring with each other may miss the point where their casual emotional or physical "play" or "games" move beyond casual or playful for at least one of them, while perhaps still seeming to be games. Especially if there is abuse of any form somewhere in a relationship, then crossing (even if unwittingly) from play into non-play games can be hurtful, harmful, even dangerous.

This confusion or distortion of reality can become quite perilous for all involved.

WHEN RELATIONSHIPS KILL

The majority of abusive, violent relationships do not end in death by accident, murder, or suicide. Yet, ultimately, there is always a risk of actual physical harm once an abusive relationship becomes physical. By degrees, some relationships are so out of control that murder is an actual risk, and where it is not, death by accident during violence is. And where severe depression and or other psychological problems result from exposure to violence, there may be risk of suicide.

Swimming in the murky waters where intent and consent are blurred by those who are engaged in not-seeing what these are, some people drown. Face it, being repeatedly beaten repeatedly over time, with the risk of serious injury increasing, involves risk of death. To deny this risk is to not see the problem. To be in a violent relationship where this risk is not acknowledged is to be in a dangerous mix of denial and physical danger. There is no guarantee or prediction regarding when out of control abuse may go too far.

This is not a book about the spirit or spirituality per se. Were it, this would be the moment to refer to the killing of the spirit, of the will of a person who is being abused. This is a kind of death, a painful living death which many persons experiencing abuse and violence come to. In this way of seeing intimate partner violence, some of those who do survive may be surviving more than one form of murder, at least two—the physical and the spiritual.

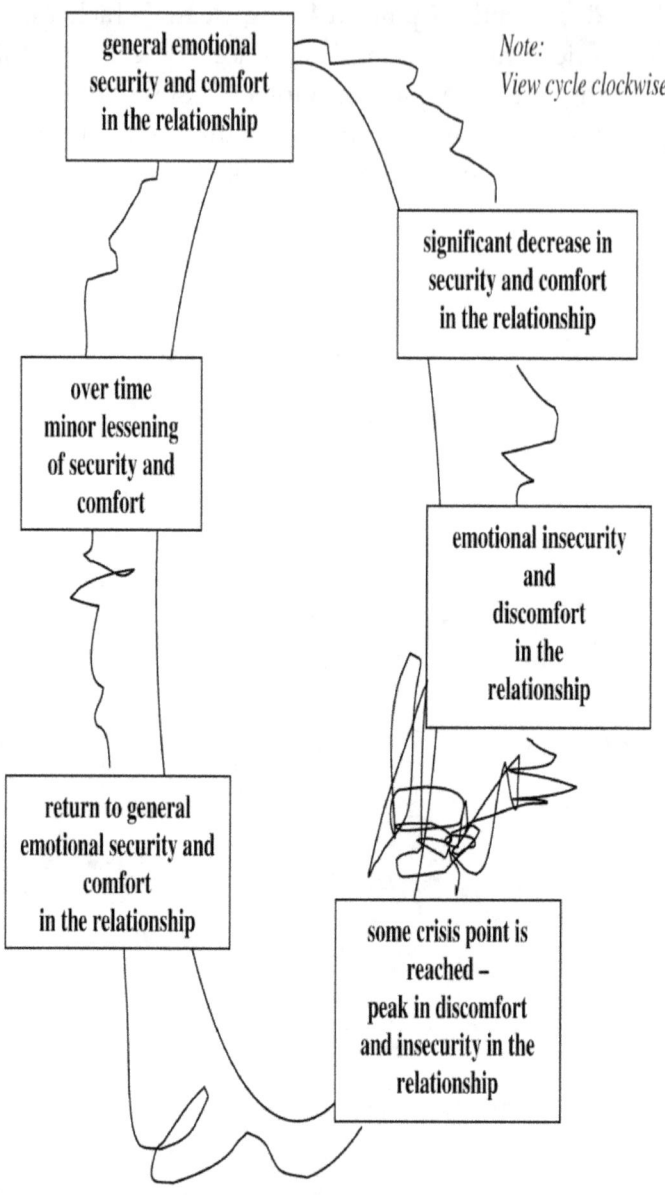

Figure 33.8.
Sample discomfort-comfort cycle.

Note:
View cycle clockwise.

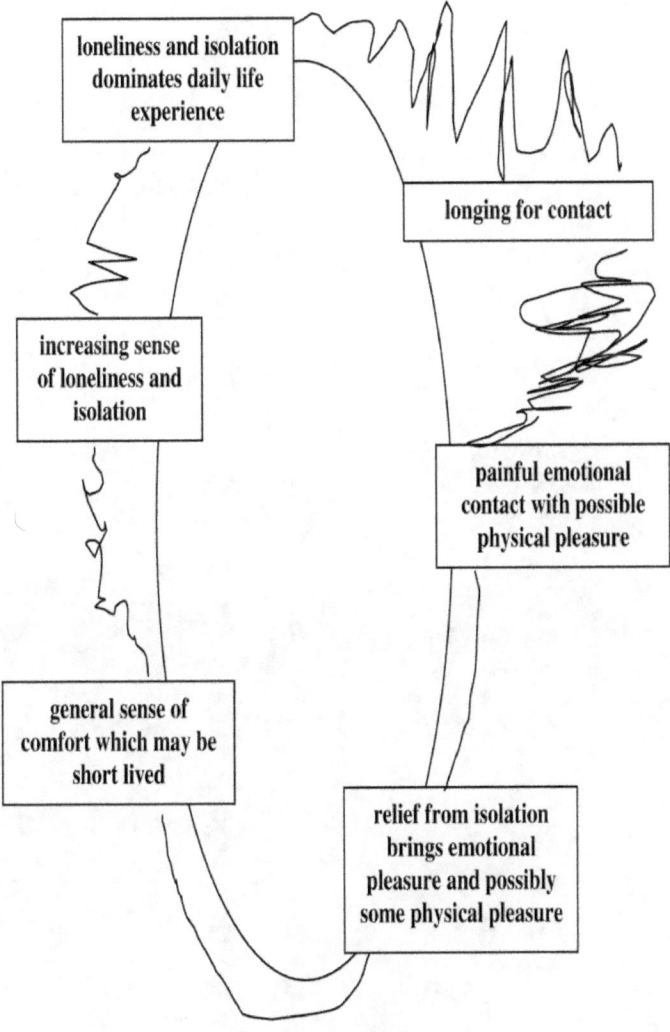

Figure 33.9.
Sample longing for contact cycle.

Part Four

34
Cage Story

She used to ask Douglas why he could not just call a few hours in advance and let her know, one way or the other, whether he was eating at home that night.

Douglas had always found this request an insult. "My work is so unpredictable and so demanding, I often don't know when and where I'll next get to urinate let alone when and where and even whether I'll have dinner," he would explain in a hurt voice.

"But why make me suffer for this, Doug?" Sophia would inquire righteously.

"Suffer?" Douglas would say. He would wave his arm pointing around at the view from and the furniture in their very upscale home. "You call this suffering?" he would shout. "You live so well because I work so hard," he would shout at Sophia.

"Well, I work hard too. I don't make as much money as you do, but I do work hard. And I would gladly live in a smaller place with fewer things and a smaller overhead. I would trade all this away for happiness, Doug," Sophia would tell him sadly but calmly.

"Happy?" Douglas would shout and stomp. "This is happy. Are you so sick, such an ingrate, that you don't acknowledge this?" Doug would continue to stomp and pace. He would yell, "Are you so out of touch with things that you think we're not happy?"

At that point, Sophia would try to hold his hand, in hopes of getting through to him, of talking to his heart. "Doug! Doug! No, this is not happy. Please, Doug, please," she would beg, "we have to sit down and try to communicate. We have to try to connect somehow," Sophia would shout to be heard over Doug's yelling. "It's my life too, you know! It's the time of my life too!"

Doug would push her away and say, "Who cares? Who cares whether you missed a hair dresser's appointment or you didn't get your little article into the paper on time? Who cares if you lost a little consulting job that might have made you a few thousand puny little dollars? For God sake, what do you contribute here? What makes your needs, your schedule, your dinner menu more important than my work? Where do you get off making demands on me?"

Sophia would always feel deeply degraded by such comments from Douglas. It was as if he could, in one fell swoop, erase all of her contributions to their finances, to his career, to their family life, to their house-hold, to their social standing in the community where she had been at his side all the way as the wife, half of the public face of the great attorney and future candidate for Senate—the public face of Douglas Hansen completed so beautifully by her presence.

"Doug, I'm part of all this. I've worked very hard, too."

"On what?"

"On everything I've contributed to our family enterprise and to the Douglas Hansen show."

At this point, Douglas would usually sputter and sometimes sound as if he were suppressing an urge to vomit.

About now, Sophia would feel the insult rushing through her nervous system like hot acid. "You are a pig! How dare you *invalidate my contributions like that?"*

Douglas would come and stand over her and yell down into her face, his saliva flying at her as he yelled, "Because you are a nothing, a no one, a little meaningless consultant and bad housewife and you have no right to tell me when to come and go or report in. Having dinner ready in case I want it is the least you can do. You owe me at least that much!"

"Owe you?" she would shout up into his face. "Owe you? I owe you nothing!" And then she would shove him away before he started to again yell into her face and in so doing again spray his saliva into her face.

Once he was shoved, he would somehow manage to feel that he had his license to kill—or to just about kill—to hit, to beat, to throw Sophia, to grab her by the throat and press in on her airways, which he often did at that point. Then he would walk out. On his way out, he would shout at her that it was her fault, "If you had the brains to stop yourself from pushing me, you wouldn't be on the floor now."

Sophia would try not to cry. She hated herself for being hated so much by her husband.

35
Brutal Fiduciary

When members of intimate partner relationships share or mingle their money, they are compounding their intimacy in a multitude of ways. This is of course quite common and can add to both efficiency and trust between partners as they deal with the financial realities of life. And where the partners have children, the sharing of resources where there is a sharing of responsibility makes still more sense.

Note that when power in the relationship becomes lopsided in any way, which it quite naturally and frequently does (oft for good reason), then this power difference must be addressed all along the way, carefully and clearly. Members of the relationship should talk to be clear with them-selves and with each other regarding any and all financial agreements.

Too often, this sort of issue is not discussed until there are questions or issues arising. Many partners never think of discussing these things until they are faced with marked problems. Time goes by, givens are set in stone so to speak. Arrangements, whether or not the best arrangements, become givens in the eyes of one or both partners.

In some relationships, somewhat challenging money matters can fester into big painful issues. However, even as big issues, they may remain relatively obscure, unclear, looming just beneath the surface the way so many relationship problems do.

Waiting until something forces a discussion is not the best approach to money in relationships.

ABUSE OF DOLLAR DOMINANCE

Let's talk further about the mix of money and power issues in some troubled relationships. A relationship's mixing of abuse of power issues with lopsided control of money is indeed a dangerous cocktail. Take a sip and see the general abuse of power and control take on an extra arm or tentacle when dollars are involved. Swallow the mix in the face of ongoing emotional and physical abuse and see the relationship grow a monster.

Control over finances can sometimes become quite savage.

Remember, we are talking about the intimate partner relationship which naturally takes on a life of its own while being fed by its members. As noted earlier, when the relationship grows dominance issues, power imbalances, and problems with these, this relationship can become a very difficult one. Control of money, or of the larger amounts of money, then further fuels, continues, extends, and amplifies lopsided power as well as the imbalances that support it. *The abuse of the control of money can thus support and mingle with other abuses taking place and vice versa.*

FIDUCIARY DUTY

How partners divide up responsibilities for bringing in, managing, tracking, and spending the money that flows into and through their relationship varies and should.

Every relationship will have its own history and preferences.

For example, sometimes one partner is naturally more the monthly bill payer while the other manages the larger assets held by the partners. This decision is made for whatever reasons the relationship chooses—for example, by reason of one being more skilled at money management, or by one running a business, or by one being the one who took on one or both of these roles early in the relationship. *Automatically, and for no particularly bad reason, there can be an allocation of a bit more power to the partner managing the couples' larger assets.*

A partner managing the couple's money or assets has what is called "fiduciary duty" to the other partner. This fiduciary duty is much like the duty anyone (an accountant, attorney, broker, or other professional for example) handling information and money for someone else would have.

There are times when the fiduciary partner's *access to information* about the couple's money relates to *actual one sided access to and use of* the money itself.

Fiduciary duty is generally defined as "the duty of a person... entrusted with someone else's property to act in that person's best interest while putting aside personal interests." Clearly, the best interests of either partner are presumed to be the best interests of the other partner, as these are the best interests of the couple.

However, should divorce, or even the possibility of a break up, appear on the horizon—or even on only one of the partners' horizons (a quite common scenario) —the best interests of each of the partners may be in conflict.

In the case of the spouse or partner having the fiduciary duty, this duty does in some instances (not all but some) invite a future conflict of interest if and when the couple (or at least that partner with fiduciary duty) may be considering a break up, divorce, or other change.

It is in such times that the personal interests of the fiduciary partner may take precedence over the interests of the other partner. (Again note that this does not happen in every case, however this is an occasional development that both partners would do well to be aware of in advance, and to discuss openly and honestly throughout their relationship.)

What is less obvious, especially when a relationship appears to one or both of the partners to be working relatively well, is that there could nevertheless be subtle questions about or choices regarding the future of the relationship. Or there could be emerging plans on the part of one of the partners to leave the relationship. Where such plans are not openly discussed in great and trusting detail, subtle but dangerous forms of abuse may emerge, such as financial abuse, asset access and distribution abuse, asset hiding, perhaps even incorrect, wrong, division of assets.

For example, where one partner does have fiduciary duty to the other, yet engages in hidden plans regarding the future of the relationship, the other partner may be at a great disadvantage (even to just prove the existence of assets, let alone to access them) later. This sometime entirely hidden planning to distort, usurp, hide assets in advance of a break up or divorce is a form of partner abuse rarely addressed in full, in fact rarely addressed.

Some—*of course not all*, yet a few—partners with primary fiduciary duty do engage in **financial gymnastics** long before divorce is ever a topic of conversation.

(Note here that most persons in fiduciary roles do not engage in such financial gymnastics or other corrupt activities, however this sort of problem is a reality for some couples and divorcing couples, a problem rarely acknowledged, and must be addressed.)

Countless codes and laws do indeed regulate fiduciary duty, even the form which arises in marriage (and in some other forms of personal relationship partnerships).

However, the psychology of this fiduciary duty in relationship, especially in an environment of intimate partner abuse and violence, is something law, even divorce law, has not fully, or perhaps cannot fully, address on its own.

No legal or judicial expert can entirely gauge the range and full extent of fiduciary abuses that may be taking, or may have taken, place in an intimate partnership, marriage, or similar relationship. Knowledge of the range of IPAVTs that can be present behind the scenes must be added to knowledge of law to even begin to approach knowledge of this aspect of partner abuse.

Additionally, understanding regarding the great lack of readiness, some-times for years, of an abused or previously abused partner to strongly and safely negotiate a fair-to-self divorce settlement with an abusive partner must be held by the professions working in these realms, including by the attorneys and judges who in many cases guide and supervise these settlement processes.

The subtleties of the situation do not fully translate into legal jargon or doctrine when there is so much living so deeply in the hidden and sometimes even subconscious layers of the relationship.

FIDUCIARY ABUSE OF
FIDUCIARY POWER

It has been said that information is power. And, indeed in an intimate partner relationship, information about finances is big power. The fragile balance of power, or, better stated, powerful imbalance of power, which emerges from a partner's abuse of fiduciary duty, is insidious and likely involves some degree of secret-keeping by the fiduciary. Again, not all fiduciaries abuse their power. However the reality is that some do, and some do obscure this abuse so well that they remain largely undetected, walking away with lopsided and even illegal distributions of funds and assets, and walking away free from charges of non-disclosure and fraud.

Chronicles of financial abuse by a spousal fiduciary are reported in divorce proceedings, as this is where there have been at least some efforts to reach justice in this arena.

These chronicles, in the form of pleadings, testimony, and evidence, seek to detail what may otherwise still be, and may long have been, hidden from the other partner (and the surrounding world) by the fiduciary during the marriage.

Unearthing what went on (frequently for years) while the general power imbalance was so powerful that it allowed no questions (or even thoughts of questions about this sort of thing) is challenging.

The cryptic anatomy of the abuse of fiduciary responsibility by a spouse or relationship partner is complex. When this abuse of power merges with other abuses and violences, detecting and deciphering its (carefully camouflaged and if discovered highly denied) presence is sometimes barely possible.

LIST:
ELEMENTS OF RELATIONSHIP FIDUCIARY'S ABUSE OF RESPONSIBILITY

Some elements of this often highly purposefully calculated and cryptic abuse of fiduciary responsibility by a relationship partner are as follows:

1. The relationship partner who has the primary fiduciary duty (as per control over the larger assets or the largest amount of assets) has control over information regarding and therefore added power over these assets.

2. This fiduciary partner therefore can control what and how much the other partner knows about these major assets and finances.

3. This fiduciary partner can control the other partner's access to these major assets and finances, and even deter the other partner's ability to even wonder about access.

4. This fiduciary partner can use this control to force unreasonable trades for the opportunity to be involved in decisions regarding the couple's assets and finances, and even deter inquiry about such involvement.

5. This fiduciary partner can use this control to force unreasonable trades for access to the couple's assets and finances or any real information about these.

6. This fiduciary partner can control financially the other partner's freedom to come and go or to leave the relationship if desired, and to independently hire legal and professional assistance where needed.

A complex of potentially overwhelming pressures can be exerted by an abusive fiduciary partner and is sometimes indeed exerted, simply for the sake of maintaining the role of power and control over assets and finances, and where desired over the partner or divorcing partner.

Couples with a history of power imbalances in this area may

eventually find that, in divorce, divisions of their assets are a travesty—or at least one of the members of the relationship may find this.

The partner who controls the money, or access to the money, or information about the money, is possibly in a position to accomplish for him or herself *his or her "win" of an unfair proportion of their assets or wealth by obscure but unreasonable means*. Many of these means are very subtle actuarial and financial procedures the other spouse would never notice, never imagine being conducted, and actually know nothing about.

Ultimately, all persons in or forming an intimate partner or similar relationship should have full knowledge of both (a) the assets related in any way to their relationship and (b) the separate and joint assets in the names of each of the members of the relationship and of their businesses. This is a healthy approach and can benefit a relationship in many ways.

Anyone in an intimate partner relationship, or something similar: should of course know; has a right to always know; and has a right to know safely and without fear of asking:

- **What these assets are now.**
- **What these assets are worth now.**
- **How much their value has changed over time and why.**
- **Where these assets are now.**
- **How to access these assets now.**
- **How to access full information about these assets now.**

HOW DOLLAR DOMINANCE ARISES

The potential for a fiduciary abusing power lies not in the delegation of responsibility for managing money (especially the larger sums of money) to one member of the couple. The majority of marriages and relationship partnerships actually do this out of convenience.

Yet, the majority of couples find that money is one of the top three reasons for argument and that money is a key factor in divorce. This is the case for married couples as well as for those in other forms of intimate partner relationship.

Educational level and earning power certainly weigh in on the matter of say in a couple's household decisions. However, when there is a history of C&Ts (compromises and trades) which form and feed patterns of abuse and violence, these troubled C&T patterns dominate over the power of education and earning.

Note that where the person who is being abused and has been for quite some time increases earnings over the years, the abuse being experienced may even increase as the partner who is abusing seeks means of further establishing and securing dominance in the face of this change.

For example, let's say a wife gains increasing professional success and related earning power later in the marriage then does her husband. If this wife had, earlier in the marriage, experienced abuse at her husband's hands, this abuse could increase rather than diminish as she became more successful in her career.

The original power structure which in this instance had the husband as dominant now has balanced out professionally perhaps, but not necessarily personally. (In fact, there are countless modern cases of highly successful professionals, wives, who are secretly dealing with being abused at home by their spouses or partners.)

This is an oft missed aspect of the power and control scenario. A highly educated and or high earning partner can be just as abused (by the partner with the history of dominant control over the couple's assets) as can any other partner.

The last place intimate partners look is to their partners for the possible committing of fraud against them. In fact, even today, the concept that a relationship's primary fiduciary partner might forget about, or disguise, hide, siphon or embezzle, the couple's money is difficult to argue in court. Somehow, our system frequently prefers not to consider such crimes as crimes when these take place in a (married or intimate) couple's relationship.

Even married couples who are also business partners find it difficult to take problems with the partner managing the business's assets to any court other than family court. Quite frequently, a divorcing spouse who claims embezzlement has taken place is sent to family court while a business partner who is not married or in a personal relationship can take the very same claims to civil (and sometimes to criminal) court.

No matter who the partners are, in many traditional and even modern forward looking seemingly well-balanced marriages and relationships, things can become very lopsided without one of the spouses realizing this is taking place.

These days, although less so perhaps, many (but not all) wives still tend to do the general household and family bill paying, while many (but not all) husbands still tend to manage the larger assets if there are any (money, savings, and investments, for example) and thus control the majority of larger family assets, if any.

And in a healthy relationship where healthy C&Ts have been made, and healthy patterns of relating are sustained and nurtured, the delegation of financial responsibilities can work well.

However, in a troubled relationship environment in which numerous interlinked C&Ts are lopsided, abuse of fiduciary duty may take place yet camouflage itself amidst other more visible actions and abuses. In this way the fiduciary abuse manages to remain undetected. Thus there can be a further compounding of the abusive nature of this abuse of fiduciary responsibility. A brutal fiduciary may even use more standard forms of IPV or IPV provocation to distract all around from the reality of the abuse of fiduciary duty taking place.

INSTITUTIONAL SUPPORT OF FIDUCIARY ABUSE

Clearly this form of abuse, financial abuse by the partner who has primary fiduciary responsibility to the other, is severely compounded in relationships where there is other abuse and violence. And, there are additional, in this case external, institutionalized, compoundings of the abuse. While volumes should be written (and will be by this author) regarding inadvertent (and perhaps sometimes advertent) *institutional collusion* with abusers, this matter requires some attention here.

This is the compounding of this mixture of financial, emotional, and oft physical (or threatened physical) intimate partner abuse by the legal system, especially the judicial system. These systems, the courts for example, may not have what it takes to see what has been hidden even from the abused partner for so many years—hidden and its trail obscured via the fiduciary partner's skilled abuse of fiduciary responsibility.

At the time of the separation and or divorce, both partners are typically required to disclose the nature and value of their assets. However, when only one knows the full nature and value, and that one controls the full information regarding the assets, the other is at a significant disadvantage.

And when the one who has control commits embezzlement or fraud, the other unknowing spouse is at a compounded disadvantage. More-over, when there are to be meetings, or settlement negotiations, or other agreements negotiated during a divorce process, there is a distinct absence of sensitivity to the imbalances coming in from a relationship with a history of abuse and violence-related dominance.

For the most part, these imbalances cannot be fully detected or corrected by attorneys or courts of law. Also note that persons who have been and or are still in the process of being emotionally and physically abused (and or threatened) by their spouses may not be able to successfully negotiate with their abusers (not even for years after the marital relationship ends).

And note: Although many formal asset division negotiations take place at or near the time of a divorce, and often take place formally with attorneys and often others such as mediators present, abused persons are often not able to fully participate on their own behalf even when appearing to. The residues of the abuse they have experienced can remain acting upon them, and any implicit or explicit present time threats are quite frequently there yet invisible to others involved in the process.

Spotting such troubled situations and imbalances is more in the realm of the psychological and social sciences than the legal. And even those in these fields are not all fully aware of this issue. This key psychological factor during divorce settlement negotiations warrants full attention and research by all systems involved.

We can hope the day will come when the possible and or actual abuse of fiduciary responsibility by a relationship partner or spouse is openly addressed. Where we do see or even sense this, we must dare to scratch the surface to see what is really taking place. And we must understand that the abused partner may be in no position to stand up to, or to even begin to know about the details of, this fiduciary abuse that is or has been taking place.

Already now, countless data exist showing the virtually inexplicable and highly illogical imbalances of assets following divorces, even and especially divorces where there are known histories of other more explicit forms of intimate partner violence and abuse.

Against the backdrop of a troubled relationship's history of abuse and violence, the hiding (and mislabeling in order to hide or distort the value) of assets may be relatively easy to accomplish for the partner who has dominated asset control.

And this hiding (and mislabeling in order to hide assets or distort their value) may also be quite morally easy for that partner to do—as the financially abusive fiduciary finds a reason (or excuse) for this abuse and does not consider this to be abuse. Of course, few willingly call this a form of domestic violence, or intimate partner abuse, although it most certainly is. Instead there is massive denial about this, and even to some degree external collusion with the fiduciary in control of the assets and funds. We can only hope the various professional fields addressing this issue open their eyes to the tremendous abuse taking place at the hands of some primary fiduciary relationship partners.

However different from physical abuse and violence this may seem, abuse of fiduciary responsibility is indeed part of the continuum of IPAV abuse and violence. Abuse in this domain can have profound long term, even lifelong, effects and must be recognized for what it is—a serious form of intimate partner abuse and violence.

36
Fiduciary Story

Unbeknownst to her, this now paralyzing predicament evolved overtime. She had spent years attempting to hold together their relatively public work life (as they were in the television news business, he as a reporter and she as a news commentator and writer)—juggling colleagues, media people, and others in effort to help Bill deal with the discrepancies between his public professional image and his private self.

This world began with the almost storybook success of their early years together, yet it was, more with each year, caving inside as it disintegrated around Bill's psychological problems, impulsive rages, uncontrolled aggression, and alcohol consumption in the form of binge drinking.

By the time Bill filed for divorce, Sally was quite enmeshed in her role as the one who would protect him from public criticism—and herself from the professional damages that Bill's downfall might cause her. She was unable to adjust to—to in any way manifest the role of being--the one who would now actually be involved in the public naming of his serious problems.

And, she had, for so many years, been the most adamant member of Bill's informal but nevertheless cult-like following. This was so much so that she would need far more than the duration of the separation and day of the divorce to break out of her deep-rooted loyalty, or habit of loyalty—fostered by the brainwashing and threats she had lived with for so long—the pressure to always say wonderful things about him no matter who she was talking to, and to never (as he called it) "negate"—in any way disagree with or seem to disagree with—him in public. In fact, her coming to terms with this situation only served to remind her in a deep way of Bill's power over her, and to throw her deeper into her submission to this man who was ready and willing to destroy her along with himself.

The separation was hell. She was many times literally afraid for her safety as he grew increasingly violent and his threats more and more serious as the divorce approached. But he only did this behind closed doors, secretly, thus entirely deniably.

And now, with the divorce approaching, when information about and access to their money was going to be important, Bill sealed all doors to the information and literally held her prisoner in that she had no real funds which would allow her to leave at will.

She had seen him take revenge before—both in fits of rage and in states of cold and calculated masterminding. She knew he was capable of this sort of thing again. And indeed she realized that he was now stalking her, following her, collecting information on men he thought she might date (although she was not dating) and the names of those men's children, somehow hearing her telephone conversations and knowing the content of them and telling her so.

Amidst the chaos, turmoil, and trepidation she was now living in, she was entirely unable to see what Bill was doing. Looking back much later, she realized that he had purposely made their lives such hell so that no one, including she, would spot his elaborate, long planned, and skillfully hidden process of robbing her.

37
Related Trauma

Long after it is over, sometimes for the rest of one's life, one lives with the seen and the unseen impact of intimate partner abuse, violence and terror. This impact can never be entirely measured. While many injuries are physical and leave visible scars or even physical disabilities, other injuries, although less visible or even invisible, can be just as injurious, damaging and long lasting.

Fortunately, recovery, healing, and building a new life can be good antidotes to or reducers of these effects. Note that there is quite frequently also a need to recognize and then address and directly treat any related psychological trauma. And, this is difficult when the deeply buried elements of intimate partner violence related trauma may re-main unrecognized by the persons around the traumatized individual as well as by the traumatized individual—and even by the specialists studying this matter.

Given that intimate partner abuse and violence–related trauma is elusive, difficult to label, and *may remain dormant for many years*, persons who may be suffering from such trauma, even unbeknownst to themselves, do well to be well informed about trauma and its symptoms.

WHAT TRAUMA IS

Trauma is so very misunderstood, yet a major piece of many

people's lives. It is estimated that at least half of all adults in the United States alone have experienced at least one major trauma-producing event. Whether this sort of event will actually result in trauma is dependent upon a number of factors including distress at the time of the trauma, psychological history, family history, and more.

Being a survivor of intimate partner abuse and violence means it is possible one is a trauma survivor as well. Possible, as not all persons subjected to intimate partner abuse and violence are traumatized by it. Traumatization takes place when the resources of the person exposed to the traumatic event are insufficient both internally (psychologically and perhaps also spiritually, for example) and externally (family support, resources available to get help, and knowing to get help, for example) to cope with this exposure.

Trauma has been given a range of definitions. The word trauma has been associated with the event causing the trauma as well as with the result of the event. A trauma itself can be therefore loosely identified as either the terrible event, the threat of the terrible event, or the effects of these. Trauma is associated with events causing death and or the threat of death, injury and or the threat of injury, or serious harm and or the threat of serious harm to oneself or to a family member.

According to many definitions, traumatic events are traumatic when they result in intense feelings of fear, or helplessness, or horror, with some sort of at least vaguely distinguishable effect on the behavior of the person exposed to the traumatic event. IPAVT terrorization experiences usually do result in some form of trauma. (Note that childhood sexual abuse is included in the definition of trauma even when it does not match this definition entirely and even when it does not involve other forms of threatened or actual physical injury.)

Among the categories of trauma causation which are generally included in its definition are war, torture, natural disaster, mass interpersonal violence, emergency worker exposure to trauma, motor vehicle accident, child abuse, rape, stranger assault, and well as partner battery (which is largely intimate partner violence).

Some research says that exposure to trauma can bring about structural and functional changes in the brain. These potential and actual changes in the brain must be recognized and respected. Although promoting recovery from trauma must always be the goal, this must be done with the understanding that the person recovering is likely forever changed on some level.

Amidst much debate over the definitions and categories of trauma, a great deal of thinking about this condition has been done. Certainly, catastrophic events such as exposure to war are traumatic. In fact, the study of the effects of exposure to war on the psyche has been key in advancing understandings of trauma, and its treatment and has led to great insights regarding various stress conditions and so-called "dis-orders" such as posttraumatic stress "disorder" (also known as PTSD), or what this book prefers to describe as *posttraumatic stress condition and or injury and or disorder, allowing for this range of post traumas:*

posttraumatic condition/injury/disorder.

And there have been numerous advances in recognizing the types of and causes of trauma. A range of specialists have joined in on the expanding of the definition of trauma so far as to include as causes of trauma, war and cataclysmic events such as: exposure to torture, natural disaster, severe automobile accidents, kidnapping, extreme childhood abuse, and neglect—but also other more so-called "social disasters" which do include intimate partner violence as well as exposure to violence in the media, inadequate pain management, and common risks.

Some also add the effects of exposure to violence in utero, in the womb, such as fetal exposure to stress hormones when the mother is under extreme stress (which may include the stress of intimate partner abuse and violence), or when there is fetal surgery, or traumatic birthing procedure, or some other extreme condition.

INTIMATE PARTNER VIOLENCE CAN BE TRAUMATIZING

By some strict definitions of trauma, undergoing and surviving intimate partner relationship abuse and violence may not absolutely be traumatic. However, many agree that while perhaps the impact of violence upon the psyche is to some extent definable and measurable in scientific standards, the actual effects run so deep that they can hardly be accurately and entirely measured or tested.

> **Like powerful unseen undercurrents driving a river from deep below…**
>
> **…the trauma of abuse and violence settles and flows deep inside.**

Sometimes the trauma of abuse and violence settles and does not appear for a long time. Other times, this trauma settles and gets to work immediately but is unrecognized for what it is. Intimate partner abuse and violence trauma may haunt some of its victims (survivors, witnesses, and others) for the rest of their lives. Addressing this trauma (both obvious and hidden) in a truly appropriate and effective way is the challenge.

EFFECTS OF TRAUMA

Abuse and violence are stressors, which basically means they generate stress. When exposure to abuse and violence is traumatic, the stress which results is more severe than a mild passing stress. Trauma can have a range of effects which include stress described as acute stress, posttraumatic stress—and also other more general and perhaps more vague stress making itself known more indirectly, through other reactions to the traumatic event. Our understandings of what stress is continue to evolve. We can generalize here this way:

Acute stress generally appears immediately after the traumatic event with symptoms such as intensified reaction to the stressor (hyper-arousal). Posttraumatic stress generally shows up some time after the event. Although the best time to treat posttraumatic stress is relatively soon after the event, treatment if taking place at all typically occurs long after the event. This is because the symptoms or the severity of these symptoms is not apparent to the traumatized individual until much later, especially if the symptoms have remained not only undiagnosed but entirely untreated.

Among the many effects of trauma experienced by the abusee is the reaching out from the past of memories and sensations associated with the traumatic experience or experiences. At night, this experience can take forms such as nightmares, sleeplessness, physical pain, fear. During the day, this experience can include instability of mood associated with cycles of physical, emotional, and behavioral symptoms. Among the many post-partner-violence behaviors are: agitated startle reflex; fear of intimacy; seemingly random episodes of anxiety, panic, depression; and, phobic behaviors.

However, these are just some of the many behaviors and conditions that will eventually be identified by the sciences and professions addressing these issues. Even definitions of posttraumatic stress disorder (PTSD) are being added to and amended. (Note again that this book holds preferable the term, *posttraumatic stress condition/injury/disorder*, as per the note in Chapter 39.)

CANNOT ENTIRELY ERASE THE MEMORY

The understanding of trauma and its effects continues to evolve. Thus the treatment of trauma is evolving as well. Sadly, the world around us produces such a great deal of exposure to trauma that there will be ongoing traumatic reactions to study for generations to come. Hopefully, understanding of the traumatized person—including one traumatized by intimate partner abuse and violence—will deepen. And, hopefully, the treatment of trauma will expand to include additional expertise in therapeutic releases which may help soften, integrate, and perhaps complete and or even heal, the experience.

Perhaps the various fields responding to intimate partner abuse and violence can rise to the occasion and fully embrace the concept of **completion**. Complete here does not mean that the traumatic experience entirely disappears from memory; however, it does mean that we can take steps to feel increasingly complete and "over" (less vulnerable to reliving) the experience.

Although some new psychotropic drugs may eventually offer one form of this possibility, their effective memory-erasing is more a lofty goal than a reality. Memory-erasing–type drugs have not shown broad applicability or hugely effective results.

Moreover, erasing memories is chancy in that we can never ensure that a memory and all of its deposits around the brain and nervous system are entirely gone. Therefore effects of memories may haunt us while not being attributable to their sources.

While this could be problematic and even dangerous, the notion that someday we may be able to entirely erase the memory and effects of exposure to trauma is powerful. Among the problems posed by this sort of treatment is the challenge of leaving no dangerous hidden residues of the trauma which may creep forward unexpectedly at some later date, and then be dangerously unexplained. In a sense, this can resemble a reliving of the traumatic event, even when the event itself is not recalled. *(For additional discussion of other aspects of this possibility, see subsection "Dangerous Response Delay and Exacerbation" in Chapter 2; and sub-section, "Nuances of Suppressed Fight or Flight Response" in Chapter 4.)*

Completing a healing process, no matter what approach to this is utilized, must take into account that no one can guarantee that all deep effects have been removed. What might appear at a later time and be more difficult to explain as it is not specifically attached to specific memories but just as troubling and harmful?

STAGES OF CHANGE

Models such as the SOC (Stages of Change) Model have been proposed to describe stages people experience as they recover from conditions, moving (frequently quite gradually) from engaging in harmful behaviors, to engaging and maintaining engagement in healthy behaviors.

These stages of change, most frequently focused on stages of overcoming and or recovering from addictive behaviors such as drinking, smoking, and drug use, are labeled as pre-contemplation, contemplation, preparation, action, and maintenance. By their very names, we see that these stages weigh heavily on the lead-in side of action. This makes sense, as the decision to break a habit or addiction is usually made in steps, long before related action is taken. We often see similar lead-ins to self-protective action among persons being abused.

Although there are indeed significant differences between intimate partner abuse (for both its recipients and its perpetrators) and sub-stance addiction, these stages of change can be useful in understanding the process of overcoming (and or recovery from) this abuse and violence, especially given that ongoing abuse and violence cycles them-selves tend to be habitual.

This model tells clinicians and others working with those experiencing intimate partner abuse that behavior change occurs in steps.

An abrupt intervention into a habitual situation including ongoing intimate partner abuse is not necessarily effective and in fact is often counter effective (unless partners are completely separated until truly wise to be together again).

To move as quickly as possible toward behavioral change and away from habitual or compulsive behaviors, we actually must first slow down to help people explore the why of changing before trying to impress them with the how. *(Of course, where safety issues are front and center, safety must always and immediately come first.)*

BEING TRAPPED IN AN UNFINISHED EXPERIENCE

Ideally, there will be a deeper understanding of therapies that help recognize and release trauma in safe settings, allowing persons who have experienced trauma to understand its deep impact and know the signs and triggers of response to and expression of this impact.

Too many victims of trauma experience a deep lack of closure (which is often unseen for years). Even when having been treated for the trauma, there can be a lingering sense of being stranded in a space which suggests closure—says that closure has taken place—but in which actual closure has never actually occurred.

Too many persons who have experienced trauma, including traumatic intimate partner abuse and violence, **remain profoundly affected for life**, with the effects reappearing or taking new forms sometimes years later. *Furthermore, too often, the effects of this sort of trauma surface in forms not identified with partner violence trauma. This makes the effects all the more difficult for persons experiencing them to address.*

A sense of free-floating anxiety, fear, disconnection from natural emotional sequences, and other lingering emotional and addiction conditions can haunt and be triggered for no clear reason, even years later.

Hence, when we think the memories of intimate partner abuse and vio-lence are healed, and we are years past the problem, the <u>dead hand of this abuse and violence</u> may reach out and touch us. Perhaps it even reaches out and beats us, re-victimizing us.

LACK OF CLOSURE

The conscious and subconscious sense of being trapped in an unfinished experience, stuck in a lack of closure state, troubles many persons who have experienced intimate partner violence and abuse.

The sense that the trauma is not complete, that the impact of the trauma lingers…

> **…and is relived at the slightest reminder, must be addressed.**

We must see these sometimes vague but nevertheless profound effects as a serious outcome of intimate partner abuse and violence. Certainly, there is a profound posttraumatic stress component here, and in this case, a component with many faces. The ghosts of intimate partner vio-lence, wearing many masks, can indeed float through the subconscious forever. Raising those ghosts to the conscious realm helps us deal with them, and helps us prevent their doing us unforeseen harm.

COMPLETING THE CIRCLE

The need for closure, and noting where closure cannot truly be attained, must be addressed. Whether it be absolute closure or paths to the sensation of closure, effective efforts to provide the sense of full closure are essential.

Helping the person who has experienced intimate partner abuse and violence to heal requires: sensitivity to the need for closure; a completion of the experience; and a clarifying of the self as per the experience:

**This trauma is not my identity.
I am me.**

Let's therefore depict the self as a circle, and the traumatized self as a circle which has been hurt, or broken, or shattered, or fractured (as in Figure 37.1). We can talk in terms of healing the circle so that it becomes complete (as in Figure 37.2).

The traumatized self or circle has weak points, breaks in the protective boundary through which abuse reaches. Now triggers bringing back the trauma, calling forth memories that act like or generate old or new trauma, can intrude.

The goal of treatment can be to help the individual understand that the injured boundary can be fortified and healed and that it is important to watch for signs that additional fortification and healing are needed over time.

FORGETTING AS COPING

Numbing while enduring abuse and violence is a coping mechanism (as described in Chapter 29). Here, in this discussion of abuse and violence–related trauma, we add additional coping mechanisms.

Forgetting can be coping; however, this forgetting of the experience is actually burying the experience deep in the subconscious mind. It lingers there, perhaps blocked but not erased, hidden but not entirely deactivated.

Forgetting serves as a barrier to remembering what has taken place, provides a profound form of not-seeing, but nevertheless this is merely a not-seeing.

Such a barrier this is to disclosing abuse and violence—to <u>oneself</u>!

Understandably, we may choose to administer memories of the heartbreak, pain, and terror to ourselves in small doses, if at all.

This appears as a protective function, as so many say, "The pain is too much to feel all at once."

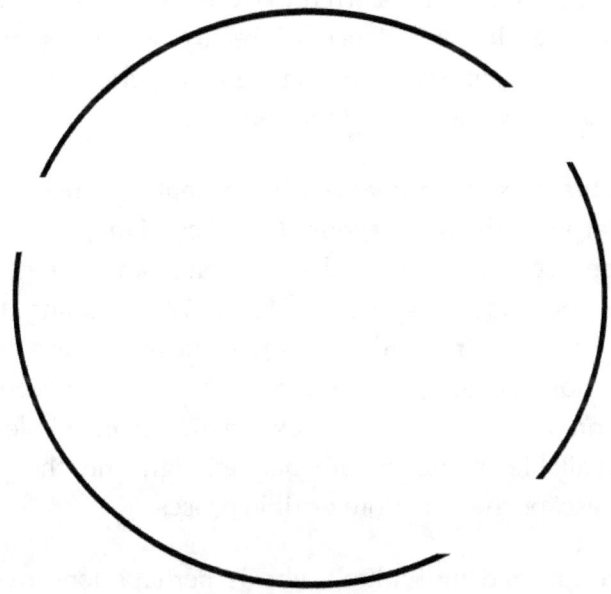

Figure 37.1.
Trapped in the incomplete, fractured, broken circle.

TRAUMA AND DISSOCIATION AS COPING

The mind deals with traumatic experience in various ways, with the processes of numbing and forgetting being two. The mind is skilled at *internal protective camouflage* and has the ability to convince, in this case, not only the outside world but also itself that the reality it serves up to its consciousness is real.

Mental processes such as dissociation, in which the mind separates out normally connected mental processes from each other and from the rest of the mind, are a way of not-seeing or not processing these as connected experiences, as whole events. Painful memories, taken apart and served back up to ourselves fractured, are possibly less painful than when served up whole. This memory fracturing process as a coping skill is then transferred to experience in the here and now, where the experience of reality is also somewhat dissociated. Memories and current experiences become incompletely perceived and reacted to.

Where the person traumatized by intimate partner violence may not be formally diagnosed as dissociating, there may likely be a certain degree of dissociation in any storage of the memory of intimate partner vio-lence. When calling up and addressing these fractured memories, the expression of them as a whole is going to naturally be more reflective of fragmented memories of the experience than whole ones. (The available memories are bad enough and the person tries to escape the still more terrible process.)

The traumatized individual, who is perhaps long over the physical pain the violence may have caused, its physical wounds and even visible trauma, may live forever with the lingering and subconscious sense of incomplete expression of something too vague to label. Being, on a deep, hidden level, frozen in this state unfinished, the person is through with it all only on the surface. There thus can be a deeply buried need for a sense of closure when living with a history of intimate partner abuse and violence, even after the visible, conscious, sense of closure has been reached. Sometimes the trauma of violent experience lingers, hidden but present, and subtly affects all aspects of one's existence for years, maybe decades.

Pretending as if this is not the case does not make this not the case, rather this pretending subjects some traumatized people to half-lives, never being entirely themselves. Given that we are indeed forever changed, on a very deep neurological level, by trauma, help to not only rebuild what can be salvaged of the self but to also construct a new self is essential. Some abuses will benefit by having this help for the rest of their lives.

TRAUMA UPON TRAUMA UPON TRAUMA IN IPAVT

This particular discussion is not only about abused people after they have left their abusers. This is also about abusees caught in ongoing cycles of relationship IPAVT. In instances of long term relationships in which intense abuse and violence is ongoing, there may be trauma upon trauma upon trauma, continuously compounding the effects of trauma-induced neurological change while burying conscious realization that one is actually traumatized.

Violence-related trauma in the face of ongoing violence is not only difficult to detect but the related need for closure, suggesting the needed closing of the shattering experience of violence and its long term effects, is buried as well.

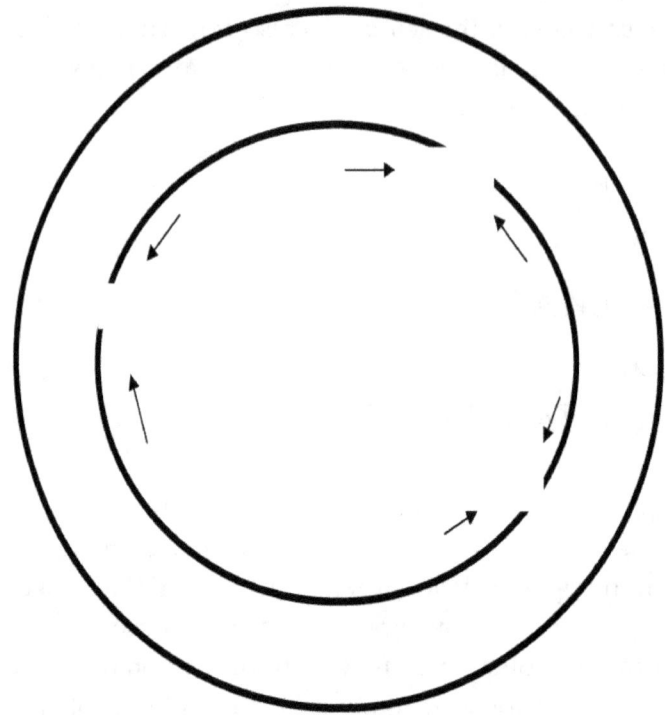

Figure 37.2.
Fortify the boundary, close the circle.

Persons who are being abused may even cling to a dangerous pattern of relationship violence, not realizing that it may be the trauma itself perpetuating the pattern and the addiction to the pattern. The hunger for closure can leave the traumatized individual stuck in a pattern whose cycles may fool the person being abused along with most or all involved.

These cycles may appear and feel somewhat like closure each time the cycle ends, takes a break from the abuse and violence and "enjoys" a sweet moment of relief. Then false, not actual, closure is experienced, leaving the abusee (along with others, sometimes even the person abusing) vulnerable to and trapped in the same cycle again and again.

LIST:
ELEMENTS OF IPAVT TRAUMA

The trauma associated with long term IPAVT (intimate partner abuse, violence and terror) falls into its own category of trauma. While many of the characteristics of other forms of trauma and post trauma are shared, there are very specific elements found in what we can call IPAVT Trauma, and also in IPAVT Post Trauma, elements which warrant separate attention and study. These of course include elements of the formally recognized Acute and Posttraumatic Stress Disorders or conditions to which we might want to make these and other special IPAVT adaptations:

1. Exposure to violence and or *threatened* emotional, physical, financial, and other abuse and violence perpetrated by an intimate, spousal, or other partner — or by oneself against such a partner.

2. Exposure to repeated incidents of such exposure — the overall length of time of this exposure can be related to ensuing and cumulative intensity and longevity of impact, whether or not this im-pact is visible or recognized as such.

3. Acute responses during or near the time (within six months) of this exposure such as intense emotional reaction to physical pain or injury, emotional distress, shame, guilt, rage, fear, terror, horror, or panic — these responses within six months are being generally defined as acute stress (as opposed to posttraumatic or other chronic stress) ... however given that when it

comes to IPAVT-related stress, the entire IPAVT stress matrix is cumulative and enmeshed, both acute and chronic stress here must be linked.

4. Similar or related responses when recollecting this exposure later (more than six months later, sometimes many years later).

5. Reactivity to cues which *trigger recollection (and even re-living)* of this exposure to violence or prolonged violence or the threat of such, and trigger panic, fear, terror, hopelessness, rage, troubled impulse control, and other reactive or coping mental states associated with this experience.

6. Inability to, or strong desire not to, recall details of this violent, abusive experience, or other aspects of one's life which were in place at the time of this experience, and or fragmented memory of this experience—sometimes coupled with occasional streams of intense and highly detailed recollection of the abuse and violence while resisting such.

7. Fragmented recollections of this experience surfacing later, more than six months later, sometimes years or decades later.

Adding the following key and quite distinct elements:

8. Fragmented or whole recollections of this experience and or of the reactions to this experience of violence, surfacing and triggering a re-living or "re-victimization" experience, to such an extent that the impacts of the original experience are not only recreated but also actually become new impacts of the new violence (albeit relived) beginning at the time of this recollection or spread across these recollections.

9. An accumulation and exacerbation of impacts and

outcomes, starting with the impacts of the original violences, and adding on the new reliving-type impacts being triggered, and over time compounding the impact of each impact and rendering the long term outcomes of this violence more complex—generating trauma upon trauma upon trauma.

10. Difficulty adjusting to the surfacing, or not yet surfacing but lingering, recollections and re-livings to such an extent that other life functions and activities (parenting, relationship-building, physical and emotional intimacy, social interaction, workplace interaction and function, career maintenance, financial maintenance, physical fitness and health maintenance, and other functions of life) are impacted.

And to this list should be added elements of the formally recognized Substance (drug and alcohol) Induced Disorder or condition. A definite sensitivity to and respect for the behavioral patterning and addictive habituation common to many relationship violence and abuse situations must be acknowledged to understand what this book describes as *Intimate Partner Abuse, Violence and Terror—Trauma and Post Trauma*:

11. Signs of addiction and withdrawal similar to those experienced when ceasing addictive substance-use-related behavior, these signs including but not limited to: the abusee craving emotional or physical contact with the person who was doing the abusing, or the abuser craving emotional or physical contact with the person who was being abused.

12. Cravings which can be intense and difficult to control (and can be emotional, physical, sexual, and sometimes cravings for the violence itself), being concurrent or not concurrent with withdrawal

conditions including but not limited to hunger for the stimulation from which the withdrawal is taking place (as well as depression, anxiety, fear, phobic sensations, anger, frustration, restlessness, changes in appetite, difficulty concentrating, sleep-lessness, replacement of object of addiction or emotional attachment with something or someone else and then reenactment of emotional, physical or financially abusive abuser-abusee actions and interactions, etc.).

13. High risk of impulse control problems.
14. Risk of impulse control issues regarding self harm, or harm to others, with this harm taking various forms, some quite invisible, some highly visible.
15. High risk of actual substance use, abuse and addiction at the time of the occurrence of this exposure to partner violence, or within six months, and or many years or decades later.
16. Risk of isolation, and of self destructive tendencies which may include suicidality or other life or health threatening conditions.

And additional awareness of health and pain impacts must be included to best capture the overall trauma:

17. Somatization of the above-listed and related impacts, and or ongoing and often increasing over time chronic physical pain, metabolic compromise, even physical illness.
18. Long term cumulative health and mental health outcomes which may surface more than six months later, and can surface years and even decades later, with no clear (to the outside onlooker) cue or trigger causation.

COMPLEX IPAVT IMPACT MATRIX

These symptoms and impacts (regarding which the above list is only partial) can be entirely or partially hidden or suppressed or denied for years. Even while hidden, these impacts can interact and then compound by interacting.

All the while, these impacts grow still more and more difficult to associate specifically with the original intimate partner abuse and violence as the time after the relationship is "over" increases. In essence, the trauma upon trauma upon trauma is buried deeply, and unless unearthed, can linger like an invisible tail wagging a visible and very troubled, confused, and hurting dog.

The complex notion of what this book describes as an *Intimate Partner Abuse, Violence and Terror Impact (IPAVT) Matrix and Diagnostic Protocol* is born. (Further publications in this area will follow this book.)

38
Altered State and Weapon Story

They had increasingly tense conversations about each other's drug and alcohol use. One was a moderate user and the other a heavy user. Of course, when under the influence they were both equally out of control and were able to see this in each other more readily, if ever, than in themselves.

Days off work were their days of use, but the hangovers and withdrawals were beginning to affect both their jobs.

Only beginning, or so they thought.

Each other's uses of drugs and alcohol were the main reason they argued; however, once they were arguing, any and every topic became a problem, including their violence, for which each of them blamed the other.

The violence while "high" was more extreme than the violence when not under the influence; however, violence had become one of their primary means of communication: a few hits here, a few hits there, sometimes a bottle or pillow or book was thrown by one of them at the other who usually but not always managed to duck.

Both of them had lost enough touch with reality to fail to see that this violence was dangerous and increasingly dangerous.

One of them had a gun, kept to have on hand when purchasing certain drugs. They had played with the gun several times, in fact this was about their only recreation, shooting at targets out in the hills where they would take a picnic and several bottles of wine, a picnic blanket and some lawn chairs, and shoot, play, and sleep all day. They usually put the gun away when they got home.

Then their arguments grew very violent. And then one of them felt the other was cheating on the relationship, a paranoid sensation induced by the drugs. So very intense was the physical violence that threats of killing were being made.

One of them grew fearful that these threats were actual threats, was very afraid when sober, and in fact was inspired to try to be sober more often to watch out for the danger of being shot.

Being sober perhaps was a life saver, perhaps was not, when yet one more "I'm gonna' kill you right now, where is that damn gun!" was shouted and the other pulled the gun out and shot in perceived or actual self defense.

39
Long Term Effects

Rates of intimate partner violence, especially physical, are likely to ebb and flow. This is in part due to changing definitions and measurements, as well as expanding understandings, of all that constitutes intimate partner abuse, violence, and terror, which is not only physical violence. Whatever the measured rates of this violence, there is more than likely additional violence which is not being reported and therefore not being counted. This is especially true when adding in the nonphysical abuses. (Refer to Chapter 18 and 19 for examples.)

And generations exposed to intimate partner violence, such as the children who have watched a parent being abused and another abusing, will come of age and be either addressing the impacts of this experience, or impacting their own children in ways we cannot foresee as a result of exposure to this experience, and doing so for years and generations to come.

TIP OF THE ICEBERG

What are the long range, lifecycle spanning health impacts of intimate partner abuse and violence? People who experience intimate partner violence and live, survive, especially those who experience this violence over a number of years, are more prone to injuries as well as to temporary and frequently ongoing troubled mental and physical (and economic) health conditions.

In fact, the serious long term effects of intimate partner abuse and violence on the mental, physical and financial health of women in particular are increasingly apparent and of increasing concern. These im-pacts are likely to be found more profound than already recognized. One of the reasons the measurement of long term impact is so challenging is that the mental, physical and even financial-economic (such as ability to earn a certain standard of living or maintain a career, or to make up for serious career damage or career obstruction by the abusing partner) impacts of this violence are not recognized for what they are.

When continuing years later (which they do in all too many cases), and sometimes not surfacing or accumulating enough to be understood as serious until years later (if ever), these impacts are too often viewed as anything but outcomes of partner violence.

The damage to a life which results from this abuse and violence is perceived as a general issue not stemming from this violence rather than an outcome of this violence. Quite often, the person experiencing these damages and others around this person attribute the condition to poor mental or physical health, poor work ethic or poor money management if the impacts are financial, generally low self esteem, or other conditions.

All too often, the person experiencing these mislabeled impacts is blamed or held responsible for resulting conditions. Now the blame the victim view is again at work and again largely unrecognized.

TIP OF THE REALITY

Again, the population of survivors of both physical and

emotional (as discussed in Chapter 2) — as well as financial and institutionally sup-ported (as discussed in Chapter 35) — intimate partner abuse and vio-lence may be a larger group than we now know. And, no matter what its size, this population may experience health impacts far more extensive than we presently see. While we may never be able to fully measure the total long term cost to a human life, or to the quality of a human life, of all forms of intimate partner violence, there is clearly room for further research in this area. And there is clearly room for further delving into the impacts of abusive behavior, including but not limited to physically violent behavior, upon overall mental, physical and financial health.

CO-OCCURRING CONDITIONS

Moreover, to allow ourselves to isolate intimate partner abuse and violence from other problems and "disorders" is to ignore the true complexity of this condition. For example, substance abuse and family vio-lence frequently appear together. The strong association between alcohol abuse and family violence requires that these behaviors be looked at together.

Physicians should be alert for the possible presence of one behavior given a diagnosis of the other. Thus, a physician with patients who have alcohol problems should screen for family violence, while physicians with patients who have signs of physical or sexual abuse should screen for alcohol use and abuse.

It is all too easy to assume that treating someone for alcohol and or drug abuse will stop any intimate partner violence taking place in that person's life, but this is not correct. It is also all too easy to assume that treating intimate partner violence in the absence of addressing any sub-stance abuse will effectively guarantee the stopping of the violence, or the stopping of the impacts of this violence.

And years later, when the long term after effects and outcomes of partner violence are being felt, drug and alcohol use, abuse and addiction mingle with these effects and outcomes, making it all the more difficult to isolate the impact of the violence. Of course, drug and alcohol use, abuse and addiction themselves are all too often part of the impact of intimate partner violence, even when such behavior surfaces years later.

DEPRESSION AND ANGER

Studies indicate that depression is found among persons, in particular women, who have experienced domestic violence, IPAVT, and that this depression diminishes to a significant extent, but in no way totally, once out of the environment in which they have been abused.

Depression itself is a strange two-faced beast, as it is to some extent basically unexpressed and or untreated anger turned inward.

Instead of striking out in response to being or having once been abused and beaten, many persons strike inward, harming or hurting themselves either emotionally or physically or both.

Years after the abusive situation has been left, the anger, if unidentified, untreated, and unexpressed, may register itself in the form of a low grade agitation or other sensation, or other more distinct and dangerous forms such as harm to self, harm to health, harm to overall well being, addiction, and sometimes suicidality.

GENERAL, POST-TRAUMATIC, AND OTHER STRESS

Although we are everywhere warned about the dangerous effects of too much stress upon us, our hearts, our healths, our minds, we know that some stress is a normal part of life. (Refer to Chapter 21.) A mild-to-moderate degree of day-to-day stress may be necessary for us to signal our bodies and minds that we are experiencing enough survival pressure to stay alert and to do what it takes to participate in life, to function and survive. However, there are many levels and types of stress that are not function- and health-promoting and are in fact detrimental and dangerous.

Any difficult situation results in its share of stress for the person or persons experiencing it. As noted earlier, abuse and violence situations are stress producing and have not only immediate stress effects but also longer term effects. Although the definitions of these terms are debated, common labels (some referred to earlier) for the long term effects of intimate partner and abuse and violence have been and are PTSD (posttraumatic stress disorder) and, in some cases, BWS (what was initially labeled as battered women's syndrome).

Note that for purposes of the discussion in this book, the recognized diagnostic term, posttraumatic stress disorder, is amended to read *posttraumatic stress condition/injury/disorder*. This allows for the understanding that much posttraumatic stress is not a disorder on the part of the victim, but is more a condition or injury the victim has sustained in being the victim/survivor of intimate partner abuse and violence.

Many other terms are emerging. Measures of recovery from these conditions are conducted both in terms of mental and emotional state and in terms of rehabilitation. In other words, does this person's recovery process restore psychological stability, health, and functional capacities, including abilities to perform daily life functions, have and pursue personal interests, form safe and healthy relationships, work and earn a living, and so on?

We know that posttraumatic stress results from one having been ex-posed to intense and likely repeated trauma on emotional, physiological, and even biochemical (neuro-endocrinological) levels, with these exposures to trauma being experienced in negative ways, in the form of suffering or other modes of registering the experience.

Note again that actual traumatization is usually defined as resulting when the person being traumatized lacks both the internal and the external resources to cope with the experience and faces the threat of (experiencing or reliving) more of the same. For many, the shock, hurt, and anger never entirely leave. Of course, the lack of internal coping re-sources, and the nuts and bolts of these, is not as readily measured as science might suggest.

So much is invisible to us that even the best tests cannot detect it all. Healing what cannot be fully recognized, or be detected at all, is a challenge. And, science is a long way from totally "curing" trauma.

ANGER AND MORE ANGER

People who have been violated in any way, including in the form of intimate partner abuse, violence, and terror, can be understandably dis-tressed, agitated, in pain, angry for years after the event, if not for the rest of their lives. Here, for the sake of simplicity, all of this is labeled anger. This particular IPAVT-related anger is beyond simple definitions of anger and is the collected tension, anxiety, and rage many abused persons carry, frequently with little outlet, and often with years of little safe outlet. Moreover, much of this anger that truly often exists is not identified even by the victims who sometimes have not developed a clear idea of what they are feeling.

This anger can be directed at the self or at others. Quite often, this anger finds no satisfactory outlet, or no outlet which exhausts this anger (exhausts this anger so that it does not later reappear in some form which may be very difficult to pinpoint and label).

This anger can linger waiting to burst forward, surprising not only others around the person but also the person displaying this anger. More likely, however, this anger bursts forward in a form not seen as anger, and or not seen as connected in any way to abuse and violence which occurred a few days, months, or years back, and is not understood. (See again subsections "Dangerous Response Delay and Exacerbation" in Chapter 2, and "Nuances of Suppressed Fight or Flight Reflex" in Chapter 4.)

ATTACHMENT CONFUSION AND RE-VICTIMIZATION

This bundle of emotion and energy labeled as anger can remain a problem in the lives of people who have been violated. This visible and invisible anger can take a form allowing a repetitive reenactment of past events. When something triggers the revival of this memory of being abused, it can virtually bring to life the long over events of abuse and violence. In the process, so-called re-victimization may be experienced, in that the memory, once it surfaces, can be relived as if it were fresh in the mind and the present-time pain still present.

Other triggers can have re-victimization effects. An unsettling or upset-ting of a current relationship situation, even a nonviolent one, may retrieve memories of a previous relationship being in distress, caught up in violence, or perhaps on the verge of a violent and painful breakup. Even comfortable present-day attachment or involvement on an emotional level can retrieve memories, and even sensations, of prior attachment to a person who abused, bringing in a reliving of the pain of being abused.

This reliving may sometimes be expressed in a new situation, in a new relationship, one in some way or ways even vaguely resembling the situation or relationship of previous abuse and violence. Know that these resemblance-triggering memories can be as distinct as the same name of someone, or as vague as the smell of someone's dinner cooking.

Recalling direct or indirect experiences of being abused (or of abusing) and or aftermaths of these experiences is quite common and frequently involuntary. Sometimes a range of unexpressed anger surfaces, anger resulting from the years of violence that may be recalled, even old anger from instances of taking abuse with no apparent alternative.

DISTORTED ATTACHMENT BONDS

It is not unusual for residuals of strong emotional ties to the person who did the abusing to linger and creep forward when triggered. This form of attachment bond, or better stated distorted attachment bond, can be confusing as it can defy the logic of onlookers as well as of the person remaining attached long after parting company with the abuser.

New experiences with new people, and new partners, can be laden with flashback triggers, even when there is no emotional or physical abuse in the new relationship.

Judgment about new love or emotional relation-ships can be affected for years.

RELIVING PAST NEGATIVES

The fight or flight reactions may appear while this re-victimization is taking place, as these were reactions experienced or visualized during violent incidents of the past. Such neurological programming may linger for decades or may wear off with age.

Nevertheless, vague reminders of past events may continue to trigger stress even when these triggers are not spotted. Old stress can thus become new stress, bringing with it other new sensations stemming from old experiences.

Although we all want to select the most positive experiences available to us, the tendency to relive past negatives and horrors remains a problem. Current stress can transform to past trauma and then produce new trauma. Even attachments to new abusers may take place, following a pattern established long prior, with scenarios playing themselves out sometimes even word for word and blow for blow.

40
After the Fact Story

G.L. is finally feeling strong again. She and her children have now gotten past the grueling divorce, the move to a different house, the selling of the house they had lived in before the divorce, the marriage of F.B. (the children's father) to S., the acquiring of a stepbrother.

Although money is tight, and the house G.L. and the children now live in is small, things run pretty well. G.L. and her children are close and they share a sense that they have survived something very painful together.

The only really difficult things that remain are the weekend visits the children have with their father. Every time they have to get ready for his picking them up to spend a weekend with him, they complain and cry and resist.

G.L. doesn't really want to force them to go, but she says, "You need to spend some time with your father." When this does not sway them (and it never does), G.L. resorts to restating the fact that the court has decreed that the children must visit their father on an agreed upon schedule.

When the father arrives, the children are usually crying, angry, and not yet packed. The father rings the bell. G.L. opens the door because the children will not.

"Are they ready?" the father asks coldly.

G.L. says, "No. I'm sorry, I can't seem to get them to want to go. It's like this every time."

He replies in a low but angry voice, "This is your fault. You've turned them against me, alienated them. I know it's you."

"No, no it's not. I tell you this every time. Now, I'll wait out front, you come in and you make 'em get ready and go. I can't deal with it anymore. It's your turn," G.L. insists.

F.B. marches right by G.L. and up to the kids' rooms. G.L. sits down outside on the steps, her face in her hands. There is shouting up there. Eventually F.B. and the kids come down packed. F.B. stands at the door. The kids tearfully kiss their mother good bye. They leave.

Then G.L. cries alone.

• •

Now, every time the children return, they are unwilling to discuss the behavior they exhibited at the time of their departure. After a while, G.L. stops trying to discuss this with them. And they won't talk about their weekend activities much.

"What did you do with Dad and S.?...Did you play with little G.?" G. is new stepmother S.'s son by a previous marriage. When the kids avoid answering. G.L. shrugs. She enjoys the peace and loving closeness she has with her children.

• •

Life goes on. Things continue calmly and happily in G.L.'s home. Or so G.L. thinks. Eventually, reports come in from teachers and other parents: the children are hitting each other and others at school.

Then, one day, a day that changes everything all over again, a letter arrives. It falls out of the pile of mail and G.L. feels uncomfortable as soon as she sees the envelope. She picks it up and takes it into the kitchen in order to read it alone: F.B. is suing for full custody of the children!!!

The nightmare begins. The divorce is relived, but now G.L.'s fitness as a mother is fiercely challenged. The files of her therapist are subpoenaed as her children had participated in some sessions. Witnesses speak against her. The relative quality of the homes and schools and toys and computers the two parents can provide is compared. F.B. has more money, a larger house, a family life which appears to be "whole" (mommy, daddy, pets, and kids). S. is at home with the younger G., so G.L.'s children would not be latchkey kids, coming home to what is described in court as a cold and empty house while the single mother G.L. is still at work. Moreover, F.B. and S. go to church and appear to offer some spiritual structure to the children's lives.

Based upon a long in the past drinking and pill problem, an old suicide attempt, her long working hours, the relative economic hardships her children experience while living with G.L., the crime rate in G.L.'s lower middle class neighborhood, and the subpoenaed testimony of her therapist, G.L. is found an unfit mother. She loses custody and becomes the parent with supervised visitation rights every other weekend.

■■

G.L. is alone. She has lost primary custody of her children. She is shattered, lost. Hopelessness sets in.

Her children are angry at her because they feel that she let F.B. win custody. They are too young to understand this is not the case.

Spending hours, days and nights alone at home with the windows closed, the phone unplugged, and no one to talk to, G.L. catches herself drinking again. She mumbles to herself that, "Maybe they're right about me."

The desperation grows. G.L. begins to sink to depths she has never known.

One morning, G.L.'s boss and old friend, C., comes to see her. C. knocks on the door again and again. When there is no answer, C. opens a side window and crawls in. She finds G.L. lying on the couch half asleep. G.L. has a hangover. "G.L., I'm going to have to fire you pretty soon. But I don't want to do this . . . You have a choice to make and NOW!"

At some point during this discussion, G.L. comes to feel that this may be her last chance to pull out of this mess and her last friend. She digs deep inside, decides to pull herself together, and to go back to work that very day, putting aside all sense that she would need to look perfect to go to work, as she once felt she was able to do. Passable would be alright for now. But first, before stepping back in to life, she throws out all the alcohol in the house, along with her wedding ring. Somehow, she relates alcohol, the drug, to F.B., the drug. She decides to be free of both. She knows she will need help and treatment. . . .

When she gets home that afternoon, she checks to be sure she has thrown out all the bottles of alcohol. She opens the windows. She plugs in the phone. She dials a number.

"I know it's late," she says, "but I hear you once lost custody of your children and that you have a lawyer who helped you get shared custody.... Yes, I'm that G.L.. . . . Yes, I lost. Totally. A few months clean and sober, well, that's not really true. I lied.... Yeah, but I'm ready to try to fix this now... Yes, I have a pencil."

G.L. trembles as she writes down the telephone number of the *suggested attorney. This is the beginning of G.L.'s transition to a stronger state of mind and a greater self esteem: she is taking action on her own behalf. She begins to put things back together, to stand up for herself. It will be a long and difficult road, but she intends to come back stronger than ever. And the first step has to be to get herself well.*

41
Child Witness and Victim

"Seeing my daddy and mommy hit each other makes me shiver."

"I hide when they start, 'cuz I don't wanna' watch."

"I hide when they start because I'm afraid."

"Sometimes my dad comes and hits me too. Then he hits my mom when she tries to make him stop."

"Thinking about it makes me want to kill someone or myself."

"I grew up watching my dad beat on my mom. I hate her for taking it. I hate myself for not stopping it."

"I am afraid if I get together with someone it will be the same way it was for my parents."

"Not me, I'll never be like either of them!"

UNADDRESSED INJURIES

Volumes can be written about the impact of intimate partner abuse and violence on children who witness it, may feel to blame for it, may find role modeling in it, and when caught in the fray are frequently hurt emotionally as well as physically. Although this book is not focused on children, this is by no means a message that what happens to these child witnesses and victims does not matter.

CARRIERS OF PATTERNS

These children are the carriers into the future of our values and knowledge. They will likely (and fortunately) want to improve upon their parents' values and expression of these, and this is good! So much can be done better. These precious people, their parents' offspring, de-serve a great deal of caring and intelligent assistance identifying, and recovering from, their exposure to adults' intimate partner violence—and their parents' pain.

To break the cycle of intimate partner violence—as well as its long term health and mental health effects, pain, and trauma—we must understand that all of this may spill from generation to generation in some form unless a conscious and visible effort to stop the violence is made!

It is also important to see that, when adults repeat patterns of emotional and physical violence and abuse around children, they are including children in these patterns. Any detrimental habits, negative addictions, played out around children bring these children right into these pat-terns.

Compulsive, destructive, and abusive cycles of intimate partners include any children on the seeming sidelines. They cannot be unaffected. Nor can they be saved from the roller coaster rides of cycles played out by adults who are likely, in some difficult to explain (to a parent let alone the child) way, addicted to the patterns they have established.

No matter how much a parent believes a child is insulated from her or his ongoing involvement in intimate partner violence and abuse, there is little protection from this reality for the child. Children see and hear—and feel—even the smallest signs of this problem.

TEACHING DENIAL

To pretend to children and teens that there is no abuse and violence is not only absurd but cruel. These young people are witnesses, they do perceive something, they feel it, usually also hear and see it or the tears and injuries.

When this feeling, hearing, and seeing is not validated by the parent, this denial of an actual reality is disturbing, confusing, and distressing. Why drive a child into denial-like patterns, teaching that denial of a serious problem is alright? *Why add to a child's confusion, fear, pain, and roller coaster experience new lessons—lessons in denial?*

HARSH AND PAINFUL REALITY

The harsh and painful reality is that these children are dependent upon these adults who are abusing and being abused. They have no way of ending the relationship with these adults, and they have no way of choosing not to need these adults.

This dependence upon these disturbed adults, coupled with the mixed messages that children in these situations typically receive (such as it is bad to hit people even though you see this happening here at home), can be highly stressful and emotionally disturbing for these children.

Riding the roller coaster of fight, feel better, fight, feel better, fight, feel better, and so on, children absorb elements of abuse and violence cycle patterning. Moreover, they absorb the ride itself—high low, high low, high low, again and again. For some children, especially those who do not know what patterning is, or what is happening to them as witnesses, these patterns can become deeply buried inside them. Many years later, or maybe not so much later, a trigger may fire the pattern into action, and the child is at risk of continuing the cycle.

Or the child is at risk of playing out the cycle of abuse and violence in another way, such as via alcohol and drug, or food or internet or other addiction, or via other detrimental and dangerous behavioral patterns.

CHILDREN HAVE A RIGHT TO THIS INFORMATION

Children have a right to know what the risks of being child witnesses might be. We do not mind children seeking information about any family tree disease that they are at risk for, do we? Why would we mind children seeking information about the possible future abuse and violence they are both at risk of being the victims of and also at risk of being the sources of? And how dare we not inform children that the detrimental behavior patterning they have witnessed may in itself be addictive—whether played out in the same form or another?

Children have a right to know what the long term health and mental health effects of being child witnesses may be. Children exposed to intimate partner, abuse, violence, and terror are at a higher risk for a number of long term health and social conditions—such as but not limited to being at risk of coming into adulthood playing out perpetrator and or victim roles.

And we are still learning about the long term effects of this nonphysical and physical violence upon children. Or maybe we know more than we want to, with the signs all around us in this violent world where adults resort to violence as a means of addressing conflict. Their children should be told and taught early what it means to see a behavioral cycle. They should be taught how to spot abusive, even problem addiction-like, behavior, and how to look closely and see the steps in relating that can be changed, redirected, and once these are identified—how to slow one's own behavior down and GO CONSCIOUS.

Adults seeking to rewrite the programming they may have instilled in their children (for example, when they allowed their children to witness emotional and physical violence) must teach their children the same thing they themselves need to learn: how to recognize and change—or get away from—patterns of abuse and violence. Not to teach these children these things out of concern that the material that will be taught is too much for children's ears and eyes is illogical. These children have already been exposed to intimate partner violence and abuse.

Now they have a right to a recapturing of this information in a way that prepares them to avoid the same experiences their parents have had. The material in this book, for example, is material young people can learn and many indeed have a hunger for. Young adults forming young intimate partner relationships are especially in need of this sort of information. Knowing all this is important:

- How relationships work.
- How to tell what is working well and what is not.
- The precursors of abuse and violence in relating.
- The signs of present time abuse and violence in relationships.
- The emotional and physical risks of abuse and violence in relationships.

- How to spot both positive and negative compromises and trades, C&Ts, as they are being made.
- The definitions of intent and consent: what is a yes and what is a no.

LOVE

Children want to see healthy love relationships. This provides a model for what good is possible and for the roles they will likely someday assume for themselves.

Parents who allow atmospheres of intimate partner violence and abuse in their homes are allowing the transmission of this sort of troubled message: it is OK to abuse someone you love; it is OK to be abused by someone you love; and it is OK to abuse yourself.

However, this is of course not OK. And that this is OK must not be taught.

Teaching children (whether teaching directly or indirectly by inference or action) that abuse of and violence against someone you love brings happiness or satisfaction can instill in these children profound confusion and serious trouble adjusting what they learn from their parents to the outside world and to rest of their lives.

Many parents are unaware of (or choose to be in denial regarding) the impact on their children of their parents' violence and abuse and terrorizing of each other (IPAVT). Too often, parents dealing with their own IPAVT situations are modeling to their children troubled ways of loving, or ways of thinking one is loving oneself and one's significant other.

Children see this modeling and incorporate this into their world views, forming a deep level of unresolved confusion and disillusionment. How can love hurt so much? Is this the way it is supposed to be? Is this the self respect my parents have for themselves? Is this low level of self esteem all that one should try for?

Children and teens are also faced with identity questions: Is all this abuse and violence because of me? What kind of person am I if I have caused this? What if I have let this happen? Why didn't I stop this? Am I doomed to be just like my mother or father? If these are my role models, will I be able to learn any other better behavior? How do I know?

Being a child witness means watching two people who purportedly love each other act as if they hate each other. This means seeing two people—who want themselves or others to think there is love there—emotionally or physically hurt each other. In a child's eyes, this does not compute. The messages are mixed and are stored in the young mind mixed.

The job of overcoming the mislabeling of acts of violence as love, and of overcoming all related confusion, begins immediately in the young mind whose tolerance for intimate partner abuse and violence is already being programmed in, whether the child or anyone watching knows this.

(It must be noted here that most all parental relationships experience moments or times when there are disagreements of some sort. Children do learn to accept that healthy relationships can include disagreements, that it is not unusual for two people to find they do not agree on absolutely everything. What is important for young people to see and learn is that when there are disagreements or even conflicts, these can be and are handled in safe and reasonable ways for all parties involved and around.)

TOLERANCE

Of course it is not only abusing and or fighting parents who teach abuse and violence as a way of life, as an acceptable medium of exchange. It is much of the media and the world around children teaching this as well.

Yes, we live in a world where many forms of abuse and violence can be (mis)understood as being virtually normal.

Everywhere they look, and a large part of what they learn in school, tells children that: violence exists (which it does of course), violence "often works," violence is "part of life," and, violence is "part of history."

The tolerance of violence can be instilled so deeply in children and yet be so invisibly there.

Children's nervous systems react to the abuse and violence and terror they witness or sense or experience directly. Their minds and memories record their reactions, of course. Repeated exposure to violence can bring a "coping" sort of tolerance of adults' abuse and violence.

Tolerance can lessen any emotional or physical response to this abuse and violence. The young person's mind can generate a mental and biochemical system of coping, of going on in life, of incorporating this reality—even of calling violence and abuse alright.

The process involved in the development of "coping" with parents' IPAVT tends to involve a ***desensitization*** of the mind to the abuse and violence being witnessed. If the highs and lows of parents' violence and abuse are ongoing, and the child is there for this emotional roller coaster ride, then the child's brain cells can open receptor sites which are receptive to, perhaps even quite desensitized to, this familiar roller coaster ride that the adults' patterns take them on.

Parents can counter this trend by visibly practicing positive conflict resolution processes and telling their children this is what they are doing. Rising above abuse and violence is possible and can become a way of life, first in the home. No, we cannot turn the hands of time back, but we can start now and teach our children well—or at least better than we have done so far.

SPECIAL NOTE:
DEPLORABLE
PARTNER ABUSE THROUGH THE CHILD

The discussion in this chapter has addressed primarily children's witnessing of the IPAVT their parents are engaging in. An additional note must be included here, knowing well that entire volumes must be writ-ten to even begin to sufficiently address this additional matter: an abusing partner abusing the other partner by abusing the child to do this. (See again subsection "Collateral IPAVT" in Chapter 2.)

Also common in this deplorable scenario are these factors: The abusing partner abusing the child while the other partner:
    (a) does not know.
    (b) knows yet cannot stop this.
    (c) is also being severely abused and or restrained.
    (d) is threatened if there is a response to this abuse.
    (e) is treated as "crazy" or not credible when trying
        to report this abuse of the child,
        even to the court or law
        enforcement.

(f) is caught between various issues such as:
- wanting to flee from the abusing partner.
- fear of being accused of kidnapping.
- fear of having to leave the child with the abuser.
- fear of loosing custody of the child to the abuser.

Whether linked with partner abuse or taking place without concurrent partner abuse, the abuse of children is indeed absolutely deplorable. Where such abuse is taking place against the backdrop of IPAVT and any related restraining order, marital separation, divorce, and or custody proceedings, the abuse is frequently lost in the "shuffle," overlooked, or even sometimes hidden.

Surrounding professional and legal processes such as divorce and custody work and motions must pay attention to what relationship partners are saying and doing as per their children's safety. This is essential where the actual safety of children is affected against the backdrop of overarching parental IPAVT.

Again note that too frequently those involved professionally seem not to know that the abuse and violence taking place between parents can distract from, cover over, hide, downplay, any underlying child abuse taking place. Where the safety of one or both parents may be in jeopardy as per IPAVT, and may be ignored or denied, the safety of the surrounding children may be entirely overlooked. We cannot allow this child abuse to be overlooked.

Education and social services must address the matter of child abuse in IPAVT environments (as well as in non-IPAVT environments.) We simply cannot look away from this reality. We cannot ignore the abuse that can take place within the all too frequently poorly informed, flawed, biased, and at times even dishonest family, social, professional, and even judicial and legal processes. Far too often these processes and their personal and professional participants actually enable the perpetration, and virtual protection of the perpetration, of child abuse and even of child sexual abuse. And too frequently this abuse of the child is indeed part of the overarching partner abuse scenario.

For the most part, society's eyes are closed to the reality that too many parents, professionals, even courts, do not protect the innocent from injury or further injury. Rather, the courts too frequently risk, and sometimes even exacerbate further, injury of the innocent. We cannot tell ourselves this sort of thing is not taking place. We cannot say that our system of justice protects us from the tragic failures of justice these misunderstandings, blurrings, and distortions promote. We are talking about human lives here.

42
Cleaning Story

She was getting out of the shower when she heard her husband shouting at their younger daughter about some toys the visiting children had thrown all over the place before they left.

Responding to her motherly instincts, she quickly pulled a towel around herself and ran out to the living room where he was yelling at the one child, demanding the child clean up immediately although it was a holiday, while the older child sat on the side and watched.

"Stop that now. This isn't fair," she said.

However he was not stopping his shouting at the child.

She began to shout as well now. "Stop I said. Why make one kid clean up and not the other? Anyway, it's a holiday. Stop, I will clean it up, let them both be," she added loudly as she reached to pull him away from the child.

He turned, yelling, "She's my child too!"

As he whirled back to the child, and raised his hand as if about to hit the child, she (the mother) leapt between them. He then grabbed her (the mother) by the hair with one hand and by the arm with the other, dragged her (the mother) out the backyard door as her towel was falling off, and threw her (the mother) down naked onto the cement step where she hit her spine on the edge of that step.

The younger child ran to stop this, shouting, "Stop, don't hurt mommy!"

Now this child was tossed out the door. The child and the mother were then both abruptly locked out of the house.

The mother tried to bring herself to run naked to the neighbors for help, or to send the child, but was not certain what to do. Frozen with indecision, she and the child cowered behind a shed in the yard.

About a half hour later, they heard him slam the door and drive away with the older child. Once certain he was gone, the mother and the younger child headed back to the house, only to find every door locked.

The child and the mother remembered a key the mother had once secretly put under a rock outside, on the other side of the house, and got back into the house.

He was gone for several days. He never called to see whether the mother and younger child were alright.

Either prevented, intimidated, or alienated, the older child never called either.

Part Five

43
Getting Out Story

"Hi, it's been a long time, how are you?"

"Fine, why?"

"You rarely call these days, so I know something's up. What is it?"

"Well..."

"Come on. Tell."

"Tell what?"

"Well?"

"Well, . . . OK, how does one know if one wants a divorce?"

"...."

"Hello? Are you there?"

"Does M.Z. know?"

"No, I don't know. I don't think so."

"So, what is it? Why now?"

"Look, I know you care about both of us, so maybe it's wrong to ask you for advice."

"No, it's OK. But exactly how does anyone know? You're asking me?"

"Yes: how?"

"..."

"Well, any ideas for me?"

"You just do. And if you aren't sure, then you definitely wait until you are very sure because even a hint of something like this can really rock the boat.... I mean, unless it's a matter of life and death."

"?"

"Oh my God, is it?"

"...."

44
When Your Skin's Too Tight

You reach back into time, wanting to touch the face of a long lost love, to look into the eyes of the one who is gone, wishing you could go back and relive the process, handle the whole thing differently. Or maybe you don't. Maybe you are happy it's over. Or maybe you never think about it at all.

But, you may know the bittersweet realization, years after a bitter break up, that the relationship could have been saved or the ending of it could have been more positively conducted. Or you may think you know.

What sort of mutual and conscious relating could have been conducted by the partners? And more specifically, what about the person being abused? What path to truth and self respect could a person being abused have followed? What different or further effort to seek help might have been made? What other path to self respect could a person being abused have followed? And, what about the person doing the abusing? What more accountability for causing injury could have been present—on the abuser's part? All in all, what could either party have done to stop the abuse and violence? Anything?

"What went wrong" questions may creep back into your mind, or these may be replaced by questions of what could have gone right. You might ask: How much good was there in that partnership? How much of the good did I miss, did we miss? What valuable connections were there? Even though these were destroyed by a joint lack of awareness, might they have been developed into a deeper more positive relationship?

How better could your investment in that relationship have been protected? That was the precious time of your life you were spending—how could the precious aspects be better appreciated?

Or was it best, safest, and wisest you got out?

PRESSURE TO SHED

Certainly, too many relationships which could be saved break up before the members look carefully at the dynamics, the spoken and unspoken compromises and trades, C&Ts, that have formed and then have reinforced troubled patterns. And certainly there are pathways to healing which many a troubled relationship never has the opportunity to travel before dismantling or shedding itself. This may be quite sad for these partners as they have invested the precious time of their lives in their relationship and now may not feel they profit enough from the investment.

But there are sometimes, even when the work, and for that matter everything imaginable, may have been done to hold partners together, that partners must part for their own as well as others' well being, stability, safety, and sanity.

Almost as frequently as we see break ups of relationships which could have been saved, which could have transcended their patterns of abuse and violence, we see the prolonging of relationships which should have concluded, as they were not going to do what it takes to stop the abuse and violence.

> **Like snakes, we can reach times when
> we must shed our old skins.**

And shedding can be good, even powerfully positive, and can allow new growth, positive change. That pivotal moment when the skin absolutely must be shed comes, and the response can be very clean and well conducted or very very messy for all involved.

Too often, the real pressure to shed an intimate partner relationship sneaks up on us. We finally, perhaps much later than we should, notice that the skin of the relationship, its behavior, its life, is far too tight—that we have outgrown it.

> **Staying in it forever might even destroy us.**

Yes, we can come to know this consciously and then finally react. How-ever, it is likely we have known this subconsciously for quite some time.

**LIST:
DETECTING THE SHEDDING POINT**

Much damage can be avoided if this shedding point and or its approach can be handled consciously. First, you, and everyone you affect, can get more out of your shedding process simply by being conscious of the fact that you are at its threshold. How do you do this?

First, watch and listen to yourself very closely. Be very alert to subtle changes in the general way you feel and act:

- Notice shifts in your ability to concentrate.
- Notice changes in your enthusiasm.

- Notice to what degree you function on automatic—mindlessly.
- Notice when you feel claustrophobic or trapped—physically, emotionally, intellectually, financially, and or spiritually.
- Notice if you are regularly exhibiting troubled behavior (which is detrimental to yourself or others).

Second, carefully look inside at identification issues:

- Notice if your life is taking on less and less meaning for you.
- Notice whether you are comfortable with your response when you stop for a moment's reflection and ask yourself, "Who am I and why am I here?"
- Notice whether you feel out of place, not identified, with yourself, your relationship, and or other aspects of your world.
- Notice to what degree you go through the motions, moving hollowly through the process of relating to your intimate partner.

Third, and most importantly, in terms of safety in relationship, take a look the safety factors:

- Are you living in a situation in which your or another person's physical safety is, or may at some point be, in jeopardy?
  - Is your or someone else's physical safety or survival at stake as a result of how you are, or someone around you is, feeling?
- Are you engaged in a mutual situation in which you

feel that you are or may be moved to, driven to, actually hit or hurt someone physically?
- Are you engaging in mutual physical assaults or attacks?
- Are there regular physical attacks being made upon you?
- Are you going to or do you feel that you might physically hurt yourself?

Fourth and equally important although the answers may be less obvious:

- Are you living in a situation in which your or another person's emotional well being is in jeopardy?
- Are you engaged in a mutual situation in which you feel that you are or may be moved to, driven to, actually negatively affect someone's emotional well being?
- Are you engaging in mutual verbal and nonverbal emotional assaults or attacks?
- Are there regular verbal and nonverbal emotional attacks being made upon you?
- Is there a potential that you or your partner will commit other forms of nonphysical abuse (such as financial abuse or abuse of fiduciary duty—as discussed in Chapter 35)?
- Are you going to or do you feel that you might jeopardize your emotional well being?

You can come to know when it is time to shed your skin. You feel caged in, boxed in, and trapped by the patterns of your life: you are losing your self and or your self control.

You are losing yourself to a pattern which is harmful for you and or for the ones around you.

You may be entirely or partially responsible for this pattern or you may not. Nevertheless, you must look at this pattern—you may be in some form of danger.

KNOWING WHAT YOU REALLY WANT TO SHED

Now, the thing to be careful of here is knowing which skin you really wish to shed: the skin of yourself or the skin or your relationship?

Note that it is all too easy to place all blame for one's own dissatisfaction with life on one's intimate partner relationship—or on one's partner in that relationship. It may be many years later before the way to identify and heal the situation is understood; however, the hands of time do not turn back.

This means that getting out may have been the wisest choice. Or, it may have been the only choice given that the tools for saving the relationship—while eliminating the abuse and violence from it—were not available to the relationship, or of interest to both of its members. Or it may have been a big mistake. So look deep inside, past layers of lies and denials, before taking this step, before leaving. You will know the truth.

GETTING OUT

Once you allow yourself to see the truth about the presence of a pattern of abuse and violence in your relationship, and if in that truth you indeed detect a true need for shedding your relationship, you must, must, must let yourself out of this skin. Your or another person's health and safety may be at stake. Here's where there is, sometimes, a strong resistance. Either you or the people around you do not want you to change. We will come back to your own resistance to change shortly. First, others' resistance.

When the people around you do not want you to change, even after you have tried to convince them that you should, then changing yourself is far more difficult. Without support to change, and with resistance to change, you may feel trapped. For your own or others' stability, safety, and sanity, you need to know if you need to get out. Listen to yourself.

When people closest to you want you to change, but do not want to change themselves in anyway, you may be similarly trapped. When the people closest to you want to change as much as they want you to change, and as much as you want to change, there is hope that the relationship, the family, and the system can grow together in a similar direction. Either way, you have to change to protect yourself and others.

Open your eyes to opportunities for change!

These are everywhere.

Do not worry if change feels a bit like dying. Something has to be shed, die off, for something new to come. Old troubled patterns need to go. Take careful steps to plan the end of the behavior you have outgrown or want to outgrow, shed, especially if this is a behavior dangerous to yourself or others. Know which levels of internal and external information and support are available to you, and utilize this support. Part of this accessing support will involve your being honest with yourself and others about any abuse and violence.

You can develop an entirely new way of seeing and being in the world. Do not let anyone tell you that you cannot get there from here. This statement reveals our deep programming to believe in severe limitations. You can get anywhere you want from here. You just need to make yourself a map, a plan.

SOME PREFER PHYSICAL DEATH TO CHANGING?

Do you resist change? If so, you are doing something quite natural. Living things are generally programmed to seek predictability and stability in their environments and to try to keep the environment (the boat) from rocking no matter how risky this may be. Change can be destabilizing, perhaps unnerving, often upsetting. Old patterns resist change.

When breaking a pattern, change happens.

So, let's say you are the one who chooses to stay in a deeply troubled abusing and violent relationship, stay hoping it will change a bit, but not too much. No matter how detrimental that pattern of abuse and violence has become, you may have grown used to it. Letting it go can feel like throwing away a whole piece of life, even a whole life. Or at least the map of a life.

This may be the only life you know anymore, the only life you think you know, and you may be deeply identified with this life. (Again see Figure 46.3.)

You may be so deeply identified with a relationship, even with an abusive one, that this life seems to you to be you, who you are, and shedding this life does indeed seem to you to be dying. (This can be the old "who am I without us" question.) If you have ever been lost and without a map, you may know the sensation of confusion, disorientation, this brings. Anticipating being lost without a map can bring on some of these same feelings. Hence, so many persons being abused stay in the face of great risk and danger.

> **Staying and surviving
> emotionally and physically
> requires a
> commitment to real change.**

Yet, breaking deep patterns of abuse and violence in one's intimate partner relationship may seem, at least at first, virtually impossible. After all, we are talking about spotting minor and major emotional and physical abuses, learning what these are and how they work, and then undergoing the changes required to break the cycle.

> **This can call for a
> complete overhaul
> of one's way of life.**

Many members of relationships are simply not up for this job and do choose to allow highly damaging and dangerous patterns to remain in place rather than try to break their cycles. And many of these people are actually addicted to the patterns of anger, fear, pain, suffering, more fear, more anger, more pain, more suffering.

They may also be hooked on the roller coaster ride itself, the moving from highs to lows and back: riding the breaks from the anger, the forgiveness, the making up, the love, the hearts and flowers, and then the anger and all that follows all over again.

(Others of course would do the work were they guided in the process of *relationship pattern overhaul*, or were they to know how to guide themselves in this process.)

Change can be difficult and frightening. It may look impossible at first. When you are without a map, or have not yet found the courage to read the map, you can stay quite stuck. You know the feeling: It's that same phase-repeating, or similar sort of closed-in, no-way-out, feeling.

When the pressure to shed one's old skin becomes unbearably great, then either a person gets help, or gets out, or gets angry, depressed, hooked on another problem pattern such as addiction to drugs, alcohol, food, compulsive sex with other people, and so on. In extreme cases when the pressure becomes far too great, there is a risk that the person may grow suicidal and or murderous.

While these emotions last, tension, even anger, even rage, can grow. Uncontrollable anger can appear: sometimes mild, sometimes fierce anger, and even death-wishing aimed either inward in the form of suicidality or outward in the form of maiming or killing. These highly unfortunate, traumatic, sad, and very dangerous predicaments are rare, yet require full attention.

Strangely enough, the extremes of self-killing (self or *sui*-cide) and of other-killing (person or *homi*-cide) are what some feel to be "cheap" ways out. Do not misunderstand this comment. These are not correct or safe, nor are they legal ways out of a trap. Uncontrollable anger, death wishing, and even considering maiming, suicide, and murder—these are highly dangerous and potentially fatal shortcuts.

Like rats trapped in a maze, with no flight option available, the fight side of the fight or flight syndrome can sweep in. Intense bursts of wild rage may briefly relieve tension;

however, these do not correct or address any of problems which generate this rage. (See Chapter 2.)

GROWING NUMB

There are those who prefer to grow numb and endure a problem pattern of abuse and violence rather than leave it, challenge it, or change it. How-ever, "preferring to grow numb" is not always an option, not always a choice, not always what is taking place.

Many persons being beaten simply detach somewhat while being beaten, or even dissociate to a great degree, to either consciously or subcon-sciously cope with what is taking place.

These people can remain trapped for a long, long time (perhaps their entire lives) and grow increasingly numb to the situation. They can be feeling there is no way out, no way to grow while staying in, no way to shed their skins, indeed feeling very trapped.

In this adaptation to abuse and violence, there also are potential time bombs. Sometimes quite abruptly and surprisingly, for numbed, detached, disassociated individuals, the tendency to express violence against themselves or others wells up, until boom—there is a shocking break!

The decision to break is usually an unconscious one, hence this may not seem to be a decision at all. Instead this "break" may be an unfortunate impulse related event. (Refer to the discussion of intent in Chapter 4. Consider how elusive intent is.)

Unfortunately, the state of numbness itself can become part of the troubled relationship cycle, the numb behavior appearing almost on cue. (You go numb while I beat you, I'll go blank while I beat you. ... You go blank while you beat me, I'll go numb while you beat me. ... We'll come back to "reality" wounded, bruised, bleeding.)

LIST:
NUMBNESS MAY MEAN TROUBLE BREWING

There are great risks to partners' numbing to, or detaching from, being abused. In long term and deeply instilled patterns of intimate partner abuse and violence, a partner going numb does not at all guarantee that the abuse and violence ends. Instead, the numbing may separate the person being abused from the pain, even when there are serious physical attacks and injuries taking place. Literally during an episode of being beaten, this person may detach while being beaten, somehow feeling that:

- There is no beating taking place although there indeed is.

- There is a much milder form of physical abuse taking place than there actually is. (*Whatever is happening to me will not result in serious injury or kill me—when it might.*)

- There is no pain to being hit, only the sense of impact when there is indeed pain.

- Somehow this beating is deserved.

Similarly, the person who is abusing may detach while abusing, seeing that he or she is hitting someone, but feeling:

- No response to being the abusing person.
- No concern that the violence may actually injure the

partner.
- No sense that the violence is as severe as it is, rather seeing the violence as minimal, minor. (*Whatever is happening here will not seriously injure or kill anyone—when it might.*)
- No sense that this beating is unfair or unjust, even feeling that somehow this beating is justified.
- A sense of blamelessness, that although one is abusive, one was made to abuse.
- A sense that one is the victim, not the abuser.
- A sense that none of the perpetration of abuse, violence and terror is taking place: dissociating while committing abusive, violent, terrorizing acts.

And, once this episode of violence is complete, the person abusing may either forget that it ever took place—or at least *say* that this has been forgotten, that there is no memory of it.

Various levels of moral, emotional, and physical *disengagement from the violence as it is taking place or after it has taken place* are quite common. Disengagement from this violence can be on the part of one member of the relationship or both. Both can be quite unaware of what is taking place—blocking it out, blanking, forgetting, or both can be in denial. However both are in dangerous territory, dangerous states of mind.

The person being beaten may not respond with self protective efforts, may feel that these efforts would be of no use, may feel that these efforts would increase the danger, or may hardly notice that a beating is being received.

The person beating may not respond by placing limits on the

damage being caused, or by noting when the abuse is becoming life threatening to one or both of the partners, or by acknowledging that a beating is being inflicted.

The state of violent and pre-violent emotional numbness can indeed be, and often is, trouble brewing. The mere reality that people can reach this place of detaching from reality during abuse and violence is an indication that the relationship has traveled to this point and now must go or change a great deal!

One of the most unfortunate developments which may take place is the moving of a deeply troubled behavior pattern from the psychological to the physical realm. This allows trapped, perhaps not yet fully expressed, energy to physicalize, to become more physical. It is not surprising that many psychological and spiritual disturbances take on a physical aspect such as inflicting or receiving intimate partner violence and may add in additional co-occurring conditions such as drug addiction, sex addiction, injury and accident proneness, and, of course, especially among persons being abused, chronic physical pain and illness.

Our tendency is to eventually, when the pressure of a "don't touch" problem is too heavy, pull whatever we can into a place where we can see it.

There is a drive to "make real" energies which are perceived but not seen. Abusers' impulsive outbursts of physical violence—uncontrolled impulsive rage—are frequently but not always responding to this drive. *(For other aspects of such outbursts of violence, see also the subsections in this book: "Dangerous Response Delay and Exacerbation" in Chapter 2; "Nuances of Suppressed Fight or Flight Response" in Chapter 4; and, "Trauma and Dissociating as Coping" in Chapter 37.)*

SEEING THE DRIVE TO VIOLENCE

It is a great and painful irony that this drive to commit (or even be the subject of) partner abuse and violence *can be valuable* when it calls conscious attention to: the energy disturbances and hidden pattern addictions that cause it *before these disturbances actually become physical, taking the form of physical violence.*

These troubled nonphysical patterns of interaction with self and others might not otherwise be seen or admitted to. With attention to this problem, help may be sought. Partners can help themselves or get help to slow the process of the problem patterns—slow the relationship's interactions down in order to see what these interactions really look like. In most cases, outside professional help to slow and see the patterns is essential.

It is important that we approach this process of slowing down with care. The land mines hiding in the twists and turns of the troubled interactive process are not readily spotted. Stumbling into these can be dangerous. *(Too many helping professionals fail to fully understand this. Too often, less than fully expert treatment professionals ignite in couples abuse and violence rather than the opposite. They do this, racing in with whatever techniques they want to employ, while not taking into account the potential dangers ignited by these too rapidly, or too rashly, or too naively applied techniques.)*

This is why couples with a history of violence do well to have a skilled and neutral third party mediate or referee the process of discovering minor but powerful aspects of their potentially or actually problematic interactions. Partners can see a (highly trained) mediator, therapist, or other guide to help them map the relationship's C&Ts which are in place and see their evolution over time.

When entirely neutral, well trained and highly experienced guides, counselors, clinicians, and therapists, can shed a great deal of light on what is taking place during interactions between partners. *(Learn how to review the qualifications of who you choose to see for help before settling on someone to be your guide, counselor, clinician, therapist.)* Such a guide can help bring the terms of the relationship into the conscious realm, and then mediate changes there. (Of course, in an ideal world, we would all be mapping these C&Ts all along the way, from the very start of our relationships, to see where we are, where we have been, and where we are going or may want to go.)

*Too often, there is no pre-emptive effort to see and change the condition which eventually leads to the **physicalization** of abuse and violence. Too often, there is no exit from the tension which is building to an invisible but nevertheless very hot boiling point where almost anything can trigger its over-boiling.*

Again and again, know that it is best to de-structure detrimental patterns before they become physical. This means that one must be conscious of these patterns, or of signs that such patterns are there, long before they make themselves visible to the physical eye. Many who wish to prevent or ward off the physicalization of relationship violence ask:

> What does it take to be so highly conscious?
> Is there a particular skill set which only some can master?

The answer is that we all carry within us the tools we need. We already carry this skill set with us, and what we need to do is slow down and pull this skill set into our consciousnesses. Simply counting slowly, to ten, before responding to a pattern can slow the process of interacting down....

> ONE, *one thousand...*
> TWO, *one thousand...*
> THREE, *one thousand...*
> FOUR, *one thousand...*
> FIVE, *one thousand...*
> SIX, *one thousand...*
> SEVEN, *one thousand...*
> EIGHT, *one thousand...*
> NINE, *one thousand...*
> TEN, *one thousand....*

THE HUMAN BRAIN CAN DO THIS. IT CAN STOP MUCH OF ITS IMPULSE BEHAVIOR. WE CAN SLOW DOWN, AND STOP AND THINK. WE CAN GO CONSCIOUS.

We can even try to visualize our places and roles in the maps we draw, perhaps via maps such as those modeled in Figure 4.1 (Blurry spectrum of partner violence intent); Figure 12.1 (Anatomy of a positive bond progression); Figure 12.2 (Anatomy of a negative bond progression); Figure 12.3 (Example of a mixed positive and negative bond progression with reversals); Figure 21.1 (Paths to violence in nonviolent and violent relationships); Figure 21.2 [Reaction to stress (even boredom can be stressful)]; Figure 33.7 (Sample pleasure–pain confusion mini-cycles or subloops); Figure 33.8 (Discomfort–comfort cycle); Figure 33.9 (Longing for contact cycle); Figure 44.1 (Stability, sanity, safety balance in and out of peril); Figure 45.1 (Stages in transcending relationship challenges: struggle, paradox, insight, and spiritual elevation); Figure 46.1 (Degrees of identity with, investment in, and dependence upon the relationship may differ for each member of the couple). Ideally, the outcome is either rising above the conflict together, as modeled in Figure 47.3, or shedding the relationship, or both.

WE KNOW THESE PATHS TO SHEDDING PATTERNS

We do know these paths to BEING MORE AWARE, and to shedding troubled relationship patterns, within the relationship and or on the way out of the relationship. Again, the within relationship shedding must be done in an environment of safety for all involved and if this is not possible, the entire relationship must be shed.

This is an awareness that we all already have, we just tend to hold it in the subconscious realm. An effort to bring this awareness forward, simply by giving the mind an order to so do, can work. Try it sometime. *We are not consciously looking for things we have not consciously told our minds to look for.*

Think about it. Look at a hill full of wild plant life. All the things growing on the hill look pretty much the same. Now study a picture book which shows types of wild plant life which grow in the area where you are. Now look at this hill again. You see so much more, so many more individual types of growing things! Similarly, upon reviewing several of the previous chapters in this book, new and even minute aspects of interactions in your relationship can become visible to you. Slow down and go conscious, it helps.

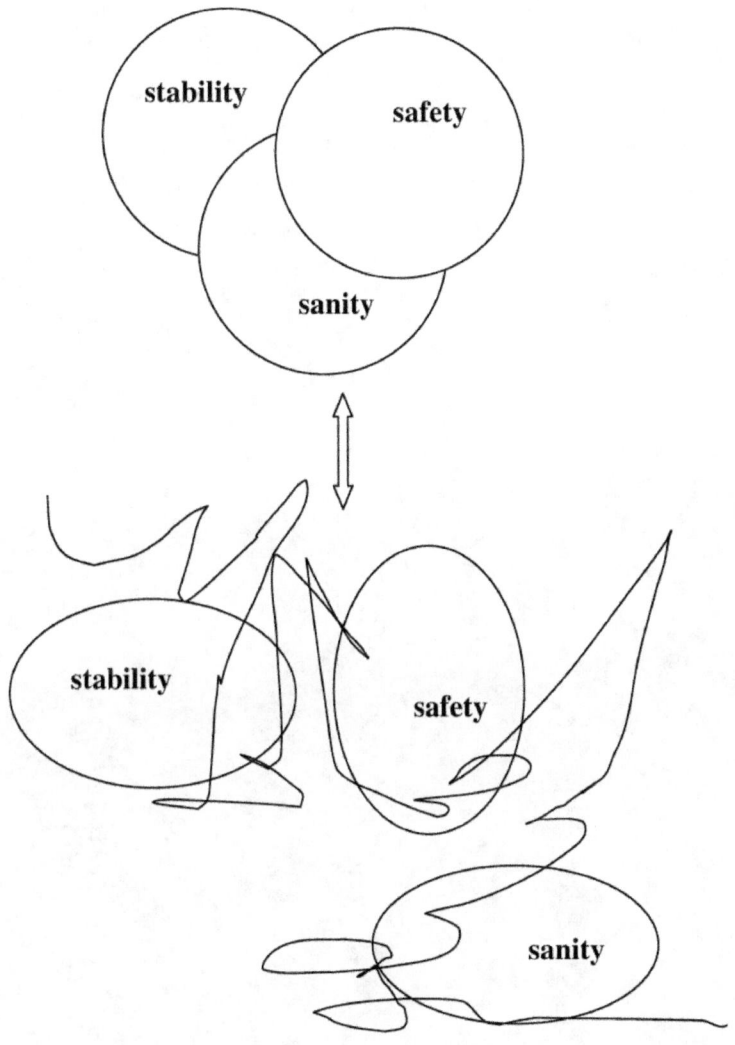

Figure 44.1.
Stability, sanity, safety balance in and out of peril.

45
Breaking Through

Have you ever seen two people fighting, yelling, throwing things, hitting, hurting each other every way they can, suddenly freeze, stop the violence a moment, and look at each other asking, "What on Earth are we doing?" This sudden dawning of awareness is likely quite rare. But wouldn't it be wonderful if it could be more frequent?

THERE IS A WAY OUT OF THIS PATTERN

Of course, violence unto death is not the only way out of a troubled intimate partner behavior pattern. Nor is leaving before attempting to see and break through problem patterns. Yet, breaking an habitual and dangerous problem pattern addiction such as one of relationship abuse, violence and terror (IPAVT) requires letting something, an addiction, die. Members of troubled and hard to break IPAVT patterns must be asked:

> Are you prepared to let a problem cycle in your life die?
> Are you prepared to release old patterns?
> Are you ready to transcend them?

This chapter shares another approach to breaking a relationship violence pattern. This approach is one which calls for a transformation of understanding on both parties' part or on at least one member's part: transformation while exiting the relationship if the other will not join in.

Under no circumstances does this material infer that an individual at risk of receiving or causing physical injury or harm should remain in the presence of this risk while practicing with the relationship partner the transformative ideas presented here. Many times it is best to separate entirely.

What is possible is a radical, complete change in behavior when a conscious decision to make this change is made. Understanding that a real shift to a new level of awareness is possible opens the door to the possibility that this new level can be achieved.

Too often, persons trapped in patterns truly do see no way out. Yet, the gift of a way out is buried deep inside, where each of us carries the map, the directions, to the shift. This may sound like a fairy tale; however, this is not a fantasy.

This does, however, require that one allow the imagination to open the door. Visualize in great detail what the pattern of relating would shift to were this shift out of a negative pattern to be made. Picture a healthy relationship and find out if this picture can be shared. It will take two to make this shift in a relationship's pattern together.

And without two, one can still go it alone. When going it alone, although the shift is still required in order to escape the pattern of relationship abuse and violence, it may not produce the same change in that saving the self becomes primary. This is entirely alright, and quite often the only wise option.

TRANSCENDING ONE'S PROGRAMMING

Think about shedding old ways of seeing things, old ways of relating to self and others, old ways of resolving conflict. Old ways can go, they are just old ways. Old patterns can go too, even if they are very deeply rooted.

You can leave a troubled pattern or you can change a troubled pattern. But if not entirely leaving that pattern, you must truly be changing that pattern to change that pattern.

If a problem pattern has become a part of you, it must go. This piece of you must die out to make room for new more positive behaviors. To die well, to bring about a worthwhile living death which will allow tremendous growth within and around you, you must break your addiction to the programming that controls the pattern you are talking about breaking.

If you are not certain that a problem pattern is part of you, an addiction which you and your partner are experiencing, then find out: Can the two of you simply decide today not to fight or argue and not to utilize emotional and physical abuse and violence as a way of resolving dis-agreements or handling communication issues?

Can this decision be made today, and can it include a plan to maintain this ban on the negative relating without a break for at least ninety days?

Perhaps you wish to try this before reading on. (If you cannot go these ninety days, this chapter may be coming too late to heal this particular relationship. However, with skilled guidance and help, this is still possible when the partners leave each other's company while working with trained experts to stop the abuse and violence, first from a distance.)

Having tried this, you may be able to extend the ninety day period on indefinitely. If so, you have achieved something very close to what is being described below, even without knowing it!

If not, perhaps what is described below can detail for you the steps to the transcendence of a negative relationship pattern—or the steps to your own personal moving to a new and better place in life—with your partner, or alone if need be.

THOSE CONCERNED ASK

Those concerned about painful and violent relationship patterns, and about possibly co-occurring disorders such as chemical dependence, chronic pain, and other crises of one's programming, ask:

> How does one break out of one's addiction to one's programming?
>
> How does one bring about in oneself a transcendence away from negative violent patterning?
>
> What type of pattern death is required to release—to free—oneself from this pattern of abuse and violence?
>
> Why does this sort of change in behavior feel like dying?

LIST:
CONDITIONS FOR TRANSCENDENCE

What truly is being shared here is another way to STOP RELATIONSHIP VIOLENCE BY TRANSCENDING IT. Partners committed to changing their relationship behaviors have the option of exploring the meaning and challenge of rising above this behavior, of transcending it. This transcending is no special elevated level of behavior and requires no special training. It does require knowing that:

1. Both partners must be committed to achieving the

awareness this calls for. ... One partner may do this alone, and this can be quite beneficial; however, this partner should not assume that the other is on the same path or comes to the same realization if the other is not involved in working to raise not only the aware-ness of the individual members of the relationship but also the awareness of the relationship itself. *(Never assume that if you have come to a realization, your partner also has.)*

2. Both partners must be absolutely safe from harming each other (emotionally, financially, physically, etc.) while this concept is being explored.

3. An outside party which both partners trust may be helpful—even essential—in setting the pace and boundaries of this process. *(This outside party must be selected for absolute neutrality, and who this outside party is must be equally agreed to by both partners.)*

4. In highly volatile situations, a long and separate cooling down period should be enacted prior to beginning this work.

Transcendence requires a new outlook on a situation. No matter how bleak and painful a situation may appear, it can be changed by being re-perceived, seen differently.

This means that, before any changes can occur, you must be convinced of the fact that you can turn things around! You must believe in the possibility of transcendence. You must also understand the phases and process of transcendence, which must be studied continually.

No matter what level of understanding you reach, there is always more to be learned.

Remember, there is no such thing as a free lunch. Setting the stage for personal transcendence is hard work. The transcendence process requires your commitment, your attention, your fortitude, and your faith in the process.

These are interactive but internal states of mind.

Much of this work is internal, even when embarking on this journey with a partner....

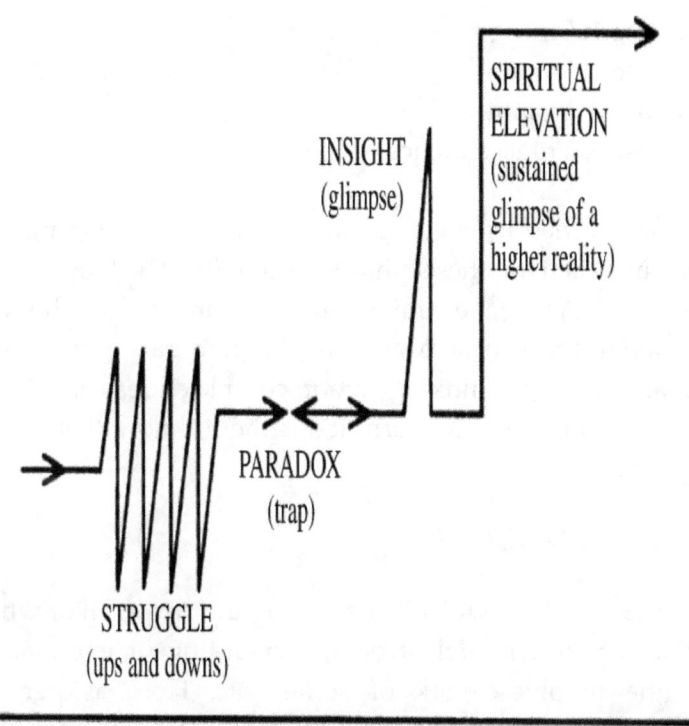

Figure 45.1.
Stages in transcending relationship challenges: struggle, paradox, insight, and elevation.

PHASES OF TRANSCENDENCE

Transcendence is a continuous process through which an individual achieves elevation to a higher emotional level (or when persons choose to call it this, a higher spiritual plane). There, this individual (you) will experience greater awareness and a higher degree of freedom. Transcendence is composed of four profound yet simple phases, each of which is necessary for the process.

These phases of transcendence are:

Phase 1: Struggle.
Phase 2: Paradox.
Phase 3: Insight.
Phase 4: Transcendence or Elevation.

Each phase has its own special characteristics. Figure 45.1 diagrams each of these phases and indicates they can be sequential. As you examine this diagram, try to think of your life in terms of it. Make this diagram part of your own mental imagery. Thinking about complex ideas in simple pictures often helps to learn about them, know them, on a deeper level.

PHASE 1: STRUGGLE

Struggle is a word which is used in many ways, all of which boil down to a model of energy spending or energy use. Struggle involves work of some sort. Here as per the discussion in this book, the work is the effort to (work to) deny, grapple, wrestle with, or escape, a challenge or hardship within a personal partner relationship. The work includes the work to get oneself to do the work itself, to expend effort, often great effort, in so doing.

(This is in no way a discussion regarding many other major struggles in life, many of which are not related to the behavior of the individual struggling.) Of course, every day contains some form of struggle on some level, even if this is so natural we do not see it as such.

We may struggle—with putting on our shoes, finding our car keys, with relationship partners, family relationships, work relationships, with ourselves, our own morality, maybe also with our cravings.

We often struggle without recognizing or seeing beyond the struggle, be-coming so deeply caught up that it becomes impossible to step back and say, "Oh, I am struggling. This must be the first phase of transcendence." But it is just this observation that will set us on the path to transcendence.

When we are struggling, we must take the time to tell ourselves that we are indeed struggling and that we can move through this first phase of transcendence.

Study the first phase of transcendence as diagrammed in Figure 45.1: STRUGGLE. This pattern illustrates ups and downs, pushes and pulls, and highs and lows so typical of the struggling phase. During a true struggle, there must be low points in order for there to be high points—both extremes are integral to it. In fact, many struggles are cyclic, repeating highs then lows then highs, again and again. Does this sound familiar? Think roller coaster!

PHASE 2: PARADOX

Paradox is the second phase of transcendence as diagrammed in Figure 45.1. Paradox is a fantastic experience. It can be gentle and easy, or it can be painful. In fact, the experience can be deeply disturbing, frightening, sometimes deadly. Paradox can produce in us a numb or zombie-like effect resulting from the no way out sensation so typical of paradox. This is the experience of being in a situation from which there seems to be no escape, no resolution. Trapped.

The more powerful the paradox, the more of a trap it feels to be, the great-er the tension and more powerful the release from it may be. The rat in the maze sensation is lived again and again when stuck in paradox.

We all have known paradox all our lives. We place ourselves in paradox and engage in mutual paradox, relationship paradox, and other forms of paradox. Sometimes parents unwittingly submit children to paradoxes in the form of double binds, something like this: "Which coat do you like?" a parent may ask a child. "The red coat or the blue one?" When the child says, "The red coat," the parent says, "That's not a good choice, you should like the blue one." And then when the child says, "The blue one," the parent says, "Well, the red one is much better."

When this happens, the child is stuck and is experiencing a double bind: LOSE-LOSE. In this case, there is nothing the child can do that would be the right thing to elicit a positive response from the parent. The child is bound by unpleasant consequence no matter which choice he or she makes. There is no escape. The situation holds, or so it would seem, no real choices. The situation also holds massive tension!

The trap of the paradoxical, or double, bind can be a learning experience, a marker on the path to transcendence, if it is understood to be this. Some double binds come from outside us but most come from within because we allow ourselves to see, or sense, them as double binds, paradoxes, traps.

In living life, both children and adults create double-bind situations for themselves with or without the help of other people. For the child with the two coats, release from the bind is seeing the folly of the parent's reasoning and not taking it personally.

This is a large job for a child. Other forms of release from the tension of the bind may be a temper tantrum, or hitting someone, or hurting the self.

One lose-lose sort of double bind that many people find

themselves in is hidden, unrecognized yet quite active, ***habit patterns of abuse and violence***. Paradoxes like this are extremely stressful and often painful. No way out. No way out. No way out. But faith in the transcendence process shows us that paradox serves a purpose. Without the tension, the feeling of being trapped is an unwinnable situation, there may be no impetus for release, for moving on, and for growing.

The tension created by your paradoxes, when used well, can generate enough energy for you to break out of them, to break the pattern as least momentarily, and to move the behavior at least momentarily to a higher level. (Note however that the tension created by a paradox can build and when there is not an awareness of this tension and its power, a release of this tension can take the form of impulse violence and abuse.)

Learn to spot your paradoxes before an explosive release damages or harms you, your partner, or others. Learn to see your paradoxes so that you can harvest the valuable energy from them in a healthy way.

Without recognizing the painful and potentially dangerous tension of the paradox, you cannot consciously direct the release from paradox—the jump or shift in perception—that is produced by consciously rising above the double bind.

Study the PARADOX phase illustrated in Figure 45.1. This shows the "stand off" or "holding pattern" in which people who need to let something of themselves die and to experience transcendence get stuck, caught, or trap themselves.

The optimal way out of this holding pattern is to break out

of it and move on, to increase your perception so that you can see beyond the limits of the double bind that holds you there.

The less desirable way out is to slip back into the struggle mode that put you there, to hit someone and hurt that someone, or to be hit and be hurt, and thus to continue to ride the struggle, the roller coaster of the highs and lows of intimate partner violence.

As seen in Figure 45.1, the paradox phase contains two arrows ending up against each other and going nowhere. These represent the stuck forces that hold a pattern addicted person or relationship in his or her or its trap.

This deadlock can hold you in its grip indefinitely. Or, if you choose to escape it, to transcend it, it can provide a takeoff point and energy to move into another level of awareness and a healing.

PHASE 3: INSIGHT

As has been explained above, when energy locked in the paradox of negative pattern addiction explodes, energy is released.

This must be done carefully and consciously—which would be the opposite of impulsively and potentially dangerously which tends to bring about abrupt impulse driven violent actions.

We may see this in some cycles of intimate partner violence, where the break from the violence, the rest, or loving moments end and then the violence begins again— sometimes to the surprise of both parties who somehow thought perhaps this loving or at least peaceful break would continue without work to hold this new behavior in place.

The same energy paradox can be released consciously to take the relationship which was trapped in paradox to a new level of relating. Partners who understand this process, can make it work. The best moment to release from the energy lock of paradox is felt by the partners locked in the problem pattern: there is suddenly an insight into a new way of relating, a relief from the stuck troubled feeling of paradox. This is the third phase diagrammed in Figure 45.1, INSIGHT.

PHASE 4: ELEVATION OR TRANSCENDENCE

Insight can be brief or can last a while. However, without a map of what is taking place, of where in the process of change and transcendence insight is (refer again to Figure 45.1 for this map), many insight opportunities may slip by unnoticed, unappreciated. Then people slip back into struggle or paradox phases.

The opportunity for insight elevation (elevation here is to hang onto the new level of understanding) cannot be consciously recognized without *conscious effort* to sustain this elevated way of being or seeing. *The pull of the negative pattern addiction can be so strong that it can yank everyone out of the insight phase right back down into the paradox or the struggle phases.*

Overcoming negative patterning, and holding onto the state the insight showed was possible, is transcending. This is the fourth phase diagrammed in Figure 45.1: ELEVATION, or what some might want to call spiritual elevation.

A strong commitment to see, understand, and then overcome stuck, struggling, addictive relationship patterns must be maintained and made again and again, likely daily, to hold the elevated state until new patterns of behavior are instilled. Then we can replace old negative patterning.

BREAKING THROUGH THE SHACKLES OF OUR PROGRAMMING

Well then, this is indeed all about breaking through the shackles of our programming. We living things are creatures of habit. So convenient and readily developed is automatic physical behavior that it merges with the nonphysical realms of often automatic or impulse driven human inter-action and emotion.

Public and private feelings, and their expressions, are often manifestations of psychological and social patterns. It is difficult to discern exactly what proportion of an individual's behavior is attributable to the larger social and cultural environment and what proportion is particular, idiosyncratic, to the individual. Nevertheless, individuals must be responsible for identifying violent and abusive behaviors and over-coming them.

Where these violence and abuse behaviors are behavior patterns, these patterns must be identified and overcome, or where unbudging and dangerous, entirely exited, walked away from. Leave.

46
Troubled Couple

We know the Troubled Couple, we see this life form all around us. And sometimes this Troubled Couple is us. Yes, the Troubled Couple is a life form, or it has at least some of the requisite characteristics of a life from. It is born, it lives, it consumes, and it dies. Most disturbing, it may pass its more troubled characteristics on to future generations—reproduce!

FIND THE TROUBLED COUPLE

Does the Troubled Couple know that it is troubled? Does it see its situation clearly, prior to getting help? Must the Troubled Couple first know who it is, that it is indeed troubled, in order to heal, transcend? Or does the process of knowing itself come later in the process, once beginning the healing or transcending of the intimate partner abuse and violence the couple is experiencing?

The Troubled Couple is of course composed of individual members. The core membership is generally thought of as being two individuals forming the couple itself. (Of course there are some variations in this model, some "couples" who choose to include more than two members. However, the most common version of the intimate partner relationship is one couple, two persons, and this is the focus of this discussion. Keep in mind that all said here can be readily adapted to variations of the couple.)

Each of the individual members of the couple has her or his own degree of relationship to this couple and to its conditions, issues, problems, and pathologies if any. And, the members of the couple are most likely not absolutely equally involved in the relationship or in the various aspects of the relationship. They may both be very involved, but there is still no real equal involvement, as every individual experiences things some-what differently. Remember, the two people sitting in a tree, K-I-S-S-I-N-G, are not necessarily experiencing the same thing. Even love, even true love, feels different for each person experiencing it.

What this means is that two partners in one relationship are actually two partners in two (or more) relationships even though they call it the same relationship. Person A and Person B are in what they think of as their relationship, which is actually what each of the two of them see as the relationship. What each of them see and experience is never exactly the same, as each partner has her or his own mind, life history, and other personal characteristics. Any discussion of a couple's relationship, no matter how long or short it is, includes a minimum of these five perspectives:

- Person A.
- Relationship Person A Sees Her or Himself In.
- Person B.
- Relationship Person B Sees Her or Himself In.
- Actual Relationship Between Person A and Person B—
    (if indeed there is one actual relationship, given how very different reality actually appears to each person—a matter that can be questioned at all times).

And, when each of these interacts with itself (with her or himself) as well as with each of these others, we have not two people in one relationship, we have a minimum of 25 perspectives interacting, as you see in the interaction chart (in Figure 46.1).

However, even this chart does not indicate the full complexity of a couple's relationship. We can see however, at least this:

→ Person A has a relationship with him or herself, plus a relationship with Person B, who has a relationship with her or himself.

→ Person A is involved with who Person A thinks Person B is.

→ And Person A is in Relationship X with who Person A thinks Person B is.

→ However, Person B is involved with who Person B thinks Person A is.

→ And, Person B is therefore in Relationship Y with who Person B thinks Person A is.

→ And then, somewhere in there are—who A really is being with B—and vice versa—who B really is being with A.

Hence, there are at least two different relationships here, as the people seen as being in them (in these relationships) are not seen the same way by the members (of these relationships). All this is to say that when healing the Troubled Couple, we are actually healing several relationships, not just one.

This being said, it may be clear that no two people will ever think that exactly the same thing is going on in their own (which is actually two or more) relationship(s). (Even when they think they think the same way, they cannot do so exactly, as they have two different minds and hearts.)

They may identify with, invest in, and depend upon whatever the relationship is that they see themselves as being in. Yet they do this quite differently from their partners who see themselves being in the same but not the same relationship. This is perhaps best described as a naturally dual- or two-faced *coupleship* (couple-ship).

Note here that this discussion is not designed to discourage any of us from intimate partner, love, and or other primary relationships. Rather, all this is to say that what is taking place between any two or more people is far more complex than we can say simply, and far more complex than words anywhere can ever entirely capture.

Ultimately, we are interacting in complex multi-layered ways we do not consciously and fully see, ways we cannot ever fully see. Yet, we are always picking up a great deal of subtle signs of and cues regarding what is taking place during interactions. So, when there are troubled interactions taking place, there are signs that these are troubled, hints of what may be perhaps greater troubles, problems, even perhaps dangers.

Still, for the most part the multitude of hints and indications are missed, or at least not consciously read, and or if read not necessarily correctly interpreted.

Additionally, as members of a couple are in the relationship(s) that they think are there, they are responding to what they think is taking place in what they think are the relationships they are in.

This is not to say we should assume that relationships we think we are in do not exist. Instead, this is to say that we must be aware at all times that we are placing our own subjective reading of what is taking place on what is truly taking place. AND SO ARE OUR PARTNERS. This is simply normal for the human brains of ourselves and all others.

IDENTITY, INVESTMENT, AND DEPENDENCE

We can and must add to this discussion the matter of identity. Identify is a powerful component that forms as the relationship forms. This is not simply the personal identities of the members of the couple. This is the identity each member of the couple has with the relationship—yes, has with the relationship that member of the couple believes she or he is in.

We can estimate degrees of identity with the relationship, investment in the relationship, dependence upon the relationship, and other elements for each member of the couple. Each of these ratings is in itself indicative of the individual member's relationship to the coupleship.

A comprehensive view of these ratings for each individual paints a picture of one piece of the couple. A comparison of these ratings between the members of the couple tells us yet more—is there an imbalance in say, identity, or investment, in the coupleship? Is one partner more involved in some areas than the other?

Or is there in some troubled cases a relatively equal investment, but with one member of the couple being more problematically or even perhaps pathologically involved than the other? Are there shifts in the dependence, investment, and identity with the relationship that can be made to balance this relationship somewhat more?

Are the partners interested in trying out new levels of identity with, investment in, and dependence upon the relationship in order to see whether this shift changes their dynamic? *And again, and ultimately, we are speaking in terms of the partners being involved in whatever they each separately see as being their shared relationship.*

From here, we can model a healthy coupleship and design pathways to reaching this form of relationship. We can also model exits from the Troubled Coupleship when one or more partners desire this. Either way, there is a mapping process that can take place, guiding the Troubled Couple to a healthier, more productive, and often safer outcome (see Figure 46.3).

TAKING FROM OTHERS

Another layer of this work must look at those surrounding the Troubled Couple, especially the children. Troubled couples are rarely troubled in isolation. They have neighbors, friends, co-workers, and relatives including children—most importantly children.

A Troubled Couple may even feed on the lives of those surrounding it, consuming their energy, time, and maybe even dollars. The concept of codependence, typically applied to the people surrounding a person addicted to drugs or alcohol, can indeed be extended to this model of relationship patterning.

The Troubled Couple requires, sucks, or seeks fuel from those living around it, especially those who have no choice but to be around—such as the children.

For children, an unspoken mandate to show up for and support the troubled patterns exists. Here is where the addictive tendencies of the Troubled Couple, its desire to live and consume what it needs to live on, are detrimental not only to the members of the Troubled Couple but also to its children and other family members.

INFINITE INTERACTIONS

We return again and again to the reality that every relationship, whether doing well or having problems, exists within a stream of infinite signals between its members. Appreciating this is important. This delicate understanding of the massive numbers of interactions and reactions in relationships can help us understanding what an intimate partner relationship is: a universe of realities and micro realities at all times, and many relationships bundled into one.

Figure 46.1.
Interaction chart for one couple in one relationship.

	Person A	Relationship Person A Sees Her or Himself In	Person B	Relationship Person B Sees Her or Himself In	Actual Relationship Between Person A and Person B
Person A	1	2	3	4	5
Relationship Person A Sees Her or Himself In	6	7	8	9	10
Person B	11	12	13	14	15
Relationship Person B Sees Her or Himself In	16	17	18	19	20
Actual Relationship Between Person A and Person B	21	22	23	24	25

Figure 46.2.

Interaction chart for one couple in one relationship where each member of the couple experiences the relationship from her or his perspective.

	Person A	Relationship Person A Sees Her or Himself In	Person B	Relationship Person B Sees Her or Himself In	Actual Relationship Between Person A and Person B	Person A is in Relationship X	Person B is in Relationship Y
Person A	1	2	3	4	5	6	7
Relationship Person A Sees Her or Himself In	8	9	10	11	12	13	14
Person B	15	16	17	18	19	20	21
Relationship Person B Sees Her or Himself In	22	23	24	25	26	27	28
Actual Relationship Between Person A and Person B	29	30	31	32	33	34	35
Person A is in Relationship X	36	37	38	39	40	41	42
Person B is in Relationship Y	43	44	45	46	47	48	49

DISENGAGING FROM PATTERNS

Disengaging from troubled, abusive, and violent patterns is similar to breaking a drug addiction. The addictive pattern has its highs and lows as well as the so-called rewards. There is a tendency for one or both members of the addictive relationship pattern to have difficulty separating from the relationship and its patterning.

The identity of the individuals can become the identity of the relationship, with one or both of the individuals knowing little of her or himself without the couple's identity. When disengaging from a troubled relationship, an over identified individual can feel danger in the possible dissolving of a prominent relationship pattern, no matter how unpleasant this pattern may be.

Here is yet another trap, a double bind, for at least one individual member of a troubled relationship pattern. The pressure to get out and be safe may be countered by the pressure to stay in and be defined.

So heavily entrenched is this self in the Troubled Couple, that leaving or changing the relationship feels like identity loss to such a great degree that this identity loss feels like death (Figure 46.3).

Healing here is, in the end, seeing what is going on, up close and personal, slowing the pace of the relationship to see its patterns, to map its patterns, to identify what parts of these patterns can be changed or eliminated—or thrown away in their entirety. (Healing is also leaving the problem situation, and there are times, as noted earlier, when this is the only wise choice.)

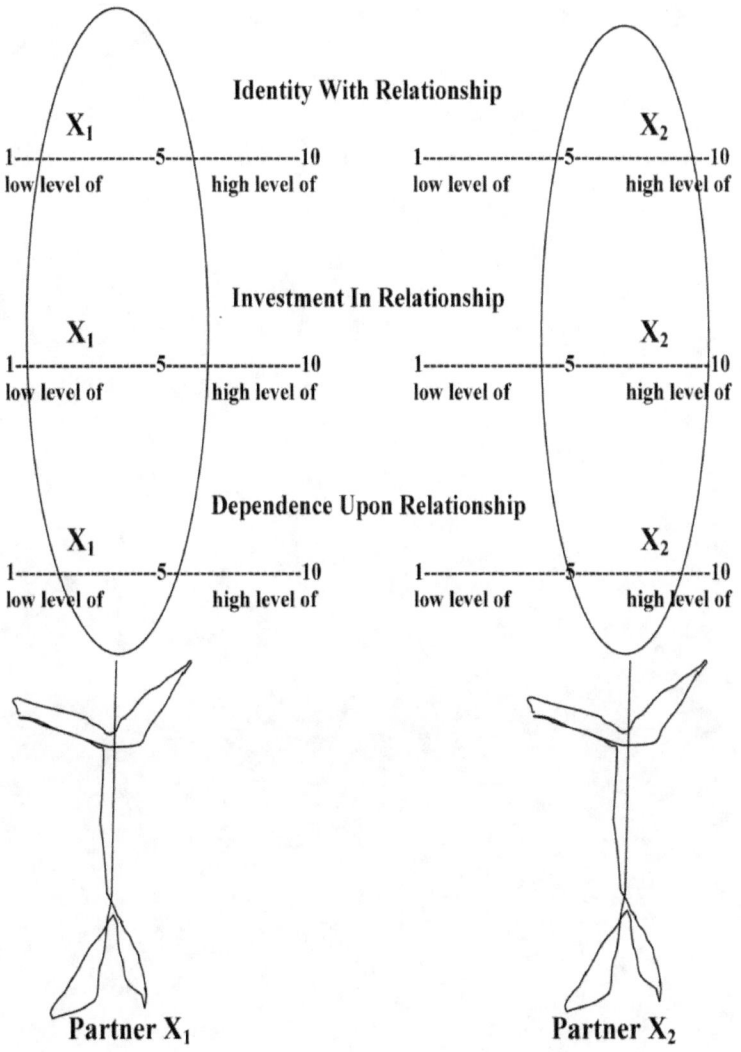

Figure 46.3.
Degrees of identity with, investment in, and dependence upon, a relationship may differ for each member of the couple.

47
Above Violence

Let's assume we want to leave a relationship's abuse and violence be-hind. As noted earlier, this is not entirely simple. Perhaps we can even visualize the transition, or transcendence, out of troubled coupledom into a higher way of relating, a higher form of relationship: *we can allow ourselves to see the path.*

Explaining in words what to do about relationships that hurt is valuable, but this involves reaching both the rational, word driven mind and the part of the brain that thinks in other forms such as pictures.

REACHING THE MIND IN MORE THAN ONE WAY

It is said that one picture is worth a thousand words, and indeed there are times when we need to get through to ourselves, to our sub-consciousnesses, in very simple-to-remember pictures. So let's stop a moment and make the words in this book secondary to picturing the concept of rising above emotional and physical violence.

Talk to that part of yourself, the one that thinks in pictures. Start by thinking about conflict after conflict after conflict, conflict repeating itself over and over, and perhaps growing more and more intense as it repeats. Have you been there? Do you have a picture of this in your mind? If so, draw this picture, taking it from your mind and putting it onto paper.

Now, take a look at the diagram in Figure 47.1. Here, an ongoing lose-lose tension looms, a problem pattern from which there appears to be no exit.

In interpersonal relating, we know that fighting conflict with conflict, conflicting conflict, will not make it go away. The type of energy used to fight conflict with conflict is more of the same conflict-oriented energy, a bit like fighting fire with fire, or stopping a flood with a huge wave of water. More of the same does not necessarily make a change. Do you have a picture of fighting conflict with conflict in your mind? If so, draw this picture, taking it from your mind and putting it onto paper. Take a look at the diagrams in Figures 47.1. and 47.2. Here, an ongoing, even escalating, effort to conflict with the conflict is diagrammed.

Conflict can be, and frequently is, managed intelligently without doing harm to participants and onlookers. Consciously conducted conflict in an intimate partner relationship can be a path of learning and development for a conscious relationship.

Sadly, not all conflict in relationship follows this path. When conflict is handled in a negative, destructive manner, it can lead to emotional and physical abuse and violence. The struggle, muddle, pain, spent energy, hurt, damage, wounds, and long term effects of negative conflict patterns in relationships are such a waste!

Why not try to turn this troubled conflict process around, perhaps to a healthy conflict process? What would this look like? Do you have a picture of turning this pattern around in your mind? If so, draw this picture, taking it from your mind and putting this onto paper. If not, take a look at the diagram in Figure 47.3. Here, the concept of rising above conflict is diagramed.

Conflict can be managed consciously. Conflict can be seen as a process *striving to rise above—to resolve itself*, to transcend the troubled even deteriorating conflict: *to change the direction of the conflict*. In fact, rising above conflict can be the goal of relationship interactions even where there is great disagreement.

Relationship partners who hold in their minds this picture of conflict resolution or conflict transcendence can aim for this result. Rules for conscious conflict can be set by partners, and partners can follow these rules. (Readers are invited to find suggested rules in a subsequent book by this author.)

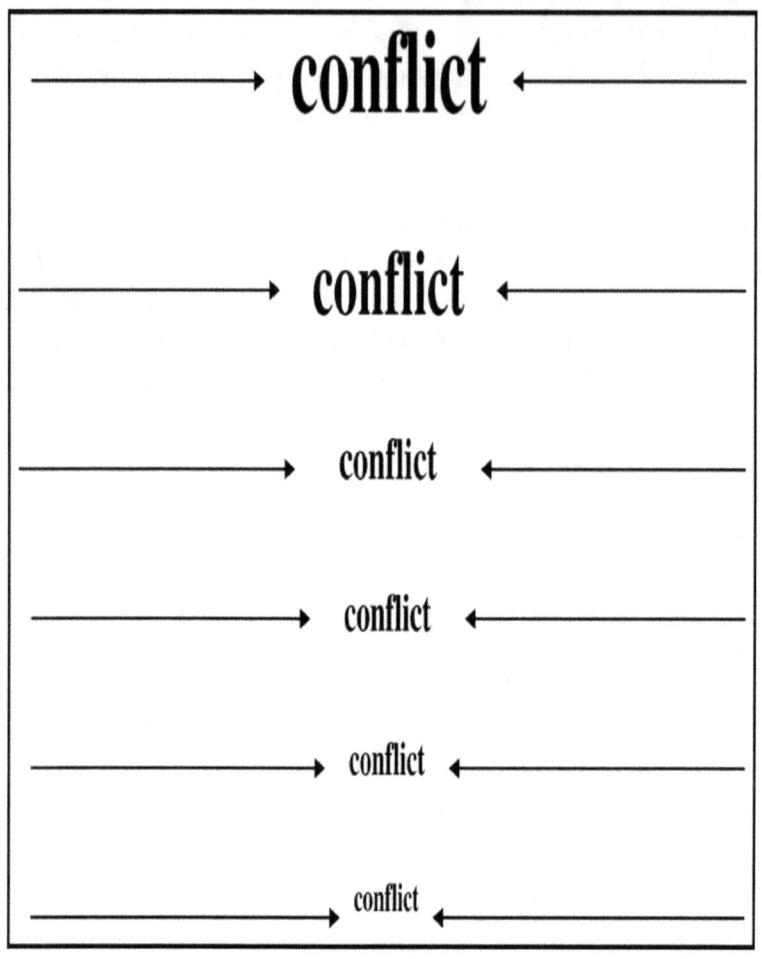

Figure 47.1
Conflict.

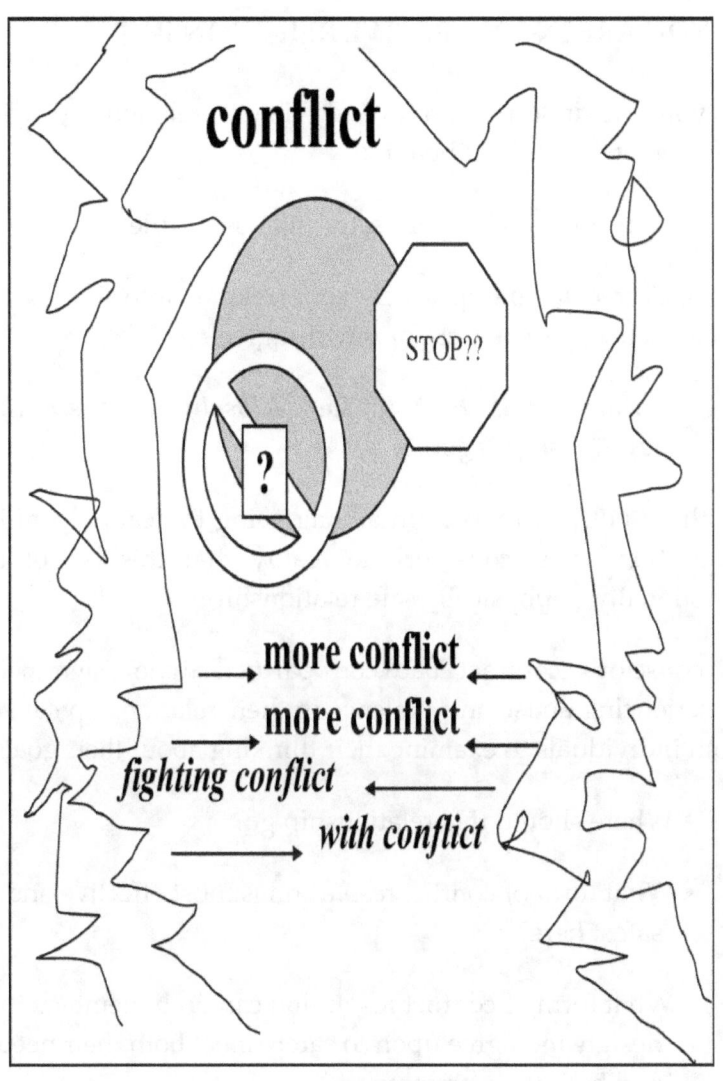

Figure 47.2
Conflicting conflict.

LIST:
IF YOU ARE IN AN ABUSIVE RELATIONSHIP

If you are in an abusive and violent relationship with someone who will <u>not</u> help to:

- Write and stick to fair, safe, and useful rules.

- Agree to and practice your relationship's rules for conscious conflict, for safe disagreeing.

   ...then, it is best to look closely at where this relationship is going.

Without both partners mutually agreeing to healthy conflict resolution rules, consider the reality that this is not an emotionally or physically safe relationship.

A conscious contract between partners who have been experiencing abuse and violence in their relationship causes both individuals to examine their thinking about their goals.

- Where should this relationship go?

- What form of conflict resolution is most effective and safest here?

- What form of conflict resolution can both members design and agree upon to safely meet both their needs and both their preferences?

Check around, not many partners will consciously write and sign an agreement explicitly allowing the use of abuse and violence to solve their relationship problems. Of course not.

Healthy agreements that will be agreed to and then kept by both parties in a relationship can help form and maintain healthy relationships. Many couples benefit by having a neutral third party mediate or supervise the writing and keeping of these agreements.

Making disagreement and conflict safe for all involved changes the texture of any interaction, even interactions between partners in love, or in other forms of emotionally and physically intimate relationship.

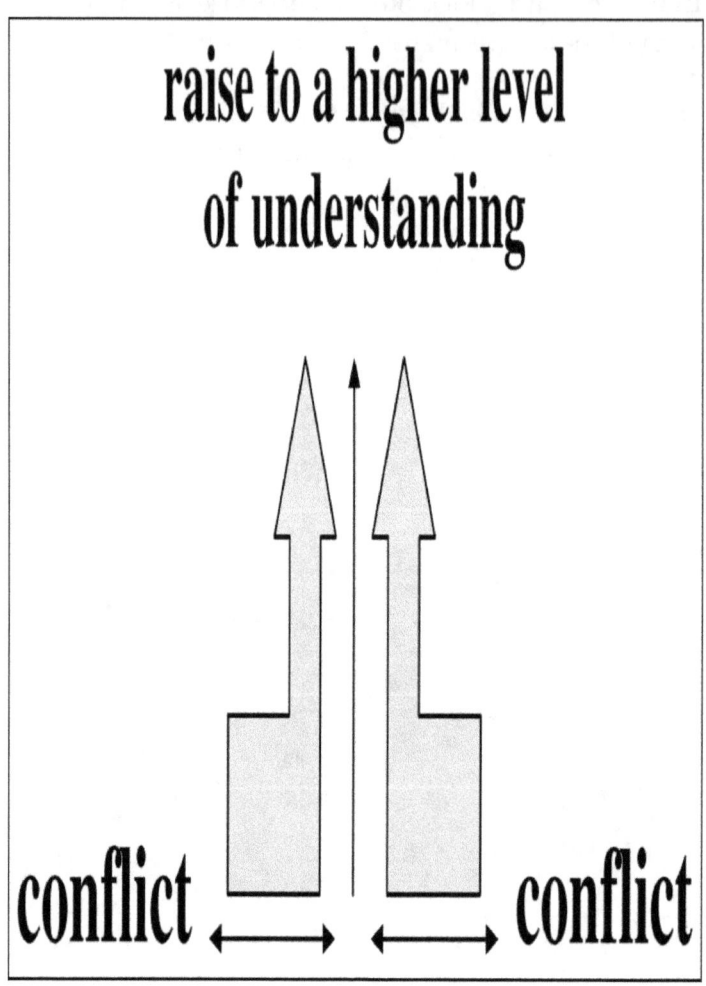

Figure 47.3
Rising above conflict.

48
Wise Elder Plan for Troubled Couple

A wise elder was very concerned about the abuse and violence in, and general instability of, a local couple's marriage. They had asked him for his advice, and he had gone away to think. He returned with a plan for them and offered to serve as the monitor he referred to in his plan.

As he presented his plan, he explained that a time of withdrawal from the external material world would be the only way the couple could strip down to who they really were as individuals and as a couple, and to what they were really doing with each other. He added that he knew how much planning for this time away this would involve, and that this planning was part of the process. Clearing a place and time to work on resolving differences, then actually showing up for the process of resolving and truly participating in this process, sets the foundation for the rest of the process. His plan went like this:

The two of you, go sign yourselves into some form of retreat where you do not know anyone and are not familiar with anything there. Wear drab baggy garments, no color, no style. No television, no telephones, no internet, no computers, no cars, no news, no alcohol, no spicy food, no watches, no street clothes, no makeup. No friends or family. Sleep on cots in separate rooms. Spend the first two days in isolation, no contact or talking to each other or anyone else.

Have someone monitor your stay, and only allow you to see each other once a day for fifteen minutes. No contact with each other or anyone else except for this monitored visitation with each other. During this monitored visitation you must be at least ten feet apart the whole fifteen minutes. You cannot touch each other, no hugging, no touching of any sort.

The topic of your conversation will be restricted to something of no interest to either of you, and if you choose not to speak during the brief visitation each day, you must nevertheless sit and face each other until this time is up.

This will continue for one week. On the seventh day, you have the option of taking a supervised one half hour walk together, on the grounds, in a circle.

You cannot leave the grounds. During this walk, the topic of the conversation will be up to you, but only if the two of you can agree on a topic within the first two minutes. If not, the monitor will provide the topic. The monitor will listen and observe during this walk. If there is any point at which the monitor chooses to stop this walk, it will end without explanation and the two of you will be separated until the next day.

The procedure of supervised visits will then continue with the fifteen minutes each day, always supervised, controlled contact. On the tenth day, you will be allowed a one hour supervised visit over a meal. The topic of conversation will be up to you two to decide, again within the first two minutes. The monitor can cancel this supervised visit at any time without explanation.

On the twelfth day, each of you will meet with the monitor, separately. At this time, you will propose to the monitor your ten step plan for a new way of communicating with each other. This plan will be shared by the monitor with the other member of the couple. New rules for relating will be designed in this fashion, with the monitor taking the information back and forth to the two of you. You can decide at any point that you want to leave the relationship for good. If you do not, you will continue in this mode until you have agreed upon the rules of relating.

A test of these rules will be conducted, with the monitor returning with the couple to its home life. If the monitor sees any reason to cancel this process and take both members of the couple back through the retreat process, the monitor will do this.

49
Coming Back from IPAVT

Beautiful and healed, as well as broken and unhealed, intimate partner relationships are everywhere around us. The broken and unhealed form a wasteland of old battlefields somewhat like those that wars between nations leave behind.

Around us we see walking wounded, and recovering survivors, bravely finding their ways back into the world and back to themselves. After years of painful relating, it is a challenge to recover, but many do. A life need not be ruined and destroyed and carry forever the damage which intimate partner abuse and violence can do. It is never ever too late to rise above the effects of abuse and violence.

If you have been there, or are there, know that you have come to one of the great challenges of human existence, the challenge of recovering from a broken heart, a broken relationship, a broken self. You may find yourself struggling in the rubble of broken dreams. You have been there a moment, a month, a decade—however long. You may feel your pain, your tears, your sense of loss and hopelessness. You may just feel con-fusion, or you may just feel nothing at all.

You say please, please someone fix this. Please please show

me a way out. Please please, someone help me.

The bits and pieces of the life you wanted to lead lie around you, shattered. You may weep or you may scream or you may sit in silence.

You tread carefully through the fragments of your fractured dreams because you hurt when you walk on them, as if they are broken glass and your feet are bare. Everywhere you see wasteland, your own personal wasteland.

But these bits are the ingredients of something new. Put them together, like pieces of a jigsaw puzzle, and you will solve the mystery of the new you. There is a secret there among those ruins, there is something new waiting for you to see: there is always time to begin again. And there is always a reason to.

A hand reaches out from somewhere, a hand you can almost see. Is it your imagination or is there someone there? Look again, the hand you see is your own. Yes, there may be others trying to help. Or you may be all alone in this. But the hand you see is your own. You are calling yourself back to life and into strength. Listen. You want to be heard. You want to come back.

The view from this seemingly rock bottom place is the best view ever. Open your eyes. From here you can truly see.

The possibilities are endless. Believe that you can resurrect yourself—believe—and you will. Get up and see your love and respect for yourself. Tap into it. This is your resource. This is you.

50
Love

We as a species have barely begun to explain what the love we feel is, or how powerful yet vulnerable love can be. While it is no surprise that love occasionally grows a little complicated, and or confused, we are a long way from explaining to ourselves exactly how and why.

Clearly, love is a powerful force, yes. And this is a force that we have yet to fully understand. Love between relationship partners is not merely romance or sexual attraction, or familial identity, or loyalty. Love is a way of communicating with and relating to ourselves and others.

The force of love must be cultivated with care and with great under-standing of the dynamics of relationships.

Especially in the case of intimate partner relationships which tend to begin in love, the care and feeding of the love is a special process which requires awareness and knowledge of the spoken and unspoken arrangements, agreements, and contracts people in close relationships make.

INTERPERSONAL AND PLANETARY PEACE

In today's world full of pressures and distractions, preserving and developing a successful love relationship may require at least some degree of conscious relating.

It may be a reach to see that planetary, or even societal, or even local community peace can be built by individuals, relationship by relation-ship. Yet we as individuals in personal relationships are in a position to model deep awareness of human exchanges, and of the messages and meanings of trades being made within these relationships.

Peace can grow from the ground up, like a seedling beginning somewhere on a forest floor and growing into a very tall and beautiful tree.

Of course, peace on the planet likely requires as much, if not more, conscious relating than do intimate partner relationships. We live in a world where violence is a common mode of expression, a common reaction to interpersonal and international problems, a common mode of conflict resolution. Just read the newspaper, turn on the television, ask children about what goes on in the world, and hear that violence is one of the key mediums of exchange and communication.

LOVE AS A MEDIUM OF EXCHANGE

Think of love as another key medium of exchange and communication. Weigh the power of love against the power of violence. Are these two mediums of exchange and communication equally powerful? Is violence resorted to because we do not believe that love can work, that love can be a solution to problems and conflicts?

Or is violence resorted to because it is within human nature to use force to gain and maintain power and control in order to achieve desired out-comes?

Violence itself comes in infinite forms.
Watch for these.
Know that abuse is violence.

Calling abuse something other than violence does not change the reality that abuse is a form of violence and adds to the violence in the world. A line or distinction drawn between physical and nonphysical violence is an artificial line, a line enabling us to deny the many faces of violence and terror in our lives and world. Look around. Is there a sharp distinction between physical violence and other abuses such as emotional and verbal cruelty, discrimination, prejudice, exclusion, hate mongering, and ostracism?

While these distinctions rightfully exist in law enforcement and courts trying to determine whether a physical assault or attack has taken place, these dimensions are not always as distinct in the mind and body of the person being abused. The experience of being abused can itself be registering physically as well as emotionally regardless of the specific form of the abuse. This is also true for the person doing the abusing. And, this is also true in instances of mutual abuse.

VIOLENCE IN CYCLES

Violence frequently appears in waves and in cycles. These waves and or cycles vary but all share a basic characteristic: violence of any form can beget violence of the same or of other forms. Violence can escalate from nonphysical to physical and from moderate physical to severe physical. Any form of violence is damaging in itself whether it escalates or not.

Violence in interpersonal relationships reflects violence in the world and vice versa. To end violence, we must each look at our own perspectives on violence and our own relationships to see what if any forms of violence are present in our personal and daily lives. Recognizing violence is the first and most important step to stopping violence. To change relationship abuse, violence, and terror, we must be willing to recognize the existence, nature, and cycles of violence we see around us. We must also know when we have no option but to leave a violent situation—or to at least seek a way to leave it.

Seeing how and where to break the cycles of violence we see in the world is a challenge. While there are many places to start...

> ...beginning with ourselves and our interpersonal relationships is one of the best. And why not?

The majority of us will be affected by intimate partner abuse and violence—either emotional or physical or both—at least once during our lives—as child witnesses, as members of our own intimate partnerships, as family or friends of troubled relationships, as neighbors, colleagues, co-workers, employers, or other persons who come into contact with couples who are troubled and couples who are doing well.

Love gets lost in the shuffle...

> ...All the hurt and pain and re-hurting and relived pain buries love in its rubble.

But we can rediscover love and share its force. We can enter and maintain conscious relationships, in which we do conscious relating to each other. This does not mean that we need endless hours of processing and reprocessing infinite aspects of each and every detail and element of our relationships. It does mean that we can choose to be involved consciously, to know: what goes on in relationships; what interactions look like; what unspoken contracts and promises we actually make; what the various checkpoints and warning signs are; and, what it takes to keep ourselves highly conscious of what we are doing with each other.

Whether or not society changes, you can.
Your changes can change the world you live in.

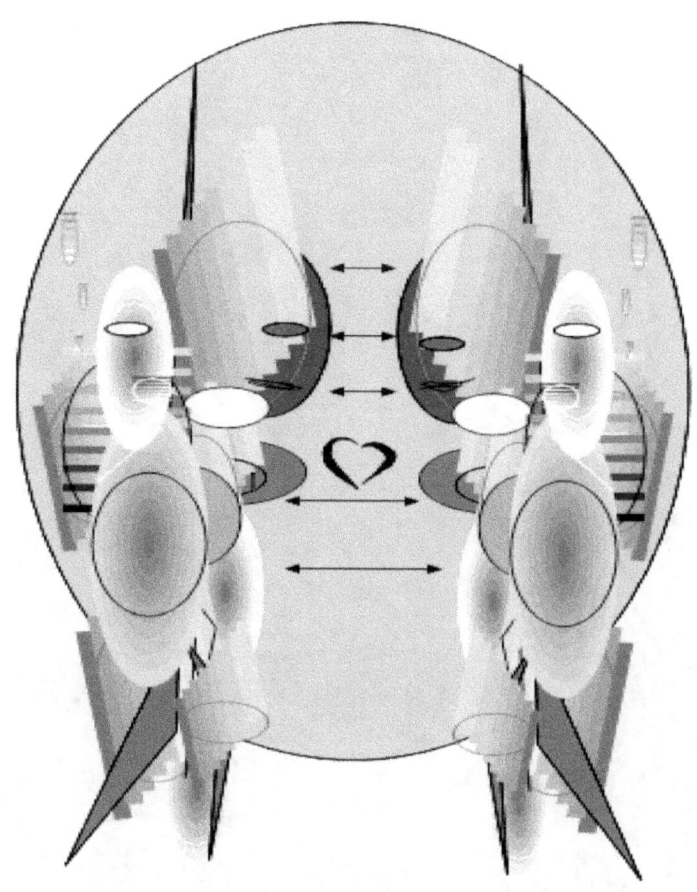

Technology of Relating
Illustration by Angela Brownemiller

About the Author

Dr. Angela Brownemiller, also known as Dr. Angela®, and known for her Ask Dr. Angela® Programs, is author of over seventy professional and lay reader books, including TRANSCENDING ADDICTION. She is also editor of the *International Collection on Addictions* and of the *Violence and Abuse in Society* collection. She is Director of the Institute for Personal, Social, and Systems Change; Director of Browne and Associates Violence, Substance Abuse, and Trauma Treatment and Prevention Program; and Director of Dr. Angela® Programs. She has been keynote speaker at conferences and events around the world on topics including violence, abuse, trauma, addiction, learning, behavior change, policy analysis, prevention, and the human mind and consciousness. Dr. Brownemiller earned two doctorates (one in social welfare and one in education emphasis psychology of learning) and two master's degrees (one in public health and one in social welfare) at the University of California, Berkeley, where she earned her doctorates with distinction and lectured in three departments for fourteen years. She has served as a National Institute of Mental Health Post-Doctoral Fellow; U.S. Department of Public Health Fellow; public relations director for Californians for Drug Free Youth; advisor to violence and abuse prevention and treatment, and addiction treatment, programs in the United States and several other countries; and project director on several California Department of Health abuse and violence prevention projects. She has served (in both clinical and educational settings) several thousand persons studying, working with, struggling with, and/or addicted to: relationships, love, sex, violent and/or abusive activities, and drugs, alcohol, gambling, gaming, food, and other objects, substances, and activities.

For Author, Consulting, Expert Service, Treatment, and
No Hurt No Harm Training Programs
Contact:
www.DrAngela.com